MOMMA'S LOST PIANO

David Madden

DAVID MADDEN

Momma's last piano

A MEMOIR

The University of Tennessee Press · Knoxville

A generous contribution from Charles B. Jones, Jr., in loving memory of
his parents and grandmother helped fund publication of this book.

Library of Congress Cataloging-in-Publication Data

Names: Madden, David, 1933- author.

Title: Momma's lost piano : a memoir / David Madden.

Description: First edition. | Knoxville : The University of Tennessee Press, [2023] |
Includes index. | Summary: "This memoir was composed after the author started
having memories of events that occurred in his early lifetime, growing up in a gritty
neighborhood in Depression-era Knoxville. The memories centered around his
mother, Emily Merritt Madden, and her experiences dealing with poverty, a sometimes
well-intentioned but never reliable husband, one son who ends up in prison, and
and another son who grows up to become one of Knoxville's greatest authors.
The style of the manuscript mimics the way memories came to the author and, in
some respects, the ways we recall the significant and insignificant events of our lives.
The memoir is at once an intimate retelling of a fundamental relationship and
a vivid evocation of an earlier place and time"—Provided by publisher.

Identifiers: LCCN 2022062239 (print) | LCCN 2022062240 (ebook) |
ISBN 9781621907824 (paperback) | ISBN 9781621907831 (pdf) |
ISBN 9781621907848 (kindle edition)

Subjects: LCSH: Madden, David, 1933—Childhood and youth. | Madden, David, 1933—
Family. | Authors, American—20th century—Biography. | Knoxville (Tenn.)—
Biography. | LCGFT: Autobiographies.

Classification: LCC PS3563.A339 Z46 2023 (print) | LCC PS3563.A339 (ebook) |
DDC 818/.5409 [B]—dc23/eng/20221230

LC record available at https://lccn.loc.gov/2022062239

LC ebook record available at https://lccn.loc.gov/2022062240

In memory of ALLEN WIER, *master of the craft of fiction.*

My mythic image of lovely Momma.

REMEMBERING AND
IMAGINING MOMMA'S LIFE
An Impressionistic Memoir

Late each night throughout a full year, just before going to bed, I shut myself up in my study and wrote a page or two of memories of my mother, Emily Merritt Madden, who had died two decades before, as my son Blake and I embraced her.

Those nights became for me an immersion in Momma's memories and my own of the relationship between mother and son over seven decades.

I wrote whatever came up out of my memory or what I imagined from what I knew about her. Like Momma herself remembering, I moved freely in time and settings, weaving back and forth, shifting within a section from my third-person to her first-person reverie, making no effort to maintain chronological order, which is the process of remembering.

Her brief memories and my own are like pictures in a family album, each complete and, separate, but generally related. And that's how they appear in these pages. I have re-arranged some, omitted others.

Momma and other family members loved to dwell on specifics, in all aspects of their lives. Their responses were keen, making everything twice as vivid and real in memory as in actual life. She always impressed me with the way she emphasized the names of people, places, and things, including my writings and jobs, almost as though they were living things.

Based on what I know about her, I sometimes imagine my mother's experiences, feelings, and memories. True to the nature of remembering, I return to some memories, sometimes more than once, but in fresh contexts. In this memoir, I have attempted to convey a sense of the constant movement and change, from place to place, among jobs and people, that was her life until later years.

The methods I employ and the shifting style here are quite different from those found in conventional, narrative-driven memoirs. Who, when, and where are sometimes ambiguous, but gradually everything becomes clear. Now and then, my voice is juxtaposed to Momma's; occasionally, our voices are meshed, so that she and I remember together.

These impressionistic passages are nocturnal "epiphanies." Just as I was isolated in my study before going to bed, Momma is often in bed about to drift off to sleep when she remembers the memories included here.

Although my full name is Gerald David Madden, "Jerry" is what family and friends call me. As a writer, I took on "David" around 1960. My two brothers and I called my grandmother "Mammy." Momma called her "Mother."

My mythic memory of Momma is of sitting in Mammy's soft chair in her house by the open front door when a green Chevrolet hove into my view across the street, paused, then glided on, revealing my mother in loving sunlight, prettier than I had ever seen her. The opening in the tall, thick green hedge framed her, and she seemed to float toward me, wearing a dark blue hat and dress, high heels, carrying a shiny purse, not smiling until she saw me looking at her, her eyes and mouth and walk conveying contentment—for the moment.

Losing her brand-new piano when she was eighteen became a metaphor for Momma's life. She devoted much of her adulthood to age ninety in pursuit of her lost piano. My memory of her quest—which included me from age five—haunts me still as I turn ninety myself.

MOMMA'S LOST PIANO

GOING FOR GROCERIES
WITH JERRY, JOHN, AND DICKIE

Dressed to go for groceries at the A&P, she opened the screen door, turned and called to Dickie, "Come on, time to go," took little John by the hand, and started down the front steps. Jerry was already in the street, walking impatiently in circles.

At the end of the cracked walkway, she turned, and here came Dickie. "What were you doing?"

"Nothing."

"Well, shut the front door and come on. Jerry. Wait. No, wait—*right where you are.*"

John pulled free from her hand and ran toward Jerry.

"John, don't you move another inch. Dickie, go take John by the hand. Yes, you have to. He's your little brother. Then don't. Jerry, you and John watch out for cars coming. Whenever you are walking without me, do as I taught you and always walk facing traffic."

She took John by one hand, Jerry by the other, Dickie traipsing on ahead out of the hollow up the hill.

She knew that when they got to the playground on Edgewood Avenue, all three boys would run for the swings. She let them, leaving her alone sitting on a huge rock, the baby in her belly.

In the last block, just before Sharp's Drugstore, remembering the sight of Chuck, and Phil now, curb-hopping, she had a firm hold on John and Jerry again, but Dickie had disappeared. She suspected he was breaking in the back door of R. T. Lyons grocery store that the Depression had forced out of business. Taking a switch to him had had no effect. She imagined him doing what Jerry had told her Dickie had done before—opening a can of pineapple with a little can opener at the lunch room table at McCampbell School, grinning that devilish grin of his.

"Mercy me, as Mother would say, what will I do with four of them, five, if you add that drunken daddy of theirs to the baby when it comes?"

Suddenly, the heavy traffic on North Broadway was zooming north and south. At least she was out of that swelteringly hot house.

COPS BRING JIMMY HOME
NEAR-ABOUT NAKED

"Momma, Momma, Momma, it's 'a tisket a tasket, a brown and yellow basket' out front." Dickie sounded thrilled to pieces.

Expecting to see a brown and yellow police car, she looked out the front door, saw a policeman open the passenger door, and watched him swagger up to the porch, and place one foot on the first step up from the flagstone walkway.

"Are you Mrs. James H. Madden?"

"What happened this time?"

"We brought you your husband, but he needs his bathrobe 'fore he can get out of the car."

Carrying his gray-mottled bathrobe, she stepped up to the back door of the police car, and tossed it in at Jimmy.

"They brung me home, Emily."

"We found him under the Gay Street viaduct, stripped of all but his shorts, and them he did number one in—scared when the other drunks stripped him, I reckon. Thought you might want him home."

"Yes, for all the neighbors to see, yes, thank you, officer. Out, Jimmy, out." John stood on the porch half naked from his bed, singing, "A tisket a tasket, a brown and yellow basket," which the kids all sang out to passing brown and yellow police cars.

"John, shut your trap, and get back in bed."

So she could get Jimmy from the curb into the living room without the neighbors seeing that he had on only his bathrobe and a hangover in the chilly Sunday morning air, she half-led, half-dragged him along the walkway, up the steps, and pushed aside John, Dickie, and Jerry, crammed into the doorway, all of them so much trouble already she feared they would trouble her the rest of her life.

2

"Don't worry, Emily. I'm sober as a judge."

"And I'm mad as hell, not that it matters a damn."

The three kids gaped at their daddy and followed him into the bedroom.

She stayed in the living room, feeling the chill, worried sick that Jimmy had taken to drink and to women at Breezy's factory, worse than ever, especially laying out with that ol' whiskey-drinking Mary, that younger woman, with a husband in Brushy Mountain State Prison, in that trashy little town of Petros, liable to bust out any day and catch them at it. She imagined herself on the lookout for that scrawny Mary, finding her with him, or alone, and smacking her into Kingdom Come for luring her no-good husband away from her.

IN QUEEN BED
WITH THREE GIRLFRIENDS

As if a curtain had gone up on a stage, Emily walked smiling toward Jerry where he was waiting at the elevator in Miller's Ready-to-Wear Department to go with her down to the basement café to have lunch together.

From before breakfast until she was ready with Ruth to step out of Ready-to-Wear into the elevator, she had tried to somehow get to a telephone and in touch with Zoe and Ruby to say, "Meet me at my house and let's go dancing tonight." Finally, she did, and they said, "Yes, yes, hell, yes."

Out of bone-chilling rain, she and Ruth stepped off the car stop platform in front of the Tennessee Theatre onto the Lincoln Park Number 2 streetcar, she aware that climbing up into streetcars calls attention to a short lady.

At the stop in front of the Union Bus Terminal Building, Zoe was among women and men just off work who got on the streetcar.

"Isn't that girl beautiful?" She felt Ruth's own beauty next to her.

She and Ruth waved, Zoe waved back, and she shouldered past the other passengers in the aisle to the middle of the streetcar.

"See my new purse?"

"Why, Zoe."

The silent type, Ruth smiled.

She and Ruth scooted over, tight, so Zoe could sit on the very edge, her slender legs stretched across the aisle.

Emily led Zoe and Ruth up the stairs to her apartment, into the ice-cold kitchen, the furnace being on the fritz, as Pearl, the skinny, bitchy young landlady, informed her as they came in. "Cold as ice up there."

"I could start a fire in the cook stove and we could huddle around it."

The three of them shivered in unison.

"Hey, hey, hey." Ruby's high, melodious voice rose from the landing.

"Ruby, you get your little butt up here."

"Here I am—in the flesh."

"We're all frozen."

"Not me, in my new fur-lined coat."

"Let's get warm until the boys come."

"I'm dead on my feet."

"Me, too."

"We all are."

"I need to get back on the streetcar and get home and get in my nice warm bed."

"I wish we could all do that very thing right now."

"Well, we're standing in the bedroom and that's a queen-sized bed."

Without another word, Emily set the example by kicking off her red high-heeled shoes she'd worked in for eight painful hours in Ready-to-Wear and, crawled under the quilts, wearing her red coat and blue, flared hat.

Wearing her new coat, swiftly dove Ruby in beside her. Shoeless, wearing her imitation fur coat and pearl gray hat, Zoe crawled over Emily and Ruby and inserted herself next to the dahlia papered wall and made a performance of snuggling.

Shy Ruth, the most beautiful and the only blond of her many girlfriends, and most elegant, more slowly and fastidiously—but not, as she expected, reluctantly, lifted what little quilt that was left and slowly swung in, as Emily, Ruby, and Zoe scooted inch by inch until she was all in, but for one foot, her fake alligator skin shoe dangling from her toes.

Their shoulders overlapped a little, but Emily felt snug, felt the all-together snug warmth of them all. She missed Ginny, though.

"Hey, you all, look." In her vanity mirror, she looked up at the image of four thirty-five-something-year-old women in coats and hats, figured quilts up to their chins. "Aren't we beautiful?"

When Ruby smiled, her perfect, slightly buck teeth lit up her exotic face, her eyes, more dazzlingly. She kissed Ruby's cheek. That started all four kissing each other's cheeks, holding their faces in their ruby-nailed hands, rubbing shoulders, then hips, then nylon stocking feet.

Someone was clomping up the stairs.

"Oh, hell, Bill said he would pick me up at about now."

Jerry appeared suddenly in the doorway between the kitchen and the bedroom, schoolbooks at his hip, exhaling clouds of cold air. He stopped and looked at the four women, shocked, quizzical, then delighted. He was going to be a writer, so she knew that he obviously loved the sight of four attractive older women in bed, under the quilts, getting warm, on display.

Pretending to dive into the bed, he caused four women to scream and shiver theatrically, all together.

They watched Jerry go on into the bathroom. In the silence, they heard him piss vigorously, and sniggered.

Jerry came out and started for the kitchen.

"Go back and flush it. And do your mother a favor, honey. Build a fire in the grate."

A car horn blared three times from down in front of the house.

"Reckon who that is?"

Going down the stairs, Emily heard Jerry on the phone say, "Iva Lee, honey, can you sneak past your mother, get out of the house, and walk over here? Not anybody here but me."

One by one, four men in cars came within thirty minutes or so for the four of them. Emily got in Bill's Studebaker convertible, just as that big-o Egyptian fellow rolled up for Ruth in an Oldsmobile.

UPCHURCH AND DAIRY QUEEN

Trying to shut Jimmy out of her mind, Emily waited in the house on Cedar Street in Lincoln Park for George Upchurch to come knocking at the door. Well, Jimmy was overseas somewhere in France or maybe Germany with General Patton. Seldom wrote, fewer and fewer words when he did, probably drunk on foreign whiskey, but she hoped not, his being an ambulance driver. He left her and three kids behind, not enough money to get by on, only her job with Breezy, who keeps telling her, "Poor little ol' Jimmy coulda been a half partner if not for that damned drinking," and left behind also that bitch Mary and her little boy to shift for themselves, except she bet he sent *her* some of his pay, too. She had to look at her in the same sewing machine room at Breezy's Sporting Goods Factory. She hoped Mary's husband would get released from Petros or escape and get a job, so one fine day Mary wouldn't be sitting there one row over from her.

George was a good man with a good job, a representative for a new type of ice cream they called Dairy Freeze that he was trying to get started in East Tennessee. She couldn't get enough of that soft serve. Maybe he would be holding a carton of it in his hand when she answered his knock. Maybe she could sweet-talk him into lending her a few bucks to pay the rent. Renting out half of the house to her old friend Rose and her husband and daughter and that addle-brained mother of hers didn't bring in enough.

She heard a car pull up out front and let him knock a time or two before she opened it. Yes, there he stood, great big grinning fellow, holding a melting cone of Dairy Freeze from the stand over on Central Avenue, must have driven lickety-split.

She was licking the last of it, his hammy hand on her bare knee, when suddenly the door of the boys' bedroom opened and there stood Jerry in his white underwear, squinting against the shine of the bulb hanging from the ceiling.

"Honey, this is my friend George, just stopping by on his way home. How come you aren't asleep?"

"I couldn't sleep and heard talking in here. Momma, you reckon God's mad at me for knocking those bird's eggs out of the robin's nest?"

George stood up and took a masculine stance. "Jerry, every boy does it, and God was a kid himself way back yonder. So, no, he ain't mad, son."

Seemingly convinced, Jerry went back to bed, and a little later on, George, bless his heart, left, a few Dairy Freeze stains on his pinstriped pant leg.

She was able to sleep, knowing she now had enough dough to pay the rent, and then some.

MIDNIGHT FUDGE CONSOLATION

She had finally gotten John and Jerry into bed, an antique iron daybed that opened up, in the kitchen by the stove that was still warm, wondering where Dickie could be, on the run, escaped from Brushy Mountain, sorely, consciously aware that this two-room apartment with shared bath in a small place on the corner of busy Atlantic and Pershing was more cramped than any of the many houses she had rented.

In her bedroom, her refuge after a long day in Miller's Ready-to-Wear, her feet killing her as usual, she shucked off her chenille robe and crawled into bed, settled snugly, and reached for *Forever Amber* by Kathleen Windsor, which Ruth had recommended and which she rented yesterday from George's Department Store on Gay, her place marked by a White Store ad for Stokely's canned pinto beans, two for twenty-seven cents, that she would also use also as a reminder tomorrow for Saturday's groceries.

Then she reached for the box of Russell Stover assorted chocolates that she had craved all the way home on the streetcar. The sight of the dark-brown little paper cups all empty made her instantly fling the box across the room, setting the window shade to rattling. Lacking chocolate made her whimper, all the day's wrecked moments condensed into tears.

She dug Granny Merritt's old hot plate out of the crammed-full bedroom closet, then marched back down the ice-cold hallway into the kitchen and quiet as a robber gathered what she needed into Mother's castoff iron pot. On the hot plate, she lovingly stirred the fudge to a boil, until she just knew, even without doing the hardball test, when it was ready. She beat it to a lustrous brown, then a dull brown, and when the spoon began to resist, she poured it onto a buttered plate, crawled back into bed, and, propped on the pillows, opened *Forever Amber*, slowly savoring the fudge she knew she so richly deserved as she read, "About the first of August Amber became convinced she was pregnant, partly because she had at least one symptom but mostly because it was forever on her mind."

From the kitchen, through the wall, came John's whining voice, then Jerry's. "Momma! Momma! I smell fudge, Momma!"

Her mouth full of fudge, she yelled back at them, "You all hush in there! You're going to wake Mrs. Yarborough and her baby, and her husband has to roll out of bed at the crack of dawn!" She sucked back up into her mouth the fudge that'd drooled.

PLAYING THE NEIGHBOR LADY'S PIANO

Finding a whole house for the family on Whittle Springs Road, no longer having to share Mother's three-room house, thrilled her to pieces.

Jimmy holding Dickie's hand, she holding John's and Jerry's, they crossed dangerous Whittle Springs Road and the long stretch of Edgewood, very cold, but the sun very bright, to Sharp's Drugstore, crossed Broadway, walked up Oglewood to Henegar, and down through the addition where houses were under construction, and up to Mother's for Sunday dinner.

Dinner went fairly well this time. No flare-ups. The kids at each other, but no more than usual.

She and Jimmy fussed all the way home in the very cold, the kids whining about this, that, and the other.

Trouble sprang on her when Dickie, then John, then Jerry got colds, and she had three kids to handle until Dickie could return to Bell Morris Elementary two blocks up on Washington Avenue. The boys spent the day in bed, or at the windows looking out, or fussing over who got to play with the two large, realistic, blue-eyed dolls from her Cleveland, Ohio, childhood, John's crying fits and bellering the loudest.

When Mother could visit and take care of the young'uns, Emily walked up the street, her sheet music of popular songs from the Cleveland years, along with such as "Claire de Lune" and "The Merry Widow," under her arm, to a house on a hill where a widow she'd met in Sharp's Drugstore allowed her to play her idle, a-little-out-of-tune piano at least once a week. Age had palsied the lady's hands, and she liked to hear live music as she struggled to bake pies for sale. Crossing the road, cars going like sixty, scared the hell out of her. But she was free, she was happy. She dreaded going back home. Sometimes, she gave in when Jerry begged to go with her and listen.

But then the day came when they could not pay the rent, Jimmy's drinking partly to blame, and they were kicked out after only four months in that better house. She turned to the For Rent section of the *Knoxville Sentinel*.

IN LOVE WITH BILL BOLES

She imagined Bill Boles sitting in his wife's ancestral mansion at the end of Armstrong Avenue. They were separated, but his daughter let it slip, when she picked up a lay-away spring outfit at Miller's, that her father sometimes visited her mother at that house, after he'd told Emily time and time again that she was the only woman in his life now who mattered a good god damn. He also declared he was not like Jimmy, that he would keep his promise to her never to take another drink as long as he lived. He'd told her he regretted that he couldn't take her dancing tonight because he had to go to Tellico Plains to his mother, who was at death's door.

"Jerry, honey, you want to do your mother a favor, honey?"

"What?"

"Jump on your bike and go by Bill's old house and come tell me whether his car is parked out front or not." She felt ashamed of herself, but . . .

"Why?"

"Just because."

"I'm right in the middle of this story I'm writing, Momma. The Cosgroves of Destiny."

"Oh, skip it." She slumped down on the couch and worked herself up to the verge of tears.

"No, I'll go. Hellfire damn it."

She saw in his face what she already knew, that for some reason Jerry didn't like Bill Boles.

Through the lacey curtains, she watched him leap onto his Western Flyer and race off.

Another drunk in my life. Another lying drunk in my life. Every man since Jimmy, in fact. Why in the world do I do it? Search me.

She flipped through an old *Life* magazine. She plucked a chocolate-covered cherry out of the Whitman's Sampler, Chocolates and Confections.

She turned on the radio. "The Shadow." "Who knows what evil lurks in the hearts of men?"

I do. What kind of a mother cajoles her fourteen-year-old son into spying on her lover? You should be ashamed of yourself, Emily Madden. I am. I am.

LOSS OF HER PIANO IN CLEVELAND

After school, opening the front door, her sweetheart, her former sweetheart, and her best friend hunched up behind her, she expected to see, *this* time, the piano Daddy had promised her.

What she saw was a gigantic wooden crate, sitting smack in the middle of the Persian rug in the living room.

"Is that *it*?" She shivered, ecstatic.

Mother said, "Yes. But your daddy said wait till he gets home so he can bust it open in front of you. Wants to see the look on your face."

"I can prize it open, Mrs. Merritt." Her ex-boyfriend stepped up to it.

"I'll handle this, Mrs. Merritt." Her new boyfriend Frankie waved her ex-boyfriend aside.

"Hell, I'll do it myself. I promised my friends I'd play 'Claire de Lune' on it for them if it came today."

"Emily, you'll show yourself in front of your friends. Your daddy bought it for you. He wants to be the one to bust open the crate, while you watch."

"He won't be home for an hour yet."

"Well, you heard me."

"Can you all stay?"

"No, they can't. Not now. I'm about to put the supper on the table."

Her friends got the hint and trailed out, Frankie blowing to her a kiss.

When Daddy swaggered in from work like a big shot, Mother shot out at him, "Charlie, that daughter of yours has tormented me to death, pacing up and down, squirming, waiting for you to come home." Mother pointed at the crate as if it were an unwelcome guest. "Well, there she sits."

Charlie set his briefcase on his chair. "Where's my crowbar?"

Holding it in her hand, at the ready, she held it out to Daddy, who took and flourished it, taking a stance before the crate, almost as tall as he. "Now shut your big blue eyes. Boys, catch her, if she faints."

She almost did. The shrieking of each board and nail thrilled her to pieces. She was aware that Mother was exiting the room, as if to be offstage.

"Mother. Come watch."

"Let her go." Daddy ripped out the last nail needed to be able to pull out the shrouded, upright piano. "It ought to be you that unveils it, honey."

Stepping up to the piano, she jerked the thick gray blanket covering it with a flourish. The dazzling shine on the upright piano made her dizzy. "I wish I could hug it."

"Why can't you?" Daddy spread his arms.

She hugged it from the side.

"Play 'Claire de Lune.' Jesse, bring me a chair from the kitchen."

"Supper's ready."

"Hell's bells." He went into the kitchen, and, holding a chair before him, came out.

She noticed again, "How short my daddy is."

Enthroned, sitting before the piano as if it were a monument, she tried to raise the lid.

"It won't budge."

"You get a key goes with it, too." Daddy stuck it in the lock. He turned his wrist, and she pushed up and opened it, revealing ivory and ebony keys, good as pearls and polished black marble.

As Daddy backed into his wicker chair to be in her view, she dove straight into "Claire de Lune," played it better than ever and knew she did, and Daddy, his working day in his office soothed, nodded as if to say, "Better than ever."

"I can't wait to play it for Frankie and Helen and . . . and . . ."

"Call 'em to run over here."

"The supper is on the table and it's getting cold." Mother's voice came clear as a dinner bell from the dining room.

"Your mother is a jealous woman, Emily."

"Of the piano? She can play it, too. Well, sort of."

"Let's eat before she pitches one of her Cherokee fits."

"Oh, brother."

"Your friends can come over later. And your little brothers, too, will want to listen to their big sister."

Late that night, to be intimately close to the piano, she slept on the divan. No longer would she have to play the pianos at her rich girlfriends' houses.

After the many people she loved, family and friends, this piano was what she already cherished the most.

Next day, after school, her gang sat all around the living room, some girls in boys' laps, watching her play her brand spanking new piano.

The sight of Daddy coming into the room, off work, made her stop, her fingers poised over the keys. "Why, Daddy, you look like death warmed over."

"You would too, if . . . Emily, go'n get your mother."

Mother came in. "You kids, we got to have a family talk. Maybe she can play for you tomorrow."

After she kissed her gang goodbye, Emily stood slack-armed in front of her father, who sank deep into his chair, the wickerwork crackling, and lit a Lucky Strike. "What?"

"What?" Mother stood stock-still.

"Mr. Lombard fired me. Out of the blue."

*Daddy, where he shot himself in Knoxville,
Tennessee, 1936.*

"Fired you?"

"Fired you?"

"Yes, fired me."

"Oh, Lord have mercy, what will we live on?"

"Sterling Wood Works Company said when I left Knoxville I could come back any time. I better call 'em."

"Charlie, I reckon we'll have to move in with your cranky mother."

"Why not *your* folks in Burlington?"

"*My* mother, she's blind, and Maudie's taking care of her out in the country."

"Your brothers and sisters . . ."

"You know Minnie ain't right, and them others are pitiful, one way or another. You've met 'em all."

"It ain't that I've not tried to forget."

"Charles Merritt, hush that talk in front of the children."

"What?" Phil piped up.

"Who done what?" Chuck batted his eyes.

Emily sat on the piano stool. "I won't go. I won't leave Cleveland. You all go and leave me behind."

"Stop showing yourself, young lady."

"Cleveland is my home."

"No, it hain't. You're a Knoxville girl." Mother crossed her arms.

"Born there, but that's all—and I remember enough of it to hate it."

"Hush that."

"Let me call Sterling's Lumber to see if they've got a position for me. Wish Momma could afford a telephone."

"If you're a-thinking of moving in with Granny, I ain't going neither." She wished Mother would quit pleating her lips like that.

"Just till we can afford a place of our own." Daddy's voice reassured nobody.

Mother saw that it was going to happen. "Well, I can't wait to get away from that awful wind off that damn Lake Erie."

About to cry, Emily ran to her room. Flung across the bed, she cried.

Two days later, when she came home from school, the crate was the only thing sitting in the living room.

Daddy had sold all their furniture, except what fit into the crate.

She spent her last evening with the gang, and finally let Frankie touch her virginity as a goodbye.

A taxi to take the family to the train station arrived at the curb.

Daddy had gotten the promise of a job at the same lumber yard in Knoxville that he had left six years before for their finer life in Cleveland, Ohio. "On Great Lake Ontario," as he'd loved to declare.

She had assumed that at least her piano would go back into the crate to go with them to Knoxville.

Daddy told her, "Honey, I had to sell it."

"The crate?"

"The piano. Man said I could keep the crate."

Mother thrust a finger at the crate. "All we can take is in the crate. Goes on the train with us."

"Mother, what did you do with my Girl Scout pin, my sheet music, and my old dolls?"

"Don't blame me. It was your precious daddy that sold it all out from under us, except what would go in the crate."

"I most certainly did not. It's all in one of the suitcases, safe, honey."

On the train station platform, Emily cringed at the sight of the piano crate, full of what of their worldly goods that could not quickly get sold.

Sitting on the train, she looked at the family she was stuck with.

Mother's hair had come undone. But she seemed not to mind, brimming with satisfaction that she was going back home to Knoxville.

Daddy's eyes looked sad, dark bags under them, and he was drawn down at the mouth. Will he ever be the same?

Look at little Phil. Puny. Fidgety Phil.

Oh, Chuck is getting handsomer than ever, like a movie star, but still a little too plump.

And me, look at my reflection in the window. Emily Luttrell Merritt, as soon as possible, you will go back to Cleveland and buy another piano, better than ever.

She was keenly aware that the crate sat in a boxcar behind her, next to the caboose.

Knoxville . . . Knoxville. Oh, lord, Knoxville!"

From the L&N Station to Broadway to Oglewood, she sat next to Daddy on the trolley, Mother in a seat behind them. They walked from the trolley stop five blocks to the three-room railroad shack on Henegar. She dreaded living crowded up with little Granny Merritt, whom she barely remembered.

Daddy told her that Granny Merritt retired from Knoxville Woolen Mill and moved into the old rest home on McCalla, in East Knoxville, but when they told her to chuck her hot plate, she bought the railroad shack on Henegar, in North Knoxville, and was content.

"Don't expect your grandmaw to welcome us with open arms, honey girl."

Granny Merritt looked severely through her screen door at the family of five, standing out on her porch.

"I'm not about to live in this trashy little house." Emily felt it in her bones.

But after hugging each one of them, Granny Merritt warmed up and smiled at Daddy, who asked her, "Who's gonna sleep where?"

Emily slept with Phil and Chuck on quilts on the bare living room floor, Mother and Daddy in Granny's bedroom. Granny snored on a canvas army cot against the wall across from the front and only window.

"I've slept on worse in my life," she'd said.

PRACTICAL NURSE FOR
THE MAYOR'S PREGNANT WIFE

To get her up and moving, Emily helped the mayor's fragile wife walk slowly, very carefully balancing, the two of them, around and around the large bedroom. Pretty Mrs. Roberts was due any day now.

Her handsome husband was too wrapped up in running the city, while also keeping his funeral home business afloat, to pay much attention to his wife, so Emily acted not only as the live-in practical nurse but as household manager, which included walking quickly down the steep hill to the White Store by the old Market House. And hiking back up the steep hill on her troublesome feet, lugging both arms full of groceries. And cooking what Mrs. Roberts was allowed to have, and what Mayor Roberts *had* to have, as a tall fellow who needed to keep his elegant figure for the public's sake.

Emily's feet had given her double trouble in each of the many jobs she'd had, but now, except for having to climb the stairs to the bedroom, she could keep her feet up, sitting now and then with Mrs. Roberts, keeping her company, and, lately, listening to her grievances about her husband's neglect. Lately, their nocturnal reproaches kept her awake too often.

She remembered screaming at Jimmy when he came in late, suspecting that he had been running with Mary, drunk, and his mild-mannered responses so infuriated her that she threw dishes at him and, when they had to live a while at Mother's that first time, causing Mother to yell from the bedroom, "That better not be one out of my favorite pink rose pattern, Emily."

Mrs. Roberts didn't throw dishes, but she was throwing the Mayor's clothes into the hallway. When Emily caught up with her, Mrs. Roberts's arms were so full of her husband's shirts, ties, and pants, that she was staggering dangerously, heading for the French doors to the outside balcony, his homburg tilted rakishly on her pompadoured head. Unable to stop laughing, Emily opened the French doors and helped Mrs. Roberts drape the Mayor's clothes, featuring his polka-dotted undershorts, over the balcony railing. She ordered Emily, in a nice way, to make a sign.

YOUR MAYOR'S CLOTHES FOR SALE CHEAP

GRANNY WILLIS'S FUNERAL

Entering the viewing room with a floating stride, Emily was surprised to see a good many relatives and friends at Granny Willis's funeral service, especially with so many of the men off to the war. She had persuaded Jerry to come, and there he sat. She sat beside Mother on her other side.

Aunt Maudie stepped away from the coffin to say hello.

"You took care of her all those years, Aunt Maudie." Emily hadn't said that before because Mother had refused to take their mother in from all the time when she was blind with glaucoma, making Maudie resentful. As a sort of buffer, Mother always took Emily with her when she visited Granny and Maudie out in the country. Maudie wanted to live it up in Knoxville—Maudie loved to dance—but her second husband was a stay-put farmer. He resented but endured having blind Mother Willis in the house.

One time, Emily corralled Dickie, Jerry, and John into going out there to see Granny Willis so they would have some memory of their great-grandmother. Dickie disappeared into the barn among the horses.

She and Jerry and John went into the dark room to see her.

"Take her hand, honey."

"Is that you, Dickie, honey?"

"It's Jerry, Grandmother, don't you remember little ol' Jerry?"

"I reckon. Did you bring the baby?"

"You mean John?"

"Lord have mercy, John, come give Granny a hug."

Emily looked around at all the faces in the viewing room.

Mother nudged her.

"There's your Uncle Ed and your cousin Hazel."

Emily despised Hazel because when she visited Mother, she showed off her latest husband and her fur coat and rings and new car parked out front, and Mother fawned over her, and when she was gone, Mother said she should visit her only living brother and her favorite niece in Florida one of these days.

No one can stand Hazel since she married that frosty old man and his white Cadillac.

Jimmy wandered half-looped into the midst of the crowded viewing room. Emily turned her head from the very sight of him.

"Mother, did you see Duck come in? Will you look at that outfit? Poor thing." She was fond of Duck, who got her name from being called "an odd duck" when she was little. She often dressed in a sailor suit, now in blue slacks and white shirt, looking mannish, but cute as ever.

She took one last look at Granny Willis, glad she had also known Granny Merritt as long as she had. Delilah Jane Carr Willis. Matilda Merritt. Charles Franklin Merritt. Ronald Dennis Madden, buried in Babyland. All in Lynnhurst Cemetery just over the city limits in Fountain City. Well, here we all are, so many, the dead and the living, and it takes somebody dying to get us together.

HANDSOME BILL WILLIAMS

She was waiting for Bill Williams, the handsomest man she had ever dated. Slender. Blond wavy hair. A smile that made Knoxville a better place for a little while. She didn't know for sure what product he sold or represented lately. Wasn't sure whether he was married or not. Good thing he didn't drink to excess like all the others, starting with Jimmy. Wine. He actually got her to taste a little wine now and then. The best dancer, and the best at kissing, she had ever known. Charming, but not put-on charming. Almost the easygoing charm of Jimmy when she married him.

Bill Williams back in town. For a while. His Studebaker so smooth running she had to look for him to arrive, not just listen. Too much a gentleman to honk for her.

Even so, as she looked out the window to watch him hove into view, she wasn't sure she'd want to be married to him, even if he ever proposed. Good thing about him was that Jerry, who didn't like any of her many boyfriends over the years, was very fond of him. Did Dickie and John ever even get a look at him?

One time she stepped off the streetcar and saw the yellow Studebaker convertible parked at the curb in front of the house and found Bill telling Jerry about one of his friends, Tom Roan, who wrote and sold a story a day to Western pulp magazines. Come to learn later on that Tom Roan was sentenced to life in prison in Alabama for murder, free to do nothing but spin off short stories.

Was Bill snowing Jerry or was he the kind who would make a good father?

No, not for John or Dickie, with their comings and goings, in and out of juvenile detention centers, reform schools, and prisons. Bill was too elegant to marry into that quagmire. Jerry only. Maybe. But not John and Dickie. Forget that.

There he is, that handsome devil in his yellow convertible. I just wish we were in Cleveland, taking a drive along Lake Erie instead of down into Gatlinburg and the Smokies. You can have them.

JIMMY SPEEDING IN A DELIVERY TRUCK

Jimmy drove Breezy Wynn's little orange and white dry-cleaning delivery truck, University of Tennessee's colors, before Breezy shifted to manufacturing sporting goods. Jerry and Dickie bounced when the truck hit a bump, and they rolled all over the back, laughing, giggling.

She kept screaming, "Jimmy, you're driving too damned fast. We're going right off that cliff into the Tennessee River."

The boys seemed scared to death by her predictions more than by the high speed and hairpin curves.

The black darkness on the round little windows in the two back doors seemed to be eyes looking her over. She had to admit it was a little thrilling, but she didn't want to be thrilled to death.

Jimmy's laughing at her was so soft she hardly heard it.

She was glad Breezy would let Jimmy use the little Vol Cleaners delivery truck over the weekend, but she hoped they made it home in one piece. Dickie and little Jerry kept on rolling around, screaming and giggling when Jimmy took a curve, just barely slowing down, and a few pieces of dry-cleaning left on the rack swung like staggering drunks.

"Jimmy, slow down. You're going to kill us all."

She had never gotten used to the way men had to show off at the wheel. No sweetheart ever made her heart beat so fast as Jimmy's speeding.

Chuck was the same way as Jimmy, but Chuck got drunk first, and Ruth didn't put up with it for long. If Daddy had taken to speeding, Mother wouldn't have put up with it for one second, either.

She finally convinced Jimmy that she was serious, and he slowed to a creep, sarcastically.

"That's better."

"But are we still moving?"

She didn't take sarcasm any better than speed, but at least sarcasm never killed anybody.

CASHIER AT LOUIE'S GREEK RESTAURANT

One of the things Emily liked about working at Louie's Greek Restaurant was watching Jerry come walking out of the Bijou, off from ushering, and stand under the marquee, looking like he was posing, then looking up and down Gay Street to cross safely, sometimes waiting for the streetcar to turn into the car barn right by Bijou Tavern, then making a run for it.

He'd come striding in, a little cocky from watching Cagney or Bogart, right up to her, where she was perched on a stool behind the cash register.

And she was glad Priscilla, the new, plump waitress, was eager to be the one to take Jerry's order for his usual hot roast beef sandwich with gravy, tangy coleslaw, and French fries, even though she was four years older and even though he seemed to've lost his mind over that Jenny Bowling, prettier than Elizabeth Taylor.

Looking out the window, recognizing so many people passing or coming in, sometimes it seemed that all of Knoxville paraded by. All those people, many she knew, some of them friends or relatives, lining up at the Bijou ticket booth across Gay, then after the movie coming out under the marquee, and faces at the windows of the streetcars passing her window going into the car barn or coming out along Gay toward Lincoln Park, where she used to live, and to McCalla Avenue where she lived now, others going out Magnolia to Chilhowee Park, near where all Mother's people lived, out to Fountain City, where Mother and Daddy first met, across Gay Street Bridge into South Knoxville, where she and Jimmy had lived in that dank basement apartment the first year they were married.

She liked Louie. He'd appreciated her suggestion that he add celery seeds to his coleslaw, because everybody complimented him on it.

Sometimes his brothers came in, but not very often. Each owned or worked in one of the other Greek restaurants, Sanitary Grill where Jimmy took her that first time they met, across from the Tennessee Theatre; Louie's at the city limits near Fountain City; the Gold Sun Café in Market Square; and, queen of them all, Regas's on North Gay and Magnolia. She counted each of those restaurants, their very names, as part of her Knoxville life, having eaten in them since the 1930s.

The only thing about old Louie was that she had to keep telling him to keep his hairy hands to himself. His feisty wife told him the same thing.

Her girlfriends came in just to see her, but they often stayed to eat. And Mother and Cap came in. And Phil and Frances. But never Dickie, who was on the lam from breaking out of Petros. Or John, who she and Cap had to take back to Kingswood, home for wayward children, far, far out in the country on Rutledge Pike at Bean Station, where folks bragged about Kingswood having once been the famous Tate Springs Hotel that attracted the Fords, the Vanderbilts, the Mellons, and the DuPonts as summer guests.

As Jerry paid the check and Emily made change, she gave him a covert, significant look and whispered, though no one could have heard, "Did you notice a woman in a flowered dress, black-haired, short young woman, come in the Bijou about an hour ago?"

"Yeah. Cute."

"I saw her through the window. Honey, that's Phil's old girlfriend, Maxine, the one that did him dirty when he was in Germany."

And poor ol' Jimmy came in, until Louie told him what she'd tried to tell him herself, that drunks were absolutely not allowed.

One time, she took Jerry aside. "Listen, if your daddy comes staggering into the Bijou drunk tonight, you tell him he better not dare come slobbering over here to Louie's."

And Jimmy's main girlfriend Mary darkened the door one lunchtime, until the sight of the one and only Mrs. James Helvy Madden sitting behind the cash register set her off at a whirl and scamper out into a downpour before she could open her umbrella again.

All Knoxville on parade, and her own people among them, Willises and Merritts and maybe some of the mysterious Carrs on Daddy's side from up in Jacksboro near Caryville and Mother's Carrs from out in Burlington.

Working at Louie's, she missed working with or just seeing her girlfriends more often, from when she worked in Miller's Ready-to-Wear. But being off her poor feet, able to sit most of the time, was her salvation.

TRYING TO GET DICKIE OUT
OF STATE PRISON

Planning to visit Governor Clement again tomorrow on Dickie's behalf, Emily rehearsed her appeal in front of the mirror in her tiny room for staff in the Maxwell House Hotel, fairly confident that she looked and sounded soulful, but, just as important, charming. People often told her she had a lovely smile, not knowing it was partly the dentures, but mostly her own lips and mouth, inspiring compliments in days gone by ever since junior high in Cleveland. Her auburn hair, the pompadour, set her off. Only thirty-eight when she got all her teeth yanked out, caused mostly from having four babies, the dentist said.

She'd gone to work in Nashville solely to be near her firstborn. She imagined sashaying into the Governor's office to plead for Dickie's early release from the pure hell of Brushy Mountain Prison. She would tell him that Dickie had already served two years of his three-year sentence. Good behavior. They made him the library assistant. Faithful Methodist now. Or so he wrote in his letters.

Little brother John serving our country in the Marines. No, the Governor's staff might check on that and discover John was about to get discharged for fraudulent enlistment.

Well, but Jerry is in the army, sir, in Alaska. All three, and their daddy and my two brothers, served their country. Explain that her ex-husband is trying to get Dickie a job where he works, with Breezy Wynn, the fullback for UT that's famous for his speed, whose factory made duffel bags for the war effort. She knew how to sell dresses to reluctant young and older women, so maybe she could persuade a governor to buy Dickie's story. If only Dickie himself could speak to him, using the talent for conning people that put him in prison in the first place.

Come to think of it, the Maddens were a family of con men and women, including herself, although a Knoxville Merritt.

And handsome Governor Frank Clement did give her a look that time he sailed into the Maxwell House and bought a La Corona at her cigar counter. The way Bill Williams looked at her. She knew she was almost too plump. Always had been, sort of. But she knew she had a certain talent for just being a woman, pure and simple.

LETTER TO JERRY IN THE ARMY

"Hi Jerry, I guess you thought I was never going to write. Honey I just can't tell you what a pace I've been going for a wk. I've run myself ragged.

"Changed jobs. Hostess in the coffee shop at the Sam Davis Hotel downtown Nashville near the Grand Ole Opry.

"Had to take about $25 less. But not so hard on me. Your old lady is now a boss and hires and fires and supervises. You know I like that, and I miss bossing you boys.

"Have been going to see Dick 3 or 4 times a wk and this official and that official about the trial, and all like that, till I am a nervous wreck. The trial is in the morning and I feel like I'll fall apart before then. I am so afraid Dick is going to get another sentence. They checked and found out about him being in that Colorado prison in Canon City that year and his army prison time in Hamburg and the dishonorable discharge, so all that goes against him. Tomorrow will tell.

"Had a letter from John. He's been sick with intestinal flu but is up now. He wrote you, he said, so take time out to ans. It is shameful how you all have drifted away from each other.

"Well, I guess I'd better turn in, have to pull out at 6 bells. Work 7 to 2 and 5:50 to 8:00 for all of $100 per mon. and meals that would choke a horse. We have to wait until the guests eat.

"Well, I'll be saying night night and write me soon. Love, Mother."

SLAPPING THE HELL OUT OF MARY

She sits in the SpinLife Lift Chair that Jerry bought for her so she could ease out of it and let her feet more firmly touch the floor, across from Mother's old chair that has a view of everything going on outside the front door and beside the antique table Mother bought on their visit to Jerry and Robbie in Boone. Imagine living past three pasture gates on a mountain farm.

She tried not to think too often of Mother being gone, stared at these four walls, dozed, dreamed, awakened, daydreamed of old girlfriends in icy cold but wonderful Cleveland.

Here I sit, chair-bound, legs hurting, unable to get out and go.

There sits the piano Mother bought for herself, lid down, greeting cards displayed along the sheet music shelf, the polished wood piano bench, chock-full of sheet music she used to play. "I Can't Begin to Tell You," "Doin' What Comes Naturally," "Oh, What It Seemed to Be."

She was aware again that it had been easier to forget her love for Jimmy than to forget that worst time she saw him huddled with Mary out of the rain in that church archway.

Her toes not quite touching the aisle floor, she'd sat in her favorite seat just behind the streetcar conductor, hugging the Saturday groceries.

"I got there just before they sold the last of the turnips, on sale for five cents a pound."

"I never could choke the darned things down myself. Maybe if *you* cooked 'em for me, Emily."

She always enjoyed riding up front behind the conductor, telling him her miseries, and he rattled off all his. Jerry said she embarrassed him when she did like that.

Victor was tonight's conductor. Sometimes she ran into him and his wife Darla out dancing. He once told her he liked her voice behind him, all the way from the car barn next to the Bijou to Atlantic Avenue in Lincoln Park.

"Always gay, that's Emily. And I just know you're smiling behind my back, so to speak."

"This rain. Looks like it's not going to let up anytime soon." Looking across the aisle and through the window over an old man's shoulder to judge how bad the rain was, she saw just up ahead, Jimmy and Mary huddled to avoid the rain in the archway of the St. Lutheran Church, the red door behind them.

"Victor, would you mind stopping a minute and letting me out, honey?"

"What in the world, Emily?"

"It'll only take me a second."

She jumped up, whirled around and set the overflowing grocery bag on the seat, lurched when the streetcar stopped, reached out and took hold of the car token receptacle, swung through the doors just as Victor opened them for her, stepped smartly without looking down the iron steps and onto the street, making a car stop with a wet screech, stomped up the three gray stone steps into the arch of the sanctuary door, slapped Mary's face, pivoted back around and down the steps and in front of another car, and stepped up into the streetcar, picked up her grocery bag, and hugged it so tight an orange jumped out and rolled toward Victor's seat at the controls.

"Have an orange, Victor." She giggled, wiped the rain off her face, then sank into a smoldering fury.

"Emily, I always thought you had a wild streak in you."

"Don't tempt me."

Jerry met her at the car stop just as he promised and took the grocery bag from her arms.

Jerry always loves to hear me tell him that story.

Under the quilts that night, recalling the shocked look of those two together, she guessed Jimmy had not really been trying to shield Mary from the rain that blew against them in the archway. Oblivious, as usual, to what people expected of him. Dickie takes after Jimmy that way. John less so. But Jerry is considerate, always has been. He can be so sweet, but he's also got a mean streak in him like the rest of us.

NEW EASTER CLOTHES FOR THE BOYS

She'd paid on a coupon book a dollar a month at Penny's to buy complete Easter outfits, blue for John, green for Jerry, brown for Dickie. Including new shoes, even underwear.

She trudged the three long blocks of Cedar Street from the streetcar stop to the house, dead tired from work, feet hot and hurting, but thrillingly imagining tomorrow morning when she'd take it all out from where she'd hidden it so well, would lay out brand-new Easter outfits and shoes on her bed for

Dickie, Jerry, and John to see when they passed through her bedroom on their way to the kitchen or the bathroom.

She'd shivered a little in anticipation as she turned the front door knob. The picture she saw was not three boys almost in rags, wearing shoes, the soles flapping and full of holes. They sat around the Warm Morning coal heater in the middle of the tiny living room, their feet, shod in shiny new shoes, up on the fenders to keep warm, their brand-new blue, green, and brown outfits making them look like rich kids turning their heads to order the maid to bring each of them a cherry smash, and smiling to beat the band. The looks on their faces. They looked so cute, even though she was mad as hell.

"You little hellions, jerk those clothes off and those shoes before I beat the living fire out of—"

But laughter that had been rising in her throat burst out and lured them away from the heater and up to her where she stood just inside the door, cold air following her in, and they posed in front of her, proudly, Dickie saluting mockingly, most likely the ring leader, Jerry imitating him, and it was John's slightly buck-toothed grin and those big innocent eyes that made her go from laughing to crying delight.

CHUCK KILLED IN ACTION

IN PALERMO, SICILY

The sight of Mother sitting by the sewing machine weeping, holding the telegram from President Roosevelt informing her that her son, Private Charles Merritt, had been killed at Palermo in the Allied invasion of Sicily, made Emily, crying, hesitate to hug her.

From the yard, Jerry peered into the bedroom through the sooty window screen. "Why you all cryin', Momma?"

She told him, and he came in and hugged her, and stood before Mother, saying, "I'm sorry," again and again. John was still out there playing with his little cars, and no telling where Dickie had gotten off to.

The memory came over her of the time two years before when they were all lying on quilts on the grass in the front yard inside the low-cut hedges, looking up at the starry sky, pointing out to each other the big and the little dipper. She'd gone into the house to make lemonade to cut down on the humidity and heat, and was coming out the front door when Chuck, coming down the alley across Henegar Street wearing blue fatigues and matching hat, jumped the hedge perfectly, AWOL. He'd joined the army cavalry partly to get sober, partly to get over Ruth divorcing him, and her joining the WACs that sent her to Alaska. And a year later, Phil was blowing up bridges in Germany. And Jimmy driving ambulances with General Patton still.

In her favorite photograph of him, Chuck, handsome as Tyrone Power, looked dashing in his cavalry uniform with its flared legs and boots and that snazzy cap.

Waiting for Mother to look as if she might welcome a hug, she saw flashes of family photographs in a dress box kept in the old wooden quilt chest of her as big sister posing for Daddy's camera with little Chuck in Cleveland in summer and winter snow settings.

Remembering the night Chuck came home reeling drunk and thought he was in the outhouse down at the alley and whupped out his do-lah-lee and pissed in a wavy arc on the lampshade where Mother sat with *Life* magazine open in her lap, Emily had to turn aside to keep from laughing.

Emily thought of her own lost child, Ronny, John calling him Baboo, and started crying. "Ronny would have been seven years old today."

"We both lost a son."

"I know. But it's not the same, Mother."

"Well, how you figure that?"

"You had yours for almost 30 years."

"Chuck was your brother, Emily."

"And I loved him to death, Mother, but it's different losing an infant child."

"Well, you've got us both crying now."

WAS BOB PRICE THE LOVE OF HER LIFE?

Was Zoe right when she figured Bob Price was the love of Emily's life? Maybe. If you went by the fact that she never came close to marrying any of the slew of other men she had gone out with in any ongoing way.

Sweet little Clyde was the only one who begged her, for six or so years, to marry him. He smelled always faintly of beer from tending bar in the Biltmore saloon, although he was not an alcoholic like Bill Boles and the rest of her lovers.

She'd divorced Jimmy when she realized he came back from the war the same ol' Jimmy. Come payday, drunk without fail.

And Bob Price finally convinced her he would give it up if he could have her. So she got on a bus to Terre Haute and met his mother and father and sister and, after a week or so, married him, and the next day got it annulled after he came home drunk as a coot at 4 a.m.

Mother infuriated her and she held it against her for years, for declaring she was never married to Bob, that she'd lived in sin with him. Mother, who never went to church or read the Bible, but whose long affair with Cap ended in marriage only after his ailing wife died.

Mother never let go of her jealousy over Daddy saying Emily was his favorite. What about Chuck obviously being Mother's favorite? Which left poor little Phil, even when a boy threw a rock at him, made him half blind in one eye, out in the cold, always doing everything he could to win her over.

Jerry never liked Bob. She came home from work when they lived on Bearden and found Bob sitting by the stove and Jerry and John sitting together a little way away from him. Drunk. They were scared of him, his being such a big man, his hair prematurely gray, his expression always serious.

And that time when she and Bob and Jerry were sitting at the kitchen table chomping on Lay's potato chips in the apartment on Central and they stopped, listening to footsteps coming slowly up the stairs.

"I'll bet it's Ginny."

"Let's go see."

Tiptoeing. Peeking.

Jimmy.

Drunk.

Needing a haircut. Shabby.

She instantly broke into her emergency charming act.

Handshaking.

"Hello, Jimmy."

"How you doing, Jimmy?"

"You Bob?"

"Yes, it's Bob, Jimmy."

She steered Bob into the kitchen again, leaving Jerry to pacify Jimmy, as he had many times.

"Is my face red?" She reckoned it was.

Bob was so cool and collected about it.

She watched Jimmy sit on her bed and loop his legs over the low foot rail.

Jerry sat in his one-armed chair that he dragged in from the stairs landing where he'd put his little desk.

Jimmy was worried about the Russians. Then he got worried about what might be happening to Dickie and then what might be happening to John.

She and Bob had their backs to Jerry and Jimmy, but she heard what Jimmy was telling Jerry. "I'm going to ask your mother to marry me again."

Jerry started in trying to handle Jimmy. "Let's go down to the street and talk."

"So, you got a few smackers you can lend me, son?"

She went to the door and watched Jerry guide his daddy awkwardly down the stairs and out the front door onto the porch and out into the wind and sunlight and sit on a curb and talk as a streetcar went by.

She went in and lay down on her bed, crying, too aware of Jimmy's whiskey odor, Bob delicately petting her shoulder.

WARNING THE BOYS TO AVOID PERCY

When she saw Percy come out of the jungle, rolling a big truck tire in front of him, guiding it with a stick, she gathered the boys together. "You all stay way away from Percy."

"Why come?" John looked up at her out of his blond curls.

"Cause he's not right."

"About what?"

"Don't get smart with your mother, Dickie."

"He comes up all of a sudden when I'm telling stories on the front steps."

"Jerry, he's just trying to get in good with you kids."

"Why for?"

"Just stay away from him, John."

"*I* know why."

"Then, keep it to yourself, Dickie. You being the oldest, you ought to be looking out for your brothers."

"Let 'em look out for their selves!"

"You sass me one more time today, Mr. James Richard Madden, and I'll smack you into next week."

Jerry turned to the window. "He's headed over to Janice's house. She's always good to him."

"I saw her go off with him one time." Dickie rolled his eyes, grinning.

Jerry got huffy. "You did not. She did not."

Emily felt Dickie had her pegged. "I wouldn't put it past her."

DANGEROUSLY ILL

Will I never see Cleveland and Lake Erie again? In Saint Mary's hospital, Emily lay on what she knew might very well be her deathbed. Five hundred miles from the eight-room house where she lived her happiest years, but only three blocks up the steep hill from little Granny Merritt's three-room house where Daddy took her, Mother, Chuck, and little Phil ten years ago. She had to watch Granny die of cancer of the rectum on her cot in the living room, where Jerry was born four years later on the opposite side of the narrow room on the squeaky pull-out couch.

After three weeks in that hospital bed, she'd gladly let herself be taken back down the hill to good ol' 2722 Henegar, where Mother lived alone now. Phil in the army overseas, and Jimmy talking about enlisting. She had to put Jerry and John in the Juvenile Home awhile, until Breezy Wynn could persuade St. John's Episcopal Orphanage to take them until, or if, she got well.

She wished Jimmy's big sister Kathleen had kept them longer, where they could play with Betty Ann and Jackie, but, no, Mr. Barbee said all of them running and yelling in and out of the house drove him out of bed after working the night shift at the rich Maddens' East Tennessee Packing House. And she'd nagged Jimmy until he arranged to send Dickie out West to stay with his big brother Uncle Elmo and Aunt Kate in Albuquerque.

She was sick so often all her life that Mother called her a hypochondriac. Maybe so. Maybe so. But I am not imagining this lingering, aching, and shooting pain. Giving birth to Ronald Dennis caused all the rest of my teeth to decay. So here am I, a toothless, thirty-five-year-old, fun-loving, high-steppin' woman. If this surgery doesn't kill me, these ill-fitting dentures will. Mother's too tired from working as a nurse's aide to come see me much, or to take care of me if I survive, despite her years at old General Hospital.

When the nurse asked, "How are we doing tonight, Miss Emily?" she whimpered, "I'd rather be on the dance floor of some old roadhouse out Clinton Pike. Or better still, swimming in Lake Erie."

THE SECRET SERVICE

CALLING FOR JOHN

When Jack Fenton from the Secret Service called and asked to speak with John, she was not surprised.

Before John showed up in Columbia where she was doing practical nursing and he stayed to live with her, he'd had been following President Johnson all over the country, asking him questions from the crowd until not only the Secret Service began to track and know him, but the President himself sometimes saw him in the crowd and called out to him by name.

"No, Jack, John's not here."

"Well, he left word that he had some crucial information about that student antiwar group he's been infiltrating for us."

"Maybe he's on the move. I'll call Jerry."

If only John hadn't created that right-wing newspaper that reported on that radical group at Ohio State University and secretly joined them to get information. That's all she knew, and Jack wouldn't tell her anything more.

Like Jerry that time refusing to sign a new loyalty oath that he said Senator Joseph McCarthy had bullied Attorney General Brownell into forcing upon the Army. She begged Jerry to keep his opinions to himself. With two ex-convicts in the family, she certainly didn't need to add a Communist. And she wasn't sure about John, why he did what he did and said what he said in that little newspaper of his, which he mimeographed in her own bathroom.

As she was about to dial, the phone rang. "Momma, John just called me from a phone booth on the interstate and told me to get you out of Columbus because that student organization's out to assassinate him and might come to the apartment tracking him down and hurt you. You're a hundred miles from me. He asked me to call Jack Fenton at the Secret Service and tell them where he is. I thought it was just John being John until Jack Fenton called me and asked if I knew where John was and I gave him the public phone number John gave me, so . . ."

"Oh, Jerry, I am at my wit's end. What am I going to do?"

"Is Dickie still coming to live with you and John when they let him out?"

"Yes, but that's after I move to Cincinnati, if Frenchie can get me that job down there."

She was glad Jerry and the Secret Service were looking after John, but she lay awake anyway with nervous leg syndrome and Elmer running up and down the furniture and leaping down on the bed the way Siamese cats do because they can't help it, and now every noise in the apartment building made her jumpy, expecting a loud knock at the door, but she felt fairly certain none of those students would come for her like the Gestapo.

SENDING THE BOYS TO SUNDAY SCHOOL

The call from Jerry she waited for each weekend finally came.

"Hello, Momma, how you doing?"

"Okay, honey, except for my legs. The rheumatism's about done your old momma in. How are you, honey, you and Robbie and Blake?"

"I've become a Christian again, Momma, after fifty years an agnostic."

"Well . . ." She was aware of using Mother's drawn-out tone of "what about that?"

She remembered putting a nickel in Jerry, John, and Dickie's hands for the collection plate and sending them off to Lincoln Park Methodist, hoping Dickie wouldn't veer off to Rose's Drugstore on the corner and spend it on ice cream, and John sooner or later following his big brother in that, too. She never doubted Jerry would drop his nickel in the plate. He never missed Sunday school because of that pretty, pretty Jonnie Lou Gilmer, especially in the summer when he couldn't moon after her all day in Lincoln Park Elementary. Lasted from second grade until the seventh. At that rate it's not exactly the puppy love we all kept telling him it was. Little did he know that the love of his life, before he met Robbie, would be the pretty girl sitting between her big sister, their teacher, and Jonnie Lou. Not beautiful Jenny Bowling after all, but sweet little Iva Lee.

He was saved on sawdust under a tent over on Atlantic Avenue, just wandered in, he said, coming home from seeing *Frankenstein Meets the Wolf Man*. Then only a few years later was when, from reading all those books, he became an agnostic, or whatever you call it.

She never went to church. Not since Cleveland. Well, now and then, when she lived and worked in Nashville, and when invited wherever she was, by men or women acquaintances.

The phone rang. "Bet that's Jerry."

"Jerry, I get so damn bored looking at these four walls all day."

"Are you still using the wheelchair and sitting in that special chair in the living room?"

"Yes, honey. The therapist comes once a week. It's so embarrassing, when he says—and him so young—that I need to exercise by squeezing my rectum."

"Well . . . I remember you going dancing every chance you could, every weekend for a good long while."

"Your mother was a good dancer, honey."

"I regret never having seen you dancing, but I knew you were."

Wonder what he thought when I stayed out all night and came back Sunday morning. 'Course he was older, going to UT by then, and so it didn't bother him. I don't think. He told me one time that Phil told him his drinking buddies down at the Watering Hole in the Broadway Shopping Center said I had a bad reputation, that's why Phil was so hateful to me allatime.

"And Robbie's director of Consumer Protection Commission here in Baton Rouge and serving on the federal Civil Rights Commission. And Blake is doing graduate work in photography at Ohio University where I used to teach."

"When you all come see me next, don't forget to bring the old home movies."

ASKING PHIL TO BABYSIT THE BOYS

"Phil, will you jump on your bike after school and come watch over the kids when they get out of school so I can help Mother at the café?"

"How much you pay me?"

"Is a quarter enough?"

"Plus a nickel?"

"I'm your sister."

"And I need me a nickel extra this time."

"I'll get Chuck to do it."

"Chuck's too old to babysit."

"I'll remind him that I used to have to babysit him for nothing when we lived in Cleveland."

"No, I'll do it for a quarter. Next time get ready to pay me thirty-five cents."

"When hell freezes over."

"Will you'uns quit it?"

"Don't worry, Mother. My little brother thinks he can get rich off of his big sister."

LEARNING SHORTHAND
AND TYPING IN NIGHT CLASS

Having always wanted to be a high-level secretary, she enrolled in a shorthand and typing class in the night school program at old Knoxville High School, where Jerry graduated in its last class in 1951. She wrote to him, to Fort Jackson, South Carolina, where he was assigned to Clerk Typist School. She realized that had she learned earlier, she could have typed Jerry's stories when they lived together. Iva Lee, the love of his life, and her sister had typed them from Christenberry Junior High through Knox High years.

Learning shorthand and typing were extremely hard on her nerves, especially after working as hostess at Howard Johnson's all day, dealing with jerks, customers, and male staff, and with bitchy waitresses, and that night hostess coming in late most nights. Then on that sluggish bus to Knox High.

But wait till she gets a highfalutin secretary position. Even Mother might show a little pride in her only daughter. Never before. Not even when she was an award-winning Girl Scout in Cleveland, a ribbon-winning swimmer, and a piano student who won the praise of her cranky teacher. Yes, she knew Mother loved her. But hell's bells, can't you fork over a nice word or two once in a while?

Maybe her class was in the very same room where Jerry and his best friend Ralph learned to type. No more hunt and peck on that old secondhand Royal

Jimmy bought for him, coming into that ward where Jerry was getting over surgery on both feet, three incisions on each, transplanting the bones to correct what Dr. Inge first thought was infantile paralysis and then most likely claw-foot deformity.

Maybe Mother was jealous. She was jealous of Daddy saying she was his best girl and favoring her in so many ways. Mother couldn't play the piano, but she bought one, saying she would learn, but it just squats in that little, low-ceilinged living room. Mother let her play sometimes, and let her keep her trove of sheet music in the piano bench. But Mother overloads the top of the piano with gaudy artificial flowers and various gimcracks and letters and bills and naughty comic post cards up on the music rack.

Well, just wait. Just wait. If only I can muster the strength to graduate from the course. It's my nerves that may do me in. Thank goodness George was coming to give her a ride home. What she would do without George, she just couldn't say.

WORKING "WHERE SMART KNOXVILLE BUYS"

She was thrilled when the prissy manager at Mayme McCampbell's Shoppe, "exclusive" millinery, hired her. She loved working in Miller's Ready-to-Wear, but the area was vast, walking from one end of the store to the other, and all around, all day long, whereas Mayme McCampbell's was about as wide as her bedroom and no longer than a motel swimming pool. Seeing the sign above, WHERE SMART KNOXVILLE BUYS, you walked up to the Frenchy art-deco façade and you knew you were entering an elegant shop under an arched tunnel-like dome.

She felt elegant most of the shift but worn to a frazzle, her feet killing her, by three in the afternoon, with three more hours to go.

She had to buy new dresses and shoes and costume jewelry to fit in with those top-of-the-line fashions. She loved what Jerry called "the ambience" of that block on Gay Street. Even getting off the streetcar where she normally didn't, right in front of the ritzy Tennessee Theatre, and passing the high-toned Farragut Hotel, named to honor the Admiral, who they say was born only a few miles west of Knoxville, she knew Phil played pool down on the basement level, next to WBIR, where Jerry wrote commercials when he was only in the eleventh grade.

Then Mayme McCampbell's Dress Shoppe. Sashaying out of it at noon, still feeling the aura of it, she strolled down to the S&W Cafeteria, the best in the South, and the tall, debonair black waiter insisted on carrying her tray to the table, even when Jerry joined her.

Jerry following her, and the two of them passing close by the tall, glamorous, black-haired lady playing the piano on the wide first landing of the staircase, looking up to smile at mother and son, following that tall black man carrying their trays up the winding staircase to the mezzanine, setting their trays down by the railing because Jerry liked looking down to see the people coming out of the revolving door to get in line, and the people eating, the ones they knew waving up at them.

Clark and Jones music store next door, where Jerry haunted the music booths, playing Chopin records. And then the Riviera Theatre where she and Jerry first saw *Gone with the Wind*. Walgreens, convenient for getting her prescriptions, then everything else as accessible as reaching across the dining room table. And very little of it too expensive for her "pitiful salary," as Mother called it.

Oh, and on the third floor above Mayme McCampbell's, some famous country music singers got started on WROL. Sometimes the music drained down into the Shoppe. She didn't really care for tacky country music, Roy Acuff, Kitty Wells, Lester Flatt and Earl Scruggs, Bill Monroe and his bluegrass outfit. So the manager lady wouldn't assume she was out of that world, she told her, "I'm from Cleveland myself."

LOOKING AT THE OLD PHOTOS

John off somewhere on one of his car trips, she thought getting out the big oval hatbox full of family pictures might maybe take her mind off being so lonesome. To avoid mingling them, she kept her own in two small Whitman's Sampler candy boxes. After Mother died, she mingled her stash of snapshots in with her own.

Striking poses time and time again for a snapshot, always with at least one other person, sometimes for a portrait in a studio, as a teenager in Cleveland, or as a thirty-two years-old mother posing between John, six, and Jerry, nine.

She loved pulling little Chuck on a sled in the snow when her life was in Cleveland. Daddy took photographs of her doing that. One of Mother doing that, too. And one or two of her and Mother standing stiffly together in the snow. When Mother took photographs of anybody, their heads were cut off sometimes. But Daddy knew what he was doing.

Daddy's in too few candid photos—in his new car, in groups at picnics, lying on the beach at Lake Erie, because it was mostly *his* eyes upon us, then CLICK.

She liked being known as an excellent swimmer, in the lake and the neighborhood swimming pool. In photographs with her friends, she smiled more than anyone else and struck a pose more often. Nicknames "Shorty" and "Dimples" under photos in the yearbooks.

Chuck was plump but sort of pretty in the photographs Daddy took, sometimes wearing a pilot helmet and goggles, one time holding a big cardboard box halfway over his head.

Back in Knoxville, Daddy loved homemade ice cream and made everybody crank it until it got hard as a brick. Then he took a chunk of hot cornbread and a dishful of the ice cream off to the wicker chair under the oak tree and beat it until it got smooth, Maraschino cherry his favorite. Why the hell didn't somebody take a snapshot of him holding his cornbread and his bowl of drippy ice cream?

Posing with Mother, she always felt they didn't look like daughter and mother having their picture taken together. The snapshots never showed them touching. She usually smiled, but not her best smile, and if Mother was smiling, her lips had barely moved, and almost never did her teeth show.

Every time she got out the pictures when she was alone in the house, she tried to find one of herself with Mother, showing Mother smiling. She knew she wouldn't. Posing with Cap or other people, Mother was relaxed, smiling, or standing alone, like that one in the backyard, wearing her flowery housecoat and nightgown, holding up a two-layer white coconut cake, beside the big ol' outdoor rocking chair. What a smile! Jerry's favorite.

Even back in Cleveland at all ages, Mother looked unwilling, or severe. "Get in the picture with your daughter, Jessie," Daddy insisted.

But she loved the pictures in the snow, especially the one with Mother holding the steering guide rope to Chuck's sled, Chuck perched on it, but not smiling.

Some of her own copies of the ones in Cleveland were singed brown from the fire Jimmy accidently started, hiding out smoking in the circus wagon Daddy pulled home from a sale and turned into a storage and coal house down at the alley. That time she got so mad at him he was ducking dishes. Poor fellow, so mild-mannered, and the look on his face showed he never understood what he'd done to deserve her flare-ups.

And a lot of the snapshots were ones that Cap or Jerry took of mother and daughter standing in front of the big flowery bushes Mother was so proud of. Now, Mother gone, Emily was in many pictures alone in front of the rhododendron and the lilac bushes.

Mother often said that her family "never had any trouble with the law until *your* children come along."

"Moth-urrrr. I can't help it."

"Well, you could have done a better job raisin' 'em. Dickie in that military prison in Germany and John in the reform school."

"And Jerry's play going to be performed at the university, and him only sixteen. And it won a statewide contest against adults. Did your kids, including your daughter, do any better than that?"

"Now, don't you breathe a word against Chuck."

"Don't cry, Mother. Seems like I never think of him dead. And I agree with you he may show up any day. *Missing* in action means only missing."

"Well, didn't I say I was going with you to see Jerry's play? He told it to me first, one Sunday while I was making a pie with apples from my tree, before you got here. I wouldn't miss it for the world. And you know I love Dickie and John to death."

With all the time and worry she spent on John and Dickie, trying to get them out of prison, she thanked God Jerry stayed out of trouble, except for getting suspended for writing stories in class and sassing his teachers.

She could tell what Jerry and Iva Lee were up to, and she hoped nothing could come of it that would ruin their lives forever. Mother always said Dickie was illegitimate, but if he was, she vowed it was not poor ol' Jimmy's fault.

"Mother, you just say that to hurt me."

RECEPTIONIST AT ALEXIAN
BROTHERS HOME CARE

She liked living and working in Chattanooga, not too far by bus from being able to visit Mother and Cap and Phil. But she didn't like the job at the cigar counter in the hotel, nor the room in that shambly house on a hill nearby. So when a regular Catholic customer told her about the opening as receptionist at the Alexian Brothers home for elderly folks, high, high above Chattanooga up on Signal Mountain, she took the bus up there in blue-sky sunny June and confidently walked into the lobby of the historic Signal Mountain Hotel that had become the Alexian Home.

The very kindly Alexian priest told her about the home and its mission. "We are a not-for-profit ministry. The Alexian Brothers follow the Augustinian rule. We are a worldwide Catholic order, Cellites, because we used to live in cells, and we have an eight-hundred-year history of humanitarian service, including the time of the Black Death. We first opened our doors to elderly men who sorely needed recuperation from war, illness, or simply a place to live. The number of residents and our services have grown to include elderly women and married couples."

She was breathlessly impressed, but she hastened to confess that she was not a Catholic, not even much of a Methodist, not much of a Bible reader either.

"Nor are all the old folks living here." The priest also assured her that being Catholic was not a requirement for the position of receptionist. She had never applied for, gotten, nor started work for any of the many kinds of places that made her feel as much eager anticipation and deep pride as this one.

She loved striding about the spacious lobby among the residents. As a very good cook, she knew that what she put in her mouth three times a day was excellent food but that hers and Mother's cooking was just a cut above.

In her clean, sunny room, nothing like a cell, she happily wrote twenty letters over the first week to family and friends, telling them that the home and the residents and the brothers were all out of this world.

John was the first to show his face, and she showed him the incredible view of the Tennessee River Valley and Chattanooga. "Hey, look, John, over yonder is Lookout Mountain, so high you can see three states."

John looked impressive in his air patrol uniform, saluting in the photographs she took of him on the ledge overlooking the view of the mountain ranges.

And Jerry came, happy to spend a few hours in a huge used bookstore on the winding road up. "I'm glad you have such a nice place to work and live on such a beautiful mountain. Is that Missionary Ridge on the other side of the city that was in the Civil War?"

And some of her girlfriends and a few loving men friends came to see her, Dickie still languishing in prison.

When she sat down in the cramped living room on Henegar Street, she said, "Mother, it feels like I died and woke up in Heaven."

"Well . . ."

TALKING TO MOTHER, AS IF . . .

Mother, Cap, Phil, Betty all gone, and most of her old friends dead, and Dickie and Gloria living way cross town in the projects with that broken-down car, my own grandchildren Greg and Cheryl Ann coming around hardly ever, Cheryl Ann less often than Greg, John living with her was all the company she had, but fitfully because he delivered for Bellew's Drugs out of the Broadway Shopping Center or the other Bellew's way the hell out on Asheville Highway, and when he *was* home he kept that dad-blamed TV full blast or, in summer, the air conditioner Jerry bought Mother years ago full blast, till she thought she might freeze to death or come down with a chest cold, and John's secondhand cigarette smoke never let up from over there on the edge of the sunken couch where he slept.

I just hope that clinical psychologist can talk John out of his constant anxiety and depression that came over him after that young girlfriend of one of his Sunshine Boys was found dead alongside the river.

But what a cook he turned out to be. Roasts and cakes, and you name it.

Yes, he took her to Kroger's and rambled around, aimlessly, smoking, impatient for her to quit chasing down those "damn bargains," he said, that she cut out of the Thursday *Knoxville News-Sentinel*.

When he wasn't working, he went out in that undependable Oldsmobile, collecting clothes from businesses and people here and there for the Eastern Kentucky flood victims and doing good deeds for kids as founder of the Sunshine Boys.

The kids. Tall, skinny, age uncertain, and took them into the back room that used to be Phil's and Betty's bedroom, and she could hear them rattling around in there on that narrow twin bed that used to be her own, where Phil and Cap breathed their last. Ask him where he was off to and he'd give a hateful answer, as if she were nagging him. She heard him in her bedroom on the phone to Jerry complaining that she was driving him crazy, and why didn't he take her to live in his mansion in Baton Rouge. John knew very well that there was no room downstairs and that she could never take those stairs, up and down, when she needed to.

But now Jerry's about to pull up and come in and take John to the car rental to sign for a fancy new car for John to take himself a jaunt. That grin on John's face when he showed it to her that time before, cruising by the house, and sailed away over the line into Kentucky to gamble.

Then Jerry was taking her to eat at Louie's, then off on one of their rides together, to House Mountain, or the Smokies, this time though, he said, to Harrogate to see the Abraham Lincoln Museum at Lincoln Memorial University and maybe over to Lafollette where Granny Merritt and Daddy were born. One time all the way to Asheville to see the Biltmore Mansion, pushing her around in a wheelchair because her feet hurt so bad and she tired out too easily walking. She knew she talked a blue streak on those trips, after days and nights of John not saying word one. Jerry talked to her, son to mother, the way he did those years they lived together, while John and Dickie were in the service or prison.

SENDING JERRY NEWS CLIPPINGS
ABOUT KNOXVILLE

She always read the *Knoxville News-Sentinel*, which Jerry used to carry on four or five different routes all over town, starting when he was only nine, as they moved from one neighborhood to another, even up along Sharp's Ridge, too. Or the *Journal*, that comes in the morning, and sometimes both, for the news, but also for the Help Wanted ads or the For Rent ads.

Up in bed usually, she cut the stories out of pages she had put by, sometimes lost, frantically hunted down, and enclosed them in her letters to Jerry because of his ongoing interest in what all was going on in the town she hated.

Human interest stories, but mainly history of Knoxville stories, or about Dave Van Vactor's activities as symphony conductor, or John Cullum that he used to act with at UT and who became a Broadway actor and singer and movie actor, too, and catastrophes such as the ferry crash on the Mississippi, great floods or snowstorms, falling bridges, or items about Hemingway or Thomas Wolfe or Knoxville's own James Agee, or something about UT.

Or news items about John running for mayor or sounding off at City Council meetings about issues and the solutions he proposed with great vigorousness. And, boy, do the five o'clock news cameras seem to love him.

To this one about Loretta Lynn in Nashville, Sunday, December 7, of all dates, 1980, headlined "Nostalgic Brush with the Past," she added her own subhead, "Rags to Riches," something she had dreamed for herself up in Cleveland. Something Jerry might reach himself, having made it big a few years back selling *Cassandra Singing* to the movies, and writing the script adaptation, the last writer-in-residence on the Warner Brothers lot, he said, but that wasn't made. And then *The Suicide's Wife*, a CBS Movie of the Week, starring Angie Dickinson. So she gave him a brush with her own past by drawing over the painting of the little log cabin where Loretta was born to make it into the three-room, slab-board cottage that Granny Merritt bought a few years before she died of cancer of the rectum across the living room from the spot where "you were born," by marking it with an x on the painting. "A window here," she wrote on the blank outside wall of Loretta's log cabin. Something about the overall effect of this story on her—including a photo of Loretta's two-story, six-column mansion, which evoked in her memory Jerry's similar mansion-like house on Park Boulevard in Baton Rouge—raked up memories of Merritt family history that she wanted to share with Jerry.

"This is very much like Granny Merritt's house on Henegar. Mammy added on to it, little by little." You had to step out of the bedroom or the kitchen door onto a fruit crate, no steps, if you wanted to go out into the backyard when we all ate on that big table outside under the old oak tree, or down to the alley to the outhouse to empty the slop jar, or do it right there in warm weather, or to pick corn or whatever from the garden.

"Had only split wooden shingles for a roof and no running water or electricity. Carried water from the big house next door. Finally had a water spigot in *our* yard.

"Your Daddy and I smooched many times on that tiny front porch. No mimosa trees back then—there was a great big oak tree in front of the big house next door—dead end of Henegar. Granny tied her hen to that old tree, baby chicks all around."

And a long letter to go with the article.

One of these days I'll sit Jerry down and tell him the mysterious story of Granny's life—Matilda Merritt from Lafollette and why she had to run off or was paid to get gone and came down to Knoxville, pregnant with Daddy.

MOTHER'S FUNERAL

As Emily stood beside Mother's casket, family members, some very distant, and friends, spoke kindly to her, as if they knew she was fragile. She enjoyed their attention. In her life, one of the constants was this broken parade of mourners. So many sick bedside events, so many funeral parlors, so many graveside tears. Her father, her own baby boy, her grandmother Merritt, her grandmother Willis, Chuck, from a kiss goodbye in the kitchen to the empty grave, her many friends, then Phil, then Cap. Now Mother. Mother. And her own many sick beds. And watching others go through the same sequences of experiences. That made her more aware of the great variety of other kinds of experiences in series. Lovers coming and going. Friends made and lost. Jobs and bosses. Landlords. Insurance collectors showing up each month. Streetcar and bus drivers she had come to know, two or three attractive, but married.

Jerry was here a week ago. Dickie was here yesterday, but a fugitive. And God knows where John is.

CAP LYING ALWAYS ON THE BED

IN THE BACK ROOM

She spoon-fed Cap as he lay on his side in the same narrow bed where Phil had died after Betty left him and went back to Kingston, the bed Phil and Betty have slept in for years before they moved out and into that very nice apartment on Thompson Place with her daughter Phil loved as his own, originally Emily's own bed in that apartment when she lived alone on Laurel next to the Children's Hospital. Her arm lately ached from stretching over from the straight chair to feed Cap, day after day, after Mother said she couldn't stand seeing him lying there like that, never getting up as he did only for a while now and then, when Greg came over or Jerry came to Knoxville.

Oh, that awful time Jerry drove him up town to the new fire station because he had become legally blind and was no longer allowed to drive himself and the Captain told him he had to stop visiting so often, reminding him that he had been Captain for only the one day he sat in for the real Captain, and that the men were tired of listening to his stories about old-time firefighting, and firemen he knew, all gone now, dead and buried, and the old main station on Commerce Avenue and State Street, torn down now. Went to bed on that narrow bed in the back room and very seldom got up.

Then one day when he did crawl out of bed and appear suddenly in the living room and told Greg to get out of his chair because he didn't want Jerry to see him lying abed that way, his back to everybody, and Jerry asked him to tell again some of his old firefighting stories and Greg had to pipe up with, "Oh, Pappy, you've told that old story a hundred times." So that was Cap's last time in his chair in the living room.

Now she had to change him and make his bed out of her long-ago experience as a practical nurse. Not so heavy now that he had lost so much weight from refusing to eat much else than soup.

Mother was a practical nurse in the old general hospital as long ago as when Jerry and John had gotten their tonsils out on the same day, Jerry in one bed and John in the other and her sitting between them. Tonsilitis. Jack from Breezy's had wrapped Jerry and John in blankets to take them there.

"I'm just not able, Emily. You're just going to have to help." That was after Mother got so frustrated with Cap's contrariness that she slapped him across the face with a wet dishrag. "You're not all *that* sick."

And his kids and grandkids didn't come by near as often, who came far, far too seldom anyway, to see a man who had visited his own ailing father every Sunday without fail until the old fellow passed. Cap. A lovable old fellow himself, who walked into Jane's Café the day Mother opened it, buying it with Daddy's life insurance money, walked into that narrow little café dripping wet just off a call to a fire, big burly fellow, and sat down at the counter, and it was love at first sight. Now look at him.

"Don't you want to take one more taste of Mother's hot vegetable beef soup, Cap?"

"No, Emmie, just let me go back to sleep, honey."

DICKIE BRINGS NUTTY GLORIA
INTO THE FAMILY

A few years back when Emily was staying with Mother and Cap, and Phil was finally living with Betty in a house of their own, Dickie and Gloria showed up at good ol' 2722 Henegar in the dead of night. Gloria was, she claimed, "a nurse by profession." Doubtful, but could be. Look at how she hung on Dickie, took care of his every need.

All the beds were full, so Dickie hit the couch, and Gloria ended up on the inside edge of Mother's queen-sized bed, Emily next to her, and Mother next to Emily. When she crawled in bed beside her, Gloria was naked as a jaybird. Always slept that way, she says. Emily wanted to wring her neck. Gloria was the stinkingest human creature she ever came in contact with. She kicked her out of bed, and the next morning Mother ordered her to take a shower and, when she refused, took a broom to her, chasing her from room to room and into the bathroom, and locked her in by jobbing a kitchen chair up under the doorknob. "And wash that hair." Gloria came out of there so meek and mild, but then she sneaked and doused too much of Mammy's favorite perfume on herself. Even Dickie'd shied away from her, and him needing the shower just as bad.

But when all was said and done, yes, she did take good care of Dickie for a good number of years, all those years in Florida in that run-down motel turned housing for drifters and the homeless and such, and that mother and father of hers living in the next room, and then along came Melissa, and when she was seven, sexual abuse, Dickie's drinking buddy, according to charges that didn't stick, because Melissa had learning disabilities and her word was only half-believed, but Family Services took her away anyhow, then released her later on to Gloria and Dickie, and then took her again not long after.

And Dickie going to jail for knifing her violent father in self-defense. After Gloria's daddy died about a year later, of pure meanness most likely, they had decided to make a move to Knoxville, where the weather difference from Florida must have been a shock. Melissa came up with Gloria and Dickie to Knoxville, and they stayed off and on in a place for folks more or less on the road, in and out, in the beautiful mansion that used to house Mann Funeral Home.

And then Melissa, only fifteen, up and married an older young man who took her out of there, but he turned out to be an addict himself, and maybe a dealer, and knocked up that child bride of fifteen quick as a wink, and he ended up in jail, leaving her with two kids, and they were taken from her, and she has never seen them again. She gets disability as her half-brother James by Dickie's third wife Mary does.

Greg drove Emily up to Fountain City to see Dickie and Gloria since Dickie didn't have a car. Seeing the squalor they lived in, Gloria's mother in there with them, in a ratty apartment complex, drugs all over and violence all the time, and babies squalling through the walls all around them, nearly broke her heart, and poor Greg seeing his own daddy in such a fix.

But that was better than where they *had* been, though Dickie and Gloria seldom see Melissa, who runs the streets with all those homeless.

"Dickie, you need to try again and harder to get into the low-income housing over in Lonsdale."

And after a year or two out in Fountain City in that awful apartment building, they are dug in over in Lonsdale in the projects. Dickie sees his third wife Mary who bore James in those mere two years after he and Naomi divorced and before Gloria came along. Glory be. Gloria. As Mother said about Elvis, "She's by herself," that is, there is none like her. Emily, and Jerry and Robbie, try to do for her, soaps and perfumes on her birthday and at Christmas, but God alone knows what she does with them. Thank God for Robbie—none like her, either.

She dreaded what she knew Dickie would get into next, asking her could they move in with her now that Mammy was gone. She fended him off with lame excuses and lies and it hurt her to do so.

For one thing, John might get enough of Los Angeles and come to good ol' 2722 Henegar, and he swore never to forgive Dickie for luring him into that bogus check con that almost got him on the Georgia chain gang and did get him put right back in federal prison in El Reno, Oklahoma, in a cell next to the assassin of Martin Luther King.

Seeing his father living that way made Greg drive her home silently sad.

"Well, Greg, that's just life with the Maddens. Don't ever forget this awfulness, Greg, you found your poor daddy in. Your grandmother's not from here. I'm from Cleveland."

VISITING JERRY IN ALL HIS HOUSES

She forgot to include a clipping about that house Jerry showed her on one of their rambling car rides. Governor Robert Love Taylor's house, "Governor's Mansion," they called it, built in 1899, only thirty-four years before Jerry was born. Fourth and Gill. Ginny lived upstairs while she and Cliff were separated, and Jerry said she lent him her key so he and Iva Lee could meet in secret.

Cliff was a dapper little fellow who sold shoes in Miller's. Feet in his hands most of his life, women his preference, and they always asked for Cliff. But imagine Jerry and Iva Lee making love in Ginny's bed in a house where a famous governor once lived? Jerry will like being reminded of the governor part. Or maybe he never knew it.

I can't believe Jimmy let Jerry and Iva Lee use his room in that trashy rooming house on the corner of Henley and Hill. Not always trashy. Very ritzy lady used to live there, but after she died it went down.

Jerry said they knocked one time and a woman's voice answered, "Jimmy's gone out to get me a Schlitz."

The women at the factory were saying "Ever' body loves sweet ol' Jimmy" even years ago when she and Mother worked at Breezy's factory when it was still uptown on Gay Street.

She loved Iva Lee, but she wasn't right for Jerry. Now, Robbie is just perfect for him. She loved her to death, told her that when Jerry talked hateful to tell him, "If you don't like my peaches, don't shake my tree." She probably never did, she's so quiet and sweet. But smart as a whip. Who would ever think of her going into politics, running for state senate and nearly won? I hardly ever even vote. Nothing to brag about. I should. I just don't, except for that handsome devil President Kennedy.

She finally got to see Jerry's mansion on Park Boulevard in the heart of Baton Rouge in Louisiana. Jerry born in a three-room shack now had a study in a two-story, twelve-room house, with columns between the living room and the dining room, for God's sake. Bought with Warner Brothers movie money.

Well, she had pictures of an even more magnificent house in Gambier when Jerry taught creative writing at Kenyon College and was an editor at the *Kenyon Review*. Once the palace of the Episcopal bishop of Ohio that Jerry told her that the bishop's mistress haunted. Four stories, built of stone. But bats, they had bats. No, thank you. She never got to visit.

Mother and Emile.

She first visited Jerry and Robbie when they lived in that basement apartment in Knoxville their first year of their marriage, and next when they were living one summer in the Van Vactors' mansion of a house where she had witnessed their marriage ceremony.

She couldn't remember whether she visited them when Jerry taught at Centre College in Danville, Kentucky, on Green Street or Caldwell Road, whichever.

But she remembered her visit to the first house they ever owned, up in the hills just outside Athens, Ohio, that farmhouse, when Jerry taught creative writing at Ohio University and Robbie finally took the courses she still needed to graduate. A good long stay.

Oh, and the farmhouse way high on a hill on Covered Bridge Road outside Louisville, Kentucky, when Jerry taught at the University of Louisville.

Jerry took movies of little Blake and me on a sled, zooming down a steep hill.

So funny when I tried to pull Blake away from a fountain in the mall and he told the police, "She's not my grandmother."

As Jerry was driving me to Corbin to catch a bus back to Knoxville, I just had to be bossy and ask him if he turned off the water hose he used to fill up the cistern, which if not would overflow. He raised hell at me all the way back—fifty miles—because he wasn't absolutely sure, and because the landlord made him promise to do it and would yell at him if he used up that much water.

All those awful houses and apartments I dragged my children through as they grew up in Knoxville. Jerry and Robbie, too, moving often, but such interesting houses, such interesting lives.

Oh, and don't forget visiting the farmhouse on Hot Holler Road high up through three gates on a steep hill in Deep Gap, outside Boone, North Carolina, where Jerry had his first teaching job—Appalachian State Teachers College—and in the summers he was a radio announcer and an actor in that outdoor drama *Horn in the West*, with Robbie having to wrap meat at Winn-Dixie to make ends meet.

And Blake came along when Jerry quit teaching there to go to Yale Drama School.

What a life. Of course, I've traveled and lived all over creation myself. And John. And Dickie. The call of the wild goose.

POSING IN HER NEW
GIRL SCOUT UNIFORM

Alone in her second-floor bedroom in the Cleveland house, she enjoyed the flouncing motion of her brand-new dress when she first put it on, then when she rose from her desk and began to walk out of the classroom, and when she took it off.

Sometimes she was almost half undressed before she realized she was going to get a good look at herself almost naked, front and back, every which way, also using her hand mirror. She didn't mind thinking of herself as vain. She *was* vain. But she was pretty for real.

Pretty in a different way the time she put on her Girl Scout uniform for the first time, standing in front of the oval mirror above the dresser to admire how she looked in it. She liked the official stiffness of it compared with her regular dresses, knowing that the uniform made her a member of a group larger than her girlfriends, that she belonged with all the Girl Scouts in Cleveland, well, also in the whole Great Lakes and beyond. The whole world, they told her. She had already a keen sense of belonging. Among her many girlfriends, she was popular. Not a leader, but a satisfied belonger. She luxuriated in the feel of the contrast between her flowing, flouncing dress and the formal stiffness and smell of the new Scout uniform. Saluting in it felt good, but she was a flouncer at heart.

On her eighth birthday, the end of the World War seemed to be one sign that she had a brighter future. Only four when it began, she followed little of the war, but the tone of their voices when Mother and Daddy talked about it almost daily impressed her. And she liked sitting with Mother as she saved pages of the Cleveland *Plain Dealer* and of magazines, photographs and paintings, putting them in a special big department store dress box to preserve them for the future.

Photographs of the generals and of President Wilson, "our president," Mother called him, comforted her when fear that the Kaiser might show up in Cleveland made her tremble.

She heard talk of Germans living all over Cleveland, as if some of them might spring up in the dark of night and machine gun everybody on her street. If any of them tried to do that, she would shield little Chuck and baby Phil.

Mother and Daddy and others didn't call her feisty for nothing. The posters around town showing our brave soldiers killing the barbarian Germans made her shivery with patriotism.

The war spoiled a lot of things in her life, from the time before she went to school and on to the third grade. Sometimes, she mimicked the complaints of the grown-ups. Sometimes she said what Daddy often said: "It's a damned shame."

Then grown-ups all said, "Well, thank goodness it's all over now, and everybody can get on with their lives."

Soldiers coming home, showing up on the streets, was a good sign a bright future was just around the corner.

And President Wilson smiled more often. Daddy praised him.

Mother said, "Even if he is from Virginia." To her, anything worth anything came out of East Tennessee, Knoxville to be precise, more so the Burlington area where her daddy owned a good deal of land, the best part of it. "I just can't feel at home up here in this ol' bone-chilling wind."

What little she remembered about Knoxville, Emily would just as soon forget. And now she could celebrate her ninth birthday and forget that ol' World War, too.

WITH JERRY AT CRIPPLED CHILDREN'S HOSPITAL

She stormed out of Mayme McCampbell's Dress Shoppe. Although she didn't blame the manager for reproaching her for taking time off, she was already fuming over being told on the phone that she must be present when Dr. Inge examined Jerry's feet, diagnosed his problem, and informed her of the treatments Jerry must take at home.

In front of Cole's Drugstore, she caught the Highland Avenue streetcar. She got to what was an old schoolhouse that was used now as the Crippled Children's Hospital before Jerry got there from Christenberry Junior High.

Sitting on a bench in the entranceway, she tried to control her temper before talking with Dr. Inge because Jerry'd told her that when he went alone that first time, the doctor was curt and sarcastic to all the children he examined.

When Jerry got there, they were late for the appointment.

"I'm Mrs. Madden." She put on her sweet, slightly aristocratic, public voice. "My son, Jerry, has an appointment to see Dr. Inge."

"Take a seat."

"Honey, I had to take off from work to come here, so I wonder, would it be possible to speak with the doctor now? I'm terribly upset. He said something about a touch of infantile paralysis, and I think from what Jerry tells me, he's just sprained his ankle from jumping over a barbed-wire fence. At Nathan's auto yard."

"You'll have to wait your turn."

She looked the people over. "Well, they don't seem to be working women. Maybe they have more time—"

"Mrs. Madden, I can't take the time to ask them whether they're working or not, but I do know that *I* have a great deal of work to do. The rule is—"

"Well, thank *you*, very much." She pronounced each syllable distinctly, with facial enhancements, and took with a flourish the form the nurse stiffly handed her.

She and Jerry sat on the bench along the wall. She stared straight ahead into next week, then commented on the bitchiness of the nurse, then expressed disgust for the trashy women sitting in the chairs, then great pity for the children walking in braces down the right wing to the examination room as their names were called out.

Half an hour later, the snooty nurse called Jerry David Madden, slushing his names together.

At the end of the right wing of the building, a pleasant young nurse told Jerry to step into a little booth, take off everything except his "under garments," and sit on the table.

"Thank you, honey."

The examination room was a schoolroom. She and Jerry sat at the kind of desks she'd had in elementary school, with the inkwell and the groove for a pencil on the hinged-lid desktop that made her feel nostalgic for Cleveland.

Finally, *finally*, Dr. Inge came in, behind him the nice nurse and a tall, handsome blond woman of about thirty-five, who spoke in a German accent.

Dr. Inge stood over them, reproaching them for being late. She fumed as she told him she had to take time off work and lose pay to come and asked if there was a reason why he couldn't just tell Jerry and then let Jerry tell her what was what.

He accused her of taking no interest in her son's serious affliction. Sensing that her put-on hoity-toity voice provoked his sarcasm, she shut it off. Then he loosened up. A mock-severe frown, a full, black mustache, a deep, rich voice. She wondered whether Dr. Inge knew he was the very spitting image of Groucho Marx. But his joking manner was so ambiguous she was afraid that if she tried to link up to it—when she understood the wisecracks—her timing might be off, and the man might get curt instead of cute.

The tall woman stood at the doctor's side, staring straight down at Jerry's feet as the doctor handled them, telling her what he thought was wrong, but that he wouldn't know for sure until he saw X-rays.

"See to it that he washes his feet before coming in next Wednesday."

"Oh, I'm very sorry, doctor." She spoke with sarcastic sweetness. "Will you need *me* next time?"

"If you're interested in knowing what your son's trouble is."

"He *says* he sprained his ankle getting away from a man who was chasing him, and he jumped off the barbed-wire fence at Nathan's Auto Salvage Yard."

"What were you doing in Nathan's Auto Salvage Yard, young man?"

"Just fiddling around among the wrecked cars."

"A treacherous place, I can well imagine."

"Did you ever mess around in there when you were little?"

"No. I've always favored golf. And you'd better be glad you sprained your ankle, because otherwise we might not have found out whatever it is we're going to find out, until too late. Or will we?"

She spoke carefully. "Could I just talk with you on the telephone about it next Wednesday?"

"Madam, I give my time free to this clinic each Wednesday, which costs me money, frankly, and I do not, therefore, hesitate to ask the parents of children on charity to be present when their child is being examined."

She withdrew into a mock-obedient posture.

Dr. Inge told them that every morning Jerry must sit in a cold bathtub and run cold water over his bare feet and legs and that he must come to the hospital to take whirlpool baths once a week and that he must wear leather metatarsal bars attached to the bottoms of his shoes, and that he must wear steel braces. She fought back tears, so as not to give him the satisfaction.

The tall, blond lady doctor followed Dr. Inge out, but the nice nurse stayed behind to tell her where to take Jerry to get his feet X-rayed. They went out the back and crossed the alley into the basement of Fort Sanders Hospital.

Jerry seemed afraid of the X-ray layout, but when it didn't hurt, he acted as tough as Humphrey Bogart.

"But I *still* don't know whether I have 'a touch of infantile paralysis.'"

She and Jerry rode the streetcar to uptown and got off in front of the old Lyric Theatre. She went back to work at Louie's and watched Jerry cross the street to go on duty at the Bijou.

On Monday, she also had to take time off again first thing in the morning to meet with the principal of Christenberry Junior High because Jerry sassed the mustached woman who taught civics because she failed to abide by "the provision in the United States Constitution that protects free speech," as Jerry put it.

After many examinations and wearing the metatarsal bars and braces for a little over a year, Jerry finally had to have an operation on both feet to correct the tendency toward claw-foot deformity.

She and Mother and Cap stood by the bed, and in loped Jimmy, maybe drunk and maybe not, hard to tell sometimes, just as a nurse gave Jerry a shot and they wheeled him away.

Everybody told her not to worry, but Dr. Inge had told her he was going to make three incisions on both feet to transplant bones and fuse the joints in both big toes.

Mother and Cap left her alone and she and Jimmy sat silently, waiting.

Two hours later, Jerry woke up and said that he hated the ether and a red devil had chased him down a tunnel but that it didn't hurt. Then the ether wore off and he hurt bad. Jimmy had to get out of there—to get a drink, she suspected.

So she was alone with Jerry until they moved him into a charity ward with six grown-ups, and Mother and Cap came back in and they all stood around the bed until the nurse yelled, "Lights out."

TAKING THE BOYS TO CHILHOWEE PARK

As she was putting on a dress that would look good at Chilhowee Park, the boys were yelling and running and fighting and crying so fast and furious, and she was feeling still the effect of hearing from sweet Madabee that she saw Jimmy with that prissy bitch Mary and her damned kid, having the best old time at the baseball game in Caswell Ball Park, and she was still mad at Mother for taking Jimmy's side when she called and told her, and the fuss they got into wore her out, and she didn't know where the rent money was going to come from, and her boss begging her to let him feel her breasts, she screamed at the boys to stop it or they were going to stay home and miss the fireworks.

"One of these days I'm just going to jump off the Gay Street Bridge."

The effect on them when she said that was so shocking—the look of those open mouths and bug eyes, except that Dickie tried to shrug it off—she hoped she could remember to use it on them again some time. Probably more than once.

When everybody was dressed just right, she yelled, "Let's go, young-uns." The way Daddy did in Cleveland, referring to everybody as "young-uns." And off they went, as if it were a procession, almost as if Daddy was the one leading it.

Holding John's play-grimy, sweaty hand and Jerry's freshly washed hand, Dickie following at his own strolling speed behind them carrying the picnic basket, sneaking a look, Emily walked down Cedar Street sloping toward the streetcar stop, the Methodist church squarely in the middle at the dead end, feeling the dread of the ordeal of the trip to Chilhowee Park that had kept her awake before dawn. John would squirm, whine, "When we gonna get there?" Jerry would sit by the window, looking dreamily at everything out there going by, and Dickie, that grin on his face that makes you wonder what kind of scheme he would be dreaming up for winning the various games. And Emily could not keep from worrying how to pay the light and water bills, what to do if the landlord kicked them out, and whether Bill Boles was lying when he vowed to leave his bed-ridden wife for her.

Then the transfer on Gay to the Magnolia Avenue streetcar, John saying over and over what rides he would do at the park, Jerry still soaking up the scene passing by, Dickie sniffing the picnic box, but the dread diminishing a little the thrilling anticipation of seeing the boys do what each liked to do best, Emily meeting in the crowd one friend or acquaintance after another, glad to see most, hoping to dodge the ones she'd rather forget, Jimmy walking with Mary, Jimmy maybe holding Mary's little boy's hand, the sinking feeling, the shame, the rage, poor John, Jerry, and Dickie seeing their daddy that way out in broad daylight for all Knoxville to see.

Jerry said he wished Daddy'd come with them to the park.

Emily was sorry she had screamed "I'd sooner jump off the Gay Street Bridge."

Dickie made no comment, not seeming to give a damn one way or another.

Stepping down off the Magnolia Avenue streetcar, she helped John down and, when he started to run ahead, pulled him back, Jerry and Dickie following. Emily held onto John, who tried harder and harder to break her grip as they came closer and closer to the merry-go-round music.

Oh, the Ferris wheel, yes, when Mother and Daddy brought her and Chuck when Chilhowee Park was new, and she was too afraid to ride it, and Chuck went straight to the pony ride, but the Ferris wheel was what she saw when she remembered the park. Had she maybe passed Jimmy in the crowd, not knowing she would part her legs for him, causing Dickie, Jerry, and John to walk here now?

Now up there sits John rocking the Ferris wheel seat and Jerry next to it in the swings whirling higher and higher like she had that time Jimmy sat in the next swing over, holding her hand as she screamed in a terror of delight. And Dickie, where is he now? No telling. Oh, over there at the dunk-the-clown game winding up for the pitch.

And then high noon, the heat hot enough to scorch, and time for the worst ordeal, the greatest dread of all, the picnic, under the band stand if they turned out lucky, and the whining and bickering and yelling and screaming over who gets what and how many, fried chicken, deviled eggs, ham sandwiches, sweet pickles, potato salad, and baked beans, just enough to go around on what she could scrape up after calculating the paying of the bills, holding back on the rent, and whether that promise-breaker Jimmy forks over what he promised, after splurging on Mary. The bandstand is full, not an inch to spare. So she took them over by the ducks.

Now where has Dickie wandered off to?

"Jerry, go track down your big brother. One of these days, you all will wake up and find I've jumped off the Gay Street Bridge."

Jimmy.

Mother showed up unexpectedly at the front door.

"Why, Mother, I—"

"I just took a notion to come visit you, honey."

As Mother walked into the house, they heard ambulance and police car sirens. "I hope it's nothing happened to your father."

"Oh, Momma, it's probably a fight in those slummy houses next to the lumber yard."

She and Jimmy had just moved into that house on Seventeenth Street where the floors slanted, a few blocks from where Daddy was a night watchman for Sterling Wood Works. Jimmy had just gone to work when Breezy still had that dry cleaning shop on Laurel nearby. Little Dickie and Jerry were fussing over toys in the kitchen. John was just "a dishrag in heaven," as Mother put it.

Somebody knocked on the door. Two cops asked Mother to go with them to the lumber yard.

"How did you know I was here?"

"We didn't. Sterling's manager had your daughter's new address in his files."

She went with Mother in the police car while the landlady from the apartment next door looked after Jerry and Dickie.

The police led her and Mother into a little house and into Daddy's office, so full of men she couldn't see anything but Daddy's legs stretched out from his swivel chair.

"Is this man your husband, Mrs. Merritt?"

When the men stood aside, she saw Daddy slumped sideways in his chair, his pistol on the floor between his feet, a hole in his head that had stopped bleeding. She screamed, unable to stop.

Mother told them, "Yes, that's my husband, Charles Franklin Merritt."

Emily turned away, saw Daddy's brown leather holster hanging by a strap on a hook on the wall by the door.

One of the officers took a step forward and leaned toward Daddy. "Looks like suicide, if you ask me."

She remembered that a photo flashed in her memory of Daddy sitting in that office swivel chair holding a macaroon cookie in one hand and a quart jar of milk in the other, his hat cocked back, his flowery necktie loosened, that misty-eyed faraway look in his eyes, sad-like, but loveable, his suit coat hanging on a hook behind him.

JERRY'S SEVERE BELLYACHE
AT BROADWAY THEATRE

They were still living on Atlantic just behind the house where they had lived on Cedar Street below Sharp's Ridge when Mrs. Culpepper, still owner of the Broadway Theatre, called to tell her that Jerry was in crying pain from a cramp in his belly.

Cap answered the phone at Mother's and said he would go get Jerry and bring him home. She thought of Baboo dying of locked bowels and Jerry the one who ran over to Mrs. Cabbage's and got her to call the doctor.

When the nice, tall young man who rented the other side of the house carried Jerry from the car into the house, he was screaming in pain.

She knew it was the first enema Jerry had ever had, and it did the job.

"I guess it was that pecan log. I shouldn't have eaten the whole thing."

"I'm damn sure you shouldn't have. Cap, open the windows for me, will you, pretty please?"

MRS. DANCE AND HER BALD BOY
BARON AND BABOO

Autumn, in the kitchen on Dempster Street, she was cooking meat loaf for dinner while Mrs. Dance watched, drinking coffee.

She liked neighbors coming in and sitting a while, not Mrs. Dance as much as some others. But the ones who knocked on the door or called out from the front porch through the screen door were only a few. The woman who came in the house when nobody was home and took her best dress had come to see her and drink coffee. Emily'd never taken to coffee, nor had Mrs. Cabbage, who was very nice, giving advice on being pregnant.

Jerry and Dickie came in out of the cold from playing ball with the pretty Crosby girl and the Jackson boy. She saw by his expression that Jerry didn't care for Mrs. Dance. Probably because he caught their strange-looking, bald-headed little boy Baron laughing at Baboo's funeral.

"I told him I was going to beat the fire out of him, but I just haven't caught him out yet."

Nobody wanted to play with Baron. She felt sorry for him, and she knew Jerry did, too, come right down to it. But Jerry loved Baboo so much, and he told her he promised to take care of him and help him become a rich and famous doctor when he grew up, or some such. He was always with him out on the porch in the sun, looking down into his baby buggy talking to him. Once, he ran John off because he was trying to feed him a banana, treat him like a little puppy, a toy. She wondered why Dickie didn't show much interest in Baboo.

Mrs. Dance said she better be getting on, and so she left by the front door and walked up the hill to her own house, a much nicer one than the Maddens'.

"What did that old biddy want?"

"She came in here wanting to be neighborly, but hinted around that she wished you kids would be more friendly with Baron."

"I'm friendly with him, by not beating the fire out of him."

"Well, he does look strange, and he is strange, I guess, running around bald-headed."

"That's what *I* say."

PHIL AT CHRISTENBERRY JUNIOR HIGH
AND BLOWING UP BRIDGES

Jerry gathered up his notebook and his textbooks.

"Living with Mammy makes it nice you don't have to walk but a block or two and into your homeroom."

"I remember one time watching Phil stand at the kitchen window looking down the hill to Christenberry for the doors to open to let students in, and he was in his underwear and Mammy was ironing his shirt and pants and he yelled, 'Hurry up, Mother, they opened the doors! I'm gonna be late!' And Mammy was ironing lickety-split, and when Phil stuck his leg in his pants he whimpered because the pants were too hot, and he went sort of dancing fast out of the house."

She imagined what Phil was doing now in the war. "And then only a few years later he was blowing up bridges in France."

WONDERING WHETHER JOHN IS "GAY"

She was thinking how damned awful, when John's gone off to play the lottery in Middlesboro, it is to have to depend on Jack and his clan across the street. Same as when Mother was living there alone. He'll do anything I ask him but they all smell so bad I can hardly stand it. Especially Trula, bless her heart. And now her little girl is big enough to come over and sit with me and do for me, little things. I don't want to imagine who her father might be. Jack's wife dying of cancer for years, just lying in bed. And Trula would look rather pretty if she would just fix herself up a little, even sloppy fat as she is. So that Jack . . . well, I don't even want to think about it. But Jack does have a big heart. He comes running if I tell Trula I need him. And his older brother is good about fixing things, too. Mows the yard front and back for less than that outfit John called in here.

John is not very handy doing anything but smoking and driving off in that jalopy all of a sudden. And those boys he has around him, brings in here, and they giggle in the back room where poor ol' Phil and Cap died. Why does that shade keep falling down?

She was more and more often alone, John being gone more often on one good deed, rescue mission, or another. He and the free physical therapist were always after her to work harder to get out of the bed more often, to shove the wheelchair aside, and walk by herself into the living room to sit in that special chair that tips forward, and you pull a lever and it springs backward with a jolt, which scared her at first, but which she had grown to like, even enjoy. One more reason to thank Jerry.

But more credit to John for living with her, taking care of her, as she used to look after Cap, instead of roaming all over the country in one old car after another as he used to. But John needed to get out, poor fellow, among his many friends out in Knoxville, his Sunshine Boys Club, including girls recently, one of the girls found murdered. But those boys he brings home . . .

"Well, it worries me," she told Jerry on one of his visits.

"You know, Momma, when I came home one time and there you were in a bed full of your women friends, I thought maybe you all were into something."

"Oh, Jerry. Your own mother?"

I just wish my girlfriends were still close by. Dead. Gone. Or too sick to visit.

Writing to Jerry always made her feel a little less lonely.

"Dear Jerry, John is so happy you're coming to see us on your way to Chicago. Me too, of course. I get so lonesome to see you. All I see is four walls and John coming or going out quick as he can, afraid I'm going to ask him to do something. I know I run him ragged some times. Being bedridden is not what it's cracked up to be, so to speak. It is pure hell.

"Thanks for the pretty pink Bible. Sabu peed on it one time, but the cover is leather so I could just wash it right off. I reckon making you kids go to Sunday school did some good to make you a Christian again after half a century. Not that it did Dickie any good, except in prison when he must've conned everybody into thinking he was saved. But Gloria does make him go with her to her church now and then, when they can bum a ride. John won't have anything to do with them. Gloria stinks. I can't get her to wash. Dickie's not much better. But he's ours, after all.

"Now, John, with all the good works he does all over creation, it must have sunk in, not that he goes to church, except the Episcopal, because of that priest that helped him get out of prison that time. But I don't suppose religion makes much difference or John wouldn't have turned out the way he did. Jerry, all those boys who come here and go with him in the back room worry me to death. They giggle and rattle around back there something awful.

"I am not doing much better, but I am not any worse. Just my knees. That young therapist said I could walk again if I would only do the exercises he showed me to make my legs stronger. I do try. Then I let it drop and don't get back to it. But I told myself, 'You can just forget about dancing, Emily Madden.' I'm always afraid that if I got again to where I could walk, I might fall and break a hip, and then, Buddy, it's kiss tomorrow goodbye. He embarrassed the fool out of me when he described the exercises I could do to strengthen the sphincter muscle to enable me to hold in number two longer. He's only twenty something."

And she feared not being able to get to the toilet quick enough. She had already reached the stage where she couldn't reach the bedpan in time sometimes. Poor John has to be the one to empty it, which was everybody's chore in the old slop jar years. Sometimes she had to call him out of bed to come help her.

"Well, I overheard what John told you on the phone last week. 'Jerry, she's gone geriatric.' Did he cry? I thought I heard him crying on the phone."

JERRY AND FRANCES DOING IT

"Jerry, you and Frances get up out of that bed this instant."

"We're just playing like we're married for when we *do* get married."

"Frances, you are a year and a half or more older than Jerry and ought to know better. Aren't you supposed to be Dickie's sweetheart?"

"Was. He's too rough."

"She's mine now. Besides, Dickie run off."

"Oh, to hell with it. Just jump into your clothes. And you go home, Frances. Must be supper time."

"Momma said we're out of everything."

"So are we, but why don't you stay and eat with us what little we can scrape together?"

"Oh, thank you, Mrs. Madden. Can Janice and Betty eat too?"

"Sure, and why not your momma and daddy and all their kin?"

"Don't forget Freddie."

"Didn't he run off with Dickie?"

"No, ma'am. He's afraid of those circus tigers."

TAKING JOHN TO THE HOME
FOR WAYWARD BOYS

She was glad John wanted to sit up front with Cap. She felt bad enough having to make the decision to take him back to the Kingswood Home for Wayward Boys at Tate Springs, without him sitting beside her, Mother on the other side.

He just would not go to school. Nothing could keep him from running around Knoxville with that six-foot-tall half-wit Edward Dunn. Jerry did all he could to track them down, even beat up Edward. No telling what Edward made John do, or maybe even John made Edward do, not just stealing and slipping into the Broadway Theatre either.

She remembered baby John Kenneth looked so cute and sweet in curls and a pink sunsuit, and daydreaming of keeping him in curls as long as possible. That wonderful portrait seemed to make it so. And crying when she thought she better cut them finally, before kids started teasing him or jumping on him.

Two vaguely familiar ladies in Woolworth's looked down at John.

"What a beautiful baby."

She smiled and stroked John's long, golden curls. Emily wished she could show off that wonderful Public Studio photograph of John's curls, taken only a week before.

"And I see you sometimes with another little boy."

"Oh, and she has yet another boy."

"I'd love to see them all three together, playing in a sandbox, and take a snapshot of them."

"The one I saw before didn't have no curls, but he was sweet and cute."

"Yes, Jerry. No, John is the only one in curls. But all three used to carry big, lifelike dolls, one of them mine from my childhood in Cleveland, and fight over them."

"Oh, you mean you aren't from around here?"

"No, my real home is up there in Cleveland on Lake Erie."

John turned his curled head upward, wondering what she meant by that.

He still had those lovely curls when they lived in that narrow, two-story house on Copeland. That's where, one dark, rainy afternoon, the kids played pretend baseball in the huge, bare, chilly living room, dimly lit, a forty-watt bulb hanging from the ceiling, too poor for a sixty watt. Rain's pouring down loud outside, and Dickie laughs when lightning scares Jerry and little John.

Dickie, at bat, waits for Jerry to pitch the imaginary ball, John, behind Dickie, catching. She's nervous that it is dangerous.

Jerry pitches, Dickie swings back—John screams bloody murder, clutches his head, rolls around on the floor, in a spreading puddle of blood that turns his yellow sunsuit red. Emily screams, rushes to John, Jerry crying, Dickie, laughing to keep from crying, as if not understanding, just standing there, the bat dangling at his side, runs out of the house, dragging the ball bat. Blood. Blood all over John, all over the floor, on her apron, and on Jerry's hands when they hugged John.

Twenty stitches. Before the stitches could be removed, they were walking to the streetcar stop—having visited her first friend after leaving Cleveland, Ruby Wayland, on Cornell Street, where they all once shared a house—when

John ran ahead and tripped on the tracks and hit his head and broke it open again. Now his right eye was bad. Sees some, but not what he should be able to see. Like Phil, that boy hitting him in the eye with a rock, causing his pupil to run out a little, but not enough to keep him out of the army.

No more boys for me. But Ronald Dennis was a boy, nicknamed Baboo by little John. Gone after only eleven weeks. First one buried in Babyland at Lynnhurst.

Up ahead she saw the three-story building that was once the summer vacation and healing spring for high society, coming down all the way from New York. John cried and said they didn't treat him right. Were mean to all the kids. Cap pulled the car up to the high steps to the wide porch. She got out of the car and opened the door and took John by the hand and they climbed the stairs. She gave him a fat bag full of Mars Bars, Tootsie Rolls, cherry and orange suckers, Cracker Jacks, and Superman, Batman, Bugs Bunny, and Donald Duck funny books. She hugged him three different times. Going down the steps, turning to wave goodbye again, she almost tripped. It'd serve her right.

JERRY APPEARS AS SHE IS TALKING TO IVA LEE

"Well, hello, honey. You look so lovely. But you always were. You were when I first saw you when Jerry proudly showed you off to me."

"How's Jerry doing? Is he happily married?"

"Yes, looks like. Three months now."

"Does he know I come by to see you?"

"No, you said not to tell him. I hope you'll keep coming. I enjoy talking with you, Iva Lee."

She felt a little guilty not telling Jerry, knowing full well that he was still in love with Iva Lee. The love of his life. Like Frankie was the love of her life when they were kids in Cleveland.

"I love what you've done with your hair, Emily."

"Well, let's just hope some handsome, rich fellow agrees with you."

"Well, I'll keep my eyes open for you."

She saw that Iva Lee noticed the change in the look on her face, and turned to see what she saw.

Jerry himself was opening the door to the jewelry shop, and held it open for Robbie.

His face, in his eyes, let her easily imagine how he must feel.

"Hello, Iva Lee."

"Hello, Jerry."

"Iva Lee, this is my wife, Robbie."

Robbie smiled, shy, awkward. "Hello, Iva Lee. Jerry's told me a lot about you."

"Glad to meet Jerry's wife." She stood stock-still but looked awkward. "I'm on my lunch break and need to get back to work. I keep the books for the Knox County Department of Education in our old Knoxville High School building. Bye, Emily. Bye, Jerry."

Iva Lee whirled out the door.

She knew Iva Lee would never return to the shop. She might not ever see her at all ever again.

MOTHER AND THAT PISTOL
AFTER CAP WAS GONE

The night after Cap's funeral, which Mother felt too sick to go to, Emily, Greg, Phyllis, and Jerry met at the house. They worried about her living there all alone, exposed to possible home invasion—Lincoln Park had become ridden with crime.

In the middle of all that talk, Mother stood up and, without a word, went into her bedroom, making everybody wonder, and came out with a pistol in her right hand, so heavy and long her body sagged on that side, her housecoat open, awry, her slip dangling. "I got this thing to keep me company. Don't nobody need to worry about me."

Far, far more worried that she would shoot her foot off, they all jumped up and rushed to her, and Greg took the pistol out of her hand, and Jerry turned her and held her hand as she sank into her floweredy easy chair by the door. "Children, I just don't know what I am going to do."

Greg and Phyllis promised to come by every night to check on her. Jerry had to fly back to Baton Rouge to teach his classes the next day.

A few weeks later, he returned when Dr. Swan put Mother in Baptist

Robbie and Jerry. Taken early in Blake's photography career, on Park Boulevard in Baton Rouge, Louisiana, circa 1974.

Hospital on the bluff in South Knoxville at the end of the Gay Street Bridge where her daddy used to run a buggy repair shop.

After they buried Mother next to Cap in Greenwood Cemetery a mile or so east of Lynnhurst and the graves of the rest of the family, Emily told Greg that he and Phyllis could live in good ol' 2722 Henegar a while, minimum rent. She just wasn't yet up to moving out of her cramped apartment on Radford, close by so she could look after Mother and Cap, and now in with all the ghosts, Daddy's, Granny's, Chuck's, Phil's, Cap's, especially Mother's.

She always knew she would miss Mother, even her flare-ups of hatefulness, and now she was gone. They had spent *some* harmonious moments over their lifetimes, from Cleveland, where Mother was sad, and through the after-years in Knoxville while living with Cap, when she often acted gay-hearted, especially in front of Jerry, Dickie, and John, and Greg and Cheryl Ann.

One time, in a fit of anger, she'd told Mother that she had never acted as if she loved her. Mother had taken to repeating to her, "To be loved, you have to be lovable."

She'd hung up on her again.

Mother sometimes gave her a hateful response to a simple suggestion.

"Mother, Kroger's has bacon for 20 percent off this week." Smiling, she sat on the sofa, waving a coupon. "Want me to get you some?"

"Why, no, I got more bacon than me and Cap can eat, and when Phil comes over."

"Would you like me to see if Kroger's has any fresh okra?"

"I got my own okra in my own garden, thank you."

"Anything else you need or want? I'm making my list up."

"No, you can just leave me off of it."

"Why are you being so contrary? All I did was to tell you Kroger's has bacon for 20 percent off this week and offered to get you some when I go, and I don't appreciate being snapped at for no reason."

"Well, if that's the way you feel, you can just pick up and get gone."

"I do not stay where I am not wanted."

"Nobody said you wasn't wanted, Emily. I just can't stand that sassing."

"Oh, Lordy Lord . . ."

"Don't you Lordy Lord me. I'm your mother."

"Don't I know it."

"There's the door. And don't you dare slam it behind you."

"Well, excuse me for living."

"You watch your mouth when you talk to me. I'm your mother, even if you are getting to be within a hair of sixty."

She'll probably tell on me to Jerry when he makes his weekly call to her after he calls me. Even Jerry says I seem to fly off the handle more than usual. It's my nerves. Greg says the reason he doesn't come by more often is because the least little thing makes me hateful. John says the same thing. Well, to hell with all of them. I'm here alone so much, they may just find me lying in this bed unresponsive one of these days.

She had dreaded the day when Mother would die. She decided she would call her to ask her if the apple tree had blossomed yet. They were both amazed that a tree shattered in two pieces by lightning would blossom and bear fruit year after year, one half standing straight as any tree, the other sprawled out on the ground, but as fruitful as the other half.

She put her dentures in the jelly glass and turned off the lamp and tried to sleep. Restless legs again, and her arthritis kicked in. She turned the light back on and reached for James Michener's *Hawaii*. She liked it, and it sure was better than counting sheep, which never worked anyway. She reached for the Russell Stover assorted chocolates box and shook it. Empty.

TALKING WITH IVA LEE ABOUT MARRYING JERRY

Iva Lee brought over all the clothes she was going to take with her on the bus to New York to join Jerry in the Red House, where Caruso the great opera singer once lived.

"I took a little at a time to Jenny's. Jerry sends all his letters there."

"So his letters are in the suitcase, too, then?"

"The last one just came. From Valparaíso, Chile, still on that ol' ship."

"Jenny has certainly been a wonderful friend to you all. Funny that she was once Jerry's girlfriend."

"Sometimes I'm still jealous, like when he still loved her when we were first going together."

"Honey, love is more than *I* will ever understand. At least Jerry doesn't drink much. All *my* sweethearts have been drunks, from Jerry's daddy to the one I can't shake loose now. Did you pack that beautiful blue satin dress yesterday that Jerry gave you for your fifteenth birthday?"

"I sure did. He's not seen me in it but once or twice. The day he gave it to me, he sneaked me into the Methodist church, the one on Henley that looks like a cathedral by the river bridge, and I changed into it in the restroom, then he took a picture of me on the steps wearing it and on the Henley Street Bridge."

"You do know, don't you, that he might not be with you very long before he ships out again."

"I know. But . . . Well . . ."

"And don't forget the draft might get him. Korea. At least there's a truce." She just loved Iva Lee to pieces, but she felt she had to warn her again, very sweetly. "Now, honey, don't you get me wrong, but I know how your mother can get, and him helping you across state lines is definitely a violation of the Mann Act, with me and Jenny aiding it all. Your mother . . ."

"I do worry. I sure don't want him to get arrested and go to prison over us getting married in New York."

"Just you all be very, very careful. Jenny's keeping her trap shut, too, I hope."

"I trust her."

"I'll never forget you and Jerry taking a blood test and going to Maryville to get married when you were only fifteen."

"We thought I was pregnant."

"I know. And that blamed Family Services woman told on you."

Iva Lee was already late going to work at Dietch's Department Store in Market Square.

After she was gone, Emily wrote to Jerry, and told him again he was taking a chance, and that she was an accessory. "Just think about it, honey."

Lordy, Lord, Lord.

DAIRY QUEEN AND LONG JOHN SILVER

Over the decades that she'd lived in the old homestead, Emily sent Jerry, John, Greg, and whoever else would go to Long John Silver for one of her very favorite dishes, the breaded shrimp, to go, with slaw, that she doctored up to

*Iva Lee and Jerry on the Gay Street Bridge,
Knoxville, Tennessee, circa 1949.*

be more like her own. Another great pleasure was soft serve, reminding her usually, but not always, that she had carried on now and then with George Upchurch, who introduced it to East Tennessee. But she hated to ask. They always had excuses for not taking her there after Kroger's or the doctor's on the ride home. Usually whining, sometimes verging on weeping, like when they got soft serve to go and tarried along the way to the house. Licking a little of their own from the bottom of the drip on their fingers, up to the melting down the cone, finally taking finally a quick bite of it. Jerry turned his nose up at Long John Silver and wasn't crazy about soft serve, but Blake and Robbie always had some. Robbie remembers that one time she asked for two cones because she craved it so, and both melted seriously by the time she and Jerry got to the house.

Sometimes she had a few choice words for those who balked, but as she reached for the bag of shrimp or the cone of soft serve, her complaints slipped her mind.

JERRY IN SAN FRANCISCO SEEMS
THE END OF THE WORLD

She was waiting for Jerry's weekly Sunday evening call. San Francisco seemed like the end of the world, and talking long distance costs an arm and a leg.

And now he's got his graduate degree, he says he's going to teach freshman English and drama and direct the plays at Appalachian State Teachers College in Boone, North Carolina, highest-up town east of the Rockies, they say. Jerry's not only the first in our family to graduate from high school, but also the first to go to college. Wish people could say that about me.

"Guess what, Momma."

"What?"

"Before I start teaching, the Van Vactors are gonna let us stay the summer in their house on the river while they're in Spain. Then we can see you when we're back in town. Are you still traveling with Olan Mills Portrait Studios?"

"Yeah, and I'm having the time of my life. Your momma has her a new boyfriend, honey."

"Hey, Robbie. Guess what. Momma's got a new boyfriend."

REMEMBERING SWIMMING IN LAKE ERIE

Being in the water, swimming or floating, she was alone, she was herself more than usual. Being with Daddy and Mother and little Chuck and her boyfriends and girlfriends from high school, before that being among other Girl Scouts, in the woods or on the beach at Lake Erie, was usually wonderful. Just being a girl. Flirtatious, everyone said to her face.

"When you smile, Emily, you are twice as pretty. Maybe thrice, so to speak," said Helen, and Frankie, standing behind her, said, "Helen's right, Emily. Do it again, for the Gipper." That made her laugh, that and it didn't take much else back then.

Mother kept close watch on her, suspicious, sex on the brain, but Daddy was far less watchful. Even so, she went everywhere in Cleveland. Summertime, diving into Lake Erie at Euclid Beach Amusement Park. All year round on Euclid Avenue and Twelfth Street area, and the magnificent glass arched shopping gallery, full of promises. The Public Square was overflowing with possibilities.

Sometimes swimming underwater, she saw those and other places in flashes. West Side Market, its vast tiled ceiling fit for a palace. That great train station tower under construction. What would swimming, backstroking, rolling stroke, floating in that chlorinated pool or in the great lake all the days and nights of your life be like? God didn't have that in mind. Climbing the ladder up out of the pool, she relished the startling cold air on her half-naked body. Seeing handsome Frankie dog-paddle toward her, she began to flirt.

And now there's Jerry diving precisely into the pool at his favorite motel, Hall's Crossroads, north of Fountain City, instead of any place closer inside Knoxville city limits, always something odd or different, and Blake seeing how long he can hold his breath underwater, and Greg showing off, doing a big, fat belly-buster, spraying Cheryl lying on her stomach on a pink beach towel, lovely at fourteen, and Robbie poolside reading a political history, she said, for her class at Ohio U, and here I sit, wet from a dip, not fat in my tight bathing suit, plump, I prefer to say.

THE CAT CAUSES THE CAR TO WRECK

When she turned to swat her Siamese cat Elmer for clawing at the back of her seat, Emily distracted Big John so severely that he lost control of the car for all of a second or two, and she woke up in the hospital with a bleeding bang on her nose in Greensburg, Indiana, a little Podunk town sixty miles west of Cincinnati.

She and Big John were not badly injured, but the car was totaled, and they needed a way to get back to Cincinnati, so she called Jerry, three hours or so away in Gambier, Ohio, where he was teaching at Kenyon College, and asked him to come and get them, and by the time he arrived, Robbie and little Blake with him, the nurse looking in on her accidentally left the door ajar and the damned cat whizzed out and nobody could find her.

So before they could set out for home, Big John and Jerry and Robbie and Blake had to comb the area for her cat while she lay fretting in bed.

Then here come little Blake carrying Elmer purring in his arms, found him strolling outside, and she cussed him out awhile.

Then they all five set out in Jerry's secondhand green and tan 1959 Chevrolet for the trailers, leaving behind Big John's disabled Oldsmobile behind.

One trailer she lived in with Big John, and the other held all her earthly goods, out in the country in an open sedge field.

"Jerry, I know it's not much, but to Big John and your momma, it's home sweet home."

"And for the cat." She was holding Elmer when Jerry said that, as he and Robbie and Blake ducked out of the trailer, quickly shutting the door behind them.

WATCHING JOAN CRAWFORD

IN *MILDRED PIERCE*

Sitting in the balcony of the majestic Tennessee Theatre made her feel a little as if she were sitting in the grand State Theatre in Cleveland. She did not feel alone sitting by her lonesome. Memories of her friends, of sometimes even Mother and Daddy, sitting with her watching movies, let her settle into the past when she was a child, then a teenager, but simultaneously very much in the now.

Watching Joan Crawford as *Mildred Pierce* felt good, even though Mildred making and selling pies reminded her of when she had to do that on Dempster Street when Jimmy first started drinking up his paycheck worse than ever. Men coming into Mildred's life after she left her husband because he wouldn't drop that widow woman, like Jimmy and Mary, and the salesman and the rich man coming into Mildred's life was like men coming into her own life, and Mildred's talented daughter was like Jerry, but he wasn't mean-spirited like she was.

Oh, but the movies of the twenties. Silent ones with Mary Pickford and Douglas Fairbanks and that old Charlie Chaplin idiot, and seeing her first sound picture, Al Jolson singing in *The Jazz Singer*. Just when her favorite stars were beginning to speak, Daddy said we gotta move back. Then seeing movies in the Tennessee, the Riviera, and the Bijou, where Jerry is now an usher.

Her best boyfriend Frankie back then looked a lot like Buddy Rogers, who never spoke, never made it in the talkies. Where, oh, where is that sweet, sexy Frankie now? She knew now she'd never know.

LETTER TO JOHN AT STATE PENITENTIARY

"Dear John, I can't seem to get my act together to come visit you. Brushy Mountain Prison isn't so very far, only thirty miles or so above Oak Ridge, but I'm working for a Greek who keeps saying he needs me to put over a new line of jewelry. He's got another line that's nothing to do with business and is too free with his hands. Just when I think I can get away to see you, he comes up with another excuse. And I have to take care of Mother and Cap when I least expect, and the cab fare from my apartment on Morgan breaks the bank, because it's too far to walk, even if my ankles weren't swollen and sore. I could sure use those orthopedic shoes Dr. Christenberry prescribed. The store that carried them is next to the old Broadway Theatre that's been turned into a bowling alley ever since that fire. Sorry, honey, to let my mind wander when I should be dreaming up a way to get to you. I don't know that many men anymore who might give me a lift, and you know Greg, hard as hell to get him to take me to Kroger's, much less Brushy Mountain Prison.

"Greg's holding down two different radio jobs that wear him out. But you should hear that voice of his. Like there's two different Gregs. No wonder. But you'd think he would fall down all over himself to do for his grandmother. Wouldn't you? Worries, worries.

"And what really worries me is your last letter where you tell me your cell is smack dab next to James Earl Ray's. If he breaks out of there again, don't you get tempted to bust out with him now, honey. Serve your time and change your life. You've spent too many years of your life in one home for wayward boys or correction facility after another. If only they had let you stay in the Marines or the Navy one.

"Oh, and Dick is a cook on oil rigs off New Orleans. Something else to worry me to death. Those hurricanes.

"Don't give up on me, John. Look for me to show my face in Brushy Mountain before the cold weather sets in.

"Love, your mother."

COLD, SLANTED FLOORS

IN THE HOME PLACE

The floors in the home place were always very cold, until Cap had a tiny basement dug under the kitchen he had added to the little three-room cottage and insulation put in under the house. At least it has been years since the wind blew through the cracks in the walls, making the flowery wallpaper puff out at you across the room or behind you on your neck. Wind used to blow under the house, it being set on columns of bricks, and frosted your feet, and rattled the wood shingles on the roof.

At least the floors never slanted like that floor in the house old man Tilly rented out on the alley between Atlantic and Cedar Street. And that was after they moved out of the house on Oswald where the floors slanted also.

Nearby they lived awhile on the second floor of a house on Hiawassee that they moved out of the day after she started down the stairs and a rat in full sunlight through the front door looked up at her. The kids were little children still.

Later, all three boys loved to sneak into Mr. Tilly's marble-terraced garden that had a big pond down below and play on the little raft, but only Dickie sneaked into the Gypsy wagon, where Mr. Tilly kept his Charlie McCarthy dummy.

Tilly often caught them and yelled bloody murder. Jerry said he wrote a story about the time he and Phil worked a while helping the old man repair damage to the marble-tiled terraces and drain the pond.

CAP LIES TOO LONG IN BED
IN THE BACK ROOM

How can Cap be so handsome, or attractive, I guess, and his son Johnny be so homely, but sweet, really, and the only one except his sister Dot who comes to see how their father's doing, laying back there all by his lonesome in one of my old twin beds in the back room, facing the wall most of the time. Glad he'll get up and sit in his old chair a little while, at least once a month.

Johnny brings memories of the old fire department with him, and that's good, and it's bad, too, depending on Cap's mood. If I hadn't moved in to look after him, there'd be room for Dot to take care of him, but she's not really able, where I've had all those years of practical nursing, well, Mother had it too, but too long ago, quit it when she married Cap.

The rest of his folks come and go seldom as a drought, but that redheaded daughter of his is so haughty, when they aren't nothing but Vestal people. Jerry used to like her daughter, Jeanette. But much less than he did Jenny and then Iva Lee. That other daughter used to come around, Helen, the one that lives high on the ridge near where Jimmy's folks used to live. Oh, me. Poor ol' Cap, just languishing.

JIMMY MEETS THE FAMILY
AT DINNER TIME

Like other women—and most men—Mother liked Jimmy on sight. Coming at Emily on Gay Street last Friday, and then there he was framed in the screen door, his hands cupped to see in.

When Mother opened the door to let him in, Emily fell the rest of the way in love with him, even for those big ears that un-flapped when he lifted his hat.

On his way out to work as night watchman at Sterling Wood Works Company, his revolver on his hip, his black lunch pail in one hand, Daddy shook Jimmy's hand with his free hand.

Little Phil showed up in the doorway to the kitchen to take a look, Jimmy easing past him, and Chuck poured on the charm. Jimmy never had to. His charm was natural, and so it came and went and was on now.

Mother could smile and speak gaily when she willed to. "Well, supper's waiting. You hungry for fried chicken and biscuits, Jimmy?"

Shy Jimmy squinted and nodded and looked at Emily as if for the first time. She kissed his cheek, a wet one.

As they all sat down, she heard Daddy's T-Model Ford start and rattle off.

She felt good in a special way, watching everybody at the round table behave.

The kerosene lamp smoked less than usual. Mother trimmed it a little and it quit. Jimmy smiled as if he appreciated it.

"Well, Emily, why don't you pass Jimmy the taters?"

"I was going to, Mother."

"She's got her mind on you being here, Jimmy. Well, Emily, take some for yourself before you pass it to Chuck."

Chuck put on that semi-crooked smile that his girlfriend Ruth said was what did it for her.

Phil kept looking around the table at each person as if he'd never seen them before.

They weren't putting on for Jimmy's benefit. She thought more that they were glad to meet him than to figure out what he was feeling about her.

If she kept him, married him, maybe she could charm him, or con him, or persuade him to leave Knoxville and take her back to Cleveland and live happily ever after.

"Jimmy, how would you like some more mashed potatoes?" She plopped a dab of butter in the middle of the bowl, then passed it on to Jimmy who added the buttered portion to the mound he was finishing.

JERRY TAKES HER ON A TRIP
TO BILTMORE ESTATE

She took one look at the Biltmore House and told Jerry she was sorry, honey, but she would never in her life be able to walk all through and up and down that enormous place.

He rustled up a wheelchair, and off they went, sailing along from room to room, around the atrium under one vaulted dome after another, alongside the windows with the views, and the breeze coming through the open French doors, blowing the sheer drapes. And Jerry loved Mr. Vanderbilt's library, of course, where beside a set of regal chairs sat a gaming table, an ivory chess set upon it, that a little sign said used to be Napoleon's, on which his heart once sat in an alcohol-filled silver urn in a mansion called Holland House.

A member of the staff said the elevator would take her in the wheelchair up to the second floor, but the very sight of it scared her, so Jerry parked her where she had a fine view down into the well of the atrium of the exotic flowers, while he roamed upstairs and into the attic and down into the basement and saw the ritzy swimming pool and came back raving about how romantic this place was.

The Biltmore seemed to her sort of like Andrews's Folly, the house of Samuel Andrews of Standard Oil, built in 1885, almost a hundred rooms, on the Millionaire's Row on Euclid Avenue in Cleveland that Daddy'd taken her to see when she was eleven, but only all around the outside because living in it turned out to be too difficult for many reasons, so it had stood empty for twenty-five years. Then Daddy took her to watch it getting torn down in 1923, when she was thirteen.

How the other half lives, my foot. Too bad I couldn't choose which half for me.

Being in Asheville already, Jerry took her to see the Old Kentucky Home, his hero Thomas Wolfe's mother's boarding house where Tom often slept. She reminded him that she, too, rented out a room or two in some of the houses they lived in to enable her to pay the rent.

He told her again the story of his taking a bus to Asheville when he was fifteen to see the inside of the house. He led her around to the back where pillars held it up the house. "That's the brick pillar," he told her, "that Wolfe as a boy, disgusted with his mother's greed and her boarders, tried to knock down—pull, like Samson, the damned place down," said he asked a man passing in the street to take a picture of him leaning against the pillar. She had seen it a time or two.

Rain came down lightly, but when they reached the gorge on US Highway 40 toward Knoxville, it was so lashing and thick and blinding among huge trucks passing that she feared grisly death at every curve.

Safe in bed, she knew that she would always remember that trip as a high point of her life.

JUST MARRIED, LIVING
IN A BASEMENT APARTMENT

The only place they could afford on their combined paychecks in South Knoxville, where Jimmy could be close to his big sister Kathleen and his big brother Elmo, was a dark, dank basement two-room apartment on Valley Avenue, at the foot of the ridge where the Madden family's failed farm sat, high up, on the corner of Pedigo and Lincoln.

Here I sit, in South Knoxville, which the rest of Knoxville sticks its nose up at. Mother and Daddy five miles across the Tennessee River in the valley between the foot of Sharp's Ridge and the foot of the ridge where St. Mary's Hospital sits.

Just me and these four walls.

Imagining herself rubbing the dingy wallpaper with cleaning putty, she decided to ask Jimmy to bring some home.

Well, at least I'll see his folks just up the hill.

"Jimmy, when you going to take me up to visit your folks?"

"Oh, maybe some time."

"Sometime when?"

"I don't know. Ain't this nice down where we're at? Close to Uncle David at the packing house."

"Then invite your Uncle David to come see us."

"I can't."

"Why not?"

"He's rich."

Then he was off, up the hill to see his big sister Kathleen, it being daylight because he has feared going up there in the dark ever since he was eleven, the year his mother and daddy died.

She held Dickie—James Richard Madden—in her arms. She wished she had refused to take him out of Daddy's mother's house and bring him into this dark, moldy basement.

Mother came on the streetcar to visit. "Well, hit shore ain't how Charlie Merritt set us up in Cleveland. What's Jimmy going to do with himself, now he's out of a job again?"

"He's looking."

"What for—a saloon on Union?"

"Mother."

"Pardon me for living. I'm just your mother."

"What does Daddy say?"

"Nothin' worth telling."

"Don't you miss Cleveland, Mother?"

"I do miss my kitchen."

"How's Granny Merritt?"

"Dyin'. It's that cancer of the anus."

"Sometimes I feel like jumping off the Gay Street Bridge."

"Well, if you do, leave that sweet little baby with his grandmother."

"Mother!"

WORRIED ABOUT JERRY

AND THEM IN THE HURRICANE

"The wind, honey, is something awful tonight, even here. The TV said you all are right in the middle of a record-breaking hurricane. I'm worried sick."

"Oh, Momma."

"Well, I can't help it. I can't help it. I've been worried sick ever since. Are you where you can get somewhere safe?"

"Momma, New Orleans is ninety miles south of Baton Rouge."

"What's to stop it from roaring up yonder?"

"We are so safe, Robbie is setting the supper table in the backyard."

"But all those trees, honey."

"The two main problem-trees fell in the last hurricane."

"See what I mean? Well, call me if you need me."

JIMMY RETURNS FROM THE WAR

Eager to live anywhere but Knoxville, unable to get the *Cleveland Plain Dealer*, she settled for usually buying the *Baltimore Sunday American* at the newsstand. The kids liked the funny papers because the color was more vivid than in the *Knoxville News-Sentinel*. The one about that little girl's problems, especially, Little Annie Rooney, but also, of course, Prince Valiant and Flash Gordon. She had never been to Baltimore, but something about it caught her up in that city, and she was glad, every Sunday, to be there. She tried to remember how she first got into Baltimore. Oh, yes, she loved reading the HELP WANTED classifieds, inspired her to dream. The vacant positions for secretaries. Well, file clerks, since she could neither type nor take shorthand. Not the ads for the type of work she had already done—waitress, seamstress, ready to wear, clerk in a drugstore.

She had just slung the funnies from the fat Sunday paper to the foot of the bed when came a knock at the door. And it after midnight. She got into Jimmy's old gray robe and went to the door. Who stood there grinning was Jimmy in the flesh, fresh home in the middle of the night from driving an ambulance with General Patton in in the battlefields of France.

With Jimmy asleep now beside her in Mother's bed at her house while she and Cap were visiting her brother Ed in Florida, they had come back from the war, first Phil, then Jimmy.

But not Chuck. She saw Chuck go off to war. She saw Jimmy go off to war. Then Phil, leaving his job curb hopping at Sharp's Drugstore, only a few years after he rode his bike to Dempster Street to babysit the kids, then babysat them as they watched westerns when he became an usher at the Strand. All those pictures of him in the corps of engineers where they had him blowing up bridges. And Jimmy driving an ambulance. And Chuck among the last in the army cavalry, wearing those polished boots and jodhpurs. And handsome. Looked like Tyrone Power. Phil and Jimmy not so glamorous. And Chuck's ex-wife Ruth as a WAC in Alaska, beautiful. And now Dickie overseas in Germany about to marry Ann, of all the girls in the world, the daughter of a Nazi colonel. Oh, me, oh my, what a strange, strange world us plain ol' everyday Merritts and Maddens live in.

And in the old pine quilt box at the foot of the bed, those photos and paintings of World War I soldiers and battle scenes Mother clipped out of the newspapers and magazines—or was it Daddy?—when we were so well off in Cleveland that Jerry likes to look at.

Jerry showed in the doorway, then leapt over Emily, who, naked from the waist up, jerked the covers to her chin, to hug Jimmy.

"How you doing, Bub?"

Jerry snuggled under the quilt between Daddy and her. "Okay. I carry the *Knoxville Sentinel* up on Sharp's Ridge now."

"Yeah, your momma's tellin' me, son."

"Jerry, you got your knees in my belly." She pushed at his hip.

John came in yelling, leapt into bed, too, hugging Jimmy, then crawled under the sheet between them, putting his arms around both of them, grinning, like posing for a family photograph.

Jerry, shy, got under the sheet too, on the edge of the mattress, next to Jimmy.

"Daddy," said John, "read us the funnies like you used to."

"Better get breakfast started," said Emily, a twinge of jealousy in her voice, like when they lived on Dempster and she screamed at the boys all day long and took a switch to them and they'd say, "I'm gonna tell Daddy when he comes home," and he came home at dark, drunk, and they hugged his legs and jumped into his arms, and she said, "Good God, I slave here the livelong day and he stays out drunk, and soon's he hits the door, it's like the return of the king of Egypt. Makes me sick."

Like when she was screaming at Jimmy over laying out with Mary, whose husband was in the penitentiary at Petros, and she saying she hoped he'd break out and catch them, and throwing dishes at him, and Mother, from the bedroom, yelling, "Them better not be any my dishes," she screaming, "I have some dishes, too, Moth-er."

SELLING FRIED PIES, ROBBIE TOO

Jerry's got Robbie making fried pies to sell at *Horn in the West*, that outdoor play he acts in. They do need money, but I don't think either of them know what they're getting into, Robbie making them, Jerry selling them. It ain't worth it. I know. And Jerry was there, about six years old, though, when we lived on Dempster, when I made fried pies and had to have them all ready when that woman came in her car to get them and take them around to the restaurants. They were very good, and the kids loved them, and Jimmy did, but I wouldn't have had to do it if he hadn't become a drunk and drank his paycheck from Breezy's and spent God knows how much on that bitch. I had to beat the kids off of them or they'd eat every one. I hated frying them in that awful lard, and you couldn't make me eat one then or now if you put a gun to my head. Mother didn't spare the horses telling me the fried pies weren't good enough. Poor little ol' Robbie. And churning their own butter up there on that mountain farm. Not the one where I visited them last year. Another one after Yale Drama School, and Blake just born, up Hot Holler Road, for God's sake.

Sunday when they make their weekly call, I think I'll just tell Jerry, listen, honey, it's hard, too hard on Robbie. Rob a bank.

JOHN CRUSADING ON TV
AT THE COUNCIL MEETING

Wondering where in this world John Kenneth Madden had gotten to, gone so long, she switched to the ten o'clock news and there was John himself attacking the mayor again, this time for failing to get repairs on the Gay Street Bridge underway as John had often proposed, winning great support from the city council and the townspeople.

"My nephew's wife has been dead ... dead ..., for over six years, because of her car sliding on black ice to miss a bus that slid, right through that broken guard railing into the river, and when in hell do you all intend to redo that whole damned bridge? You heard me—'damned.'"

The council members applauded right along with the audience, except Mayor Ashe and his mother, longtime councilwoman, and one or two deadpan councilmen. John kept fixed on his face that look of deep, deep sadness and outrage.

Then the TV turned to advertising. "Your dollar buys *more*—at a Cas Walker *store.*"

John rushed through the front door in a shush of cold air and twisted the dial to the ten o'clock news.

"Did I miss me?"

A BEAUTY IN CLEVELAND

WEST HIGH SCHOOL

She came out of American history and walked down the hall toward chemistry, hoping her derrière was not too big, like Sally's, Mellie's, and Betty's were. Or big at all. More like Helen's, she hoped.

Then she started worrying that she might even fail chemistry. But those three boys walking toward her gave her the twice over and she just knew they turned to see how she looked from behind, as she often caught boys doing to other girls. Being popular took her mind off the mysteries of chemistry. But then, up ahead after chemistry was civics. Nothing mysterious about it, just the most boring of all. She could furtively shape her hair, adeptly, just with her fingertips, and look forward to English and Mrs. Hamilton's admiration of her penmanship and her voice reciting Byron, "She walks in beauty like the night," and Frankie's curly hair smack in front of her.

She took her seat in chemistry, close enough to watch Frankie come strolling into the room, but here came Sally and Betty first, smiling at her as they sat down, left and right of her. But where's Mellie? There she comes, Hobart the boxer right behind her, not looking at Mellie's behind. And lovely Helen last.

Did Hobart agree with Emily that her breasts were more shapely than her four girlfriends'? The idea of tapping him on the shoulder after he sat down in front of her to ask him made her giggle and that made Hobart half turn and give her a profile smile.

She liked the tenth grade very much more than the ninth had been.

LETTERS FROM ZOE AND RUTH

"November 24, 1953. Out of Zoe's Ink Well.
"Darling Emmie,

"Janice and her daddy are at West High because Janice is an angel in the school play. I'm too sick, in bed, or so I said.

"I feel sort of mean taking up with that guy when you and I have such a little time together, but I do hope you understand and will excuse it this time. You know me. These handsome men are so irresistible. But I got the run around after all. He seemed over anxious, so I asked him to stay over and get the plane home Sun. morning. He must have said well to hell with her and got someone else that night. He was cute though and nice but there was something about him that I didn't like also. I guess he felt the same about me.

"I saw Ruth for a while today. Invited her over for Thanksgiving dinner. We wished you could have been with us for one of our gab sessions. Have you met some one else new there in Chattanooga? Red is still faithful, calls every day practically day and night, when Tom's not here. Boy, I really got even. Had a man get Red on the phone for me, and Red sure was cramped to death with his wife there. Said he couldn't meet me. So I hung up. Don't you know I'm a mean one?

"I'm sending you the 25 cents I owe you in stamps. You can always use stamps. Use one to write to me. Tell Ginny hello.

"Love, Zoe."

Then she read again the one from Ruth that had slipped off the bed onto the floor.

"Dear Emmie,

"Saw Jack again Monday night. Gets better every time. (ha ha) By the way, how is that exclusive romance of yours? I am really hungry to see you. Zoe called me the other day—she wants us to come down to Chattanooga together so as to have some fun with you. What do you think? The two of us coming down. I will call first—or wire. Honey, I am going to have to give up Jack or Elmer one, and I don't want to give up Jack.

"Do you ever feel like you are a piece of driftwood, honey? Oh, well, I guess 'our roads are writ out,' as an old woman told me. Write to me.

"I love you always, Ruth."

IN THE PRINCIPAL'S OFFICE WITH JERRY

She stood on the curb, waiting, freezing.

Jerry reported to her. "I escorted John halfway to Lincoln Park Elementary, chased him the rest of the way, and threatened to throw a rock at him, if he didn't run up the walk into the main entrance."

She knew Jerry was embarrassed to be seen walking to school with his mother.

She griped viciously about having to beg him back into school after the biology teacher confiscated the story he was writing and he sassed her, and then she would have to beg Louie to let her off to go with Jerry to the Crippled Children's Hospital again.

"Your mother may be out of a job after today." Jerry looked ashamed, guilty, and angry. "I've had to run back and forth to juvenile court over Dickie, and now *you're* starting on me with Christenberry."

As they entered Christenberry Junior High, Jerry looked all around, obviously hoping Iva Lee and her gang of girlfriends weren't in sight.

In the office, Mrs. Fraker tried her North Pole freeze on her, but when she sensed that Emily was good at that act too, she eased off.

The conference with Mr. Bronson went well until he used his most severe tone. "Jerry, do you promise to stop writing stories in class?"

"I can't, sir."

"He *sure does*, Mr. Bronson." She flopped her new red purse on her lap.

Jerry refused twice again. She threatened to beat the living fire out of him, aware though that she had never even slapped him once in his life. "It don't hurt to promise."

"Hurts more than a paddling does."

Realizing only tears would do it, she broke down in front of the whole world. "You're just as much a torment to me as John and Dickie *ever* were. Jerry is not my only problem, Mr. Bronson." Tears in her eyes, her voice a little coy.

"Yes, I know. Have they tracked Dickie down yet?"

She summoned her high society voice. "Why, I'm sure I don't know what you mean, Mr. Bronson."

"Isn't he wanted by the police? Escaped from State Training School in Nashville, didn't he?"

"How did you know *that*?" She hoped he would think she was sincerely shocked. "I've not breathed it to a living soul."

"Why, it's common knowledge, Mrs. Madden. A matter of public record, so to speak."

But her tears won. Mr. Bronson left it up to her to extract finally a promise from Jerry before school tomorrow. Meanwhile, he'd be allowed to return to classes tomorrow.

Dickie.

Mrs. Fraker was resentfully reluctant to accept Emily's request that Jerry be let off school to go to the Crippled Children's Hospital with her. "He's missed enough school as it is."

"Mrs. Fraker, this child may have in-fantile pa-raly-sis."

Mrs. Fraker looked at her and looked at Jerry as if they'd cooked up a lie between them. "Permission granted."

At the Crippled Children's Hospital somebody left the afternoon paper on the bench where she and Jerry sat down to wait to be called to consult with Dr. Inge.

TWO BOYS ESCAPED FROM REFORM SCHOOL
SURVIVE ZERO TEMPERATURE AND DEEP SNOW

The story told how Dickie Madden had saved the younger boy's life by letting him wear his Mackinaw jacket.

Emily was proud but mortified; Jerry was proud but jealous.

After that time the cops rounded them all up for breaking into R. T. Lyons shut-down grocery and hauled them off to the police station—Jerry, Dickie, Buddy Smith, and Freddie Weaver—and the cops let them go without even calling her, she never had to worry about Jerry stealing, but his writing stories and radio plays in class and sassing his teachers when they confiscated his stories or tore them up got him into trouble of a different kind that caused her to have to be late for work or get off early to handle far too often.

But Jerry always had some kind of job that brought in money to live on. So . . . Sure enough, Jerry did it again, sassed the teacher who ripped up his story. She tried again to cry Jerry back into Christenberry, but Mr. Bronson said Jerry needed to be taught a lesson. So he suspended him for three days. Instead of crying in shame, he just wrote all day long on his stories.

This time she decided to try a letter on Mr. Bronson. He reluctantly accepted it, and let Jerry back in school.

"Iva Lee was sure glad to see me."

"YOU A DANCING FOOL, EMMIE"

She almost forgot. She dashed off a note. "Dear Jerry, Honey, the cops come and got John again. Now they'll send him to John Tarleton Home for Boys again.

"Bill Williams called and I begged him to take me for a ride to put Knoxville city limits behind me for a few hours. Empty the drip pan under the icebox again. Go on to sleep. Your mother."

Bill was honking his damn horn for all the neighbors to hear.

Snuggled up to Bill as he drove and being among the girls again, she felt like a new person.

"Emmie, I just want to know one thing. I see you working yourself every weeklong day to a frazzle, *to a frazzle*, and for the life of me I cannot, I cannot understand how you can get out there on that dance floor every Friday night the way you do. Tell me. Tell me."

"Why, Madabee, I—"

Starting up again, the band drew her to her feet, she stepped right into Bill's arms, and off she went into "That Old Black Magic," wishing Bill Boles could be the one leading her, even if he wasn't as handsome as Bill Williams, even if he couldn't dance as well as Bill Williams, even though whiskey laid him out so bad he had to call Madabee to tell her he was just too goddamn drunk to be seen among humans.

She knew she was a good dancer, all the men told her so in words and tones she could believe, and she knew it when her short, plump body was the cause of what she felt when Bill drew her too tightly to him.

Madabee and Ruth and Zoe and Ginny always wanted to call it a night sooner than she ever did, but when the band stopped and she saw the bass fiddler reach for his big canvas bag, she knew it was over.

Until maybe tomorrow night. Or maybe she would have to work her tail off, her feet hurting so bad in those high heels on the carpet at Miller's she sometimes ducked behind a rack of dresses and just let the tears flow.

As the girls gathered up their wraps and their pocketbooks, Ginny said, "Emily, you are just a dancing fool, honey, that's all there is to it."

GONE WITH THE WIND COMING

TO THE RIVIERA THEATRE

After *Of Mice and Men* ended, Emily sidled over into the aisle, assuming little Jerry would follow on her heels, but hearing glorious, dramatic music, she turned and saw the screen filled with words, moving across the screen, GONE

WITH THE WIND, then Jerry was walking slowly up the inclined aisle backward, mesmerized. Then there stood Vivien Leigh as Scarlett O'Hara heroically, against a lurid sunset, raising her fists to heaven, tears making her face shine. Emily went down the aisle and took Jerry's hand, but he resisted, taking only a few steps backward, until she had to drag him.

Outside, Jerry made her promise to take him to see that lady vow, "If I have to lie, steal, cheat or kill, I will never go hungry again," in *Gone with the Wind*, and thrill to that music. Having read the novel twice, she was eager to take Jerry to see the movie. Six year-olds were not likely to understand much of it, but then Jerry at six was not that young.

WITH BIG JOHN IN A TRAILER

OUTSIDE CINCINNATI

Desperately rooting around in a big box for the costume jewelry she had bought on sale when Zale's went out of business a few years ago, she thanked her lucky stars that Big John owned three trailers, this one full of her stuff, with only a little room for more. She didn't tell Mother for fear she would insist, as she had for years, that she clear her stuff out of her garage that Cap and Phil had built for the new Mercury Zephyr in the first place, but they never parked in there before they had to sell it, and by now their own stuff was stored in there mingled with hers, leaving barely room for Cap's lawn mower and such.

"Living in sin is what you're a-doing" was Mother's opinion. "Beside that, you're too old to be doing sich as that."

"I may be old, but I'm not that old."

"But, Emily, he's so much younger than you are."

"You just said that."

"Yes, and I'll say it again. You need to reel in a good man your age and get yourself a house of your own and cut out all that dancing."

"Mother, I have not danced in ages."

"See."

"No, I don't see. But yes, a house would be wonderful, and a good man. But I'd sooner find a good house than a good man to go in it."

"Well, that young man is not the only fish in the sea."

"He's not a young man, Moth-er. He's just not quite the same age as I am."

"Now, Cap and me are just right. Same age, more or less."

"I thought he was less."

"Don't you get smart with me. I won't stand for it. Now, where do you think you're a-going?"

"To get the first bus back to Cleveland and start my life over again."

"Oh, sit down, honey, and tell me what really ails you."

Well, she was ashamed that Jerry and Robbie saw her living in a trailer, that's true. Okay, John happened by, too, because his life was on the road, wandering aimlessly. And Dickie, just out of prison, was coming next week.

The cold, icy wind howling out there in the open, outside Cincinnati city limits, was so bad she had to rush it, as images welled up of all the other places where she'd stacked boxes and stored big industrial cardboard drums full of her stuff, things bought mostly on sale, towels and washcloths, and dresses, and broken hair dryers, and empty candy boxes that she might need for one reason or another one of these days. Stacked in hallways between her apartment and the next one over. Stored in dirt-floored cellars when she found whole houses she could afford.

And that earthen cellar under the back of the house on Cedar Street in Lincoln Park when she beat the fire out of Dickie for feigning a stomachache to get out of helping her, and he slinked away anyway, and General Hospital called to tell her that he'd walked three miles with a ruptured appendix, and showed up asking for a doctor, but that he was doing well, all things considered. "Come get your son, Mrs. Madden."

Never an attic, somehow. Always the garage at Mother's or a cellar or hallway in a house or even up against the bedroom wall in some of her two or three-room apartments. And always, she sadly remembered, giving up the search for yard-sale jewelry that might bring a dime or two after she cast them aside. Jerry told her about visiting Hedy Lamarr's apartment, paid for by her ex-lover, in a ritzy building, that her bedroom was so full of boxes of her stuff that she had only a narrow path to her narrow bed. And her once the world's most beautiful movie star.

Oh, that huge pine box her piano came in, into which Mother and Daddy stuck all their worldly goods for the depressing train trip out of Cleveland back down into Knoxville. She was glad she didn't have that nightmare often anymore—her nailed up in that old wooden crate inside the bench among her sheet music.

Big John's not very classy but he's good to me. Maybe even good *for* me. Wants to marry me. What he doesn't need to know is that two of my boys are behind bars and the army is about to send the other one to hell and gone. Alaska. He's been in the army himself, he says. Maybe yes, maybe no. Anyway, he might not care that much for me anymore, if he only knew. Not that I know enough about him to know he wasn't in jail a time or two his own self. Hell, my own no-good former husband spends many a Saturday night in jail because he's so loveable that one cop told me that they nab him for his own good. Like that time they brought him home stark naked and I had to go out to the curb with his housecoat. And none of the men in my family, either side, nor Jimmy's, is *not* an alcoholic. Big John is the first boyfriend not a drunk. Oh, he may drink a beer now and then. But he's a straight arrow if there ever was one. Needs a job, though.

So we watch television. Can't dance. I offered to teach him, but he sweetly begged off. I never thought I'd be content to sit all evening and watch the Ed Sullivan show and such. To him, that cafeteria nearby is high-toned. I don't mind paying now and then, but it almost makes him cry.

Him being good to me is what matters. Never a cross word. Worships me. Well, not really. But feels like it. The more I see him, the more I think I might come to love the poor fellow. That he snores is not the end of the world.

JOHN AND JERRY MISBEHAVE

"How many times do I have to tell you kids not to play with Gran'paw Charlie's holster? Where did you find it, John, in the first place? Mother said she hid it where none of my 'damned kids' could ever find it. You just better not let her catch you playing Gang Busters with that holster ever again. And stop whining, John. Go play cars under the house—and do not go anywhere near the garden. Mother will scream bloody murder that you're digging up her garden, and it's me she'll—John, do you want me to jerk a knot in your tail. Stop that bellering."

"Wish I could find the gun, too."

"Jerry, why do you let him dig around looking for it?"

"Why is it me who has to watch him? Why not Dickie, our big brother?"

"Where the hell *is* that young'un?"

"I don't know. One second he's playing with me and John and the next he's gone."

"Now, where did John go?"

"He slipped out."

"Then go see what's he's into now. I'm going to have to lie down and rest."

"Want me to look for Dickie, too?"

"No, honey, that would be a waste of time."

She lay down on Mother's bed, safe to do so until she got off work as a nurse's aide at General.

"Want me to pull the shade down?"

"Yes, honey, that would be sweet. Thank you."

"I see John out there playing horse with that snaggle-toothed boy next door."

"Then you go out and play, too, honey, be on the watch. Oh, Lordy, Lord."

DICKIE LIVING WITH HER IN COLUMBUS

She was so happy to have her firstborn living with her, come to her from years of wandering and prisons. Jerry was the one all those years when John and Dickie were wandering or locked up, until he went away, into the merchant marine and into the army, to being married and a father. John living with her off and on when he needed a place to stay, a job, then taking off when she least expected. And she knew Dickie could not stay put for long.

There he sits watching TV, full of food she cooked, and quieter than John, but sweet, and his resonant voice was good to hear when he piped up.

She went off to take care of the old lady, home nursing. Coming home, seeing him there or knowing he would turn the knob was good. Just damned good. Her firstborn. Not much talk of where all he had been in recent years now since prison, nor did she expect he'd tell her when he was about to set off again. He would just be there one day and gone the next, following "the call of the wild goose," like in that story Jerry wrote about him, and no word until she was a nervous wreck wondering.

WITH DADDY GOING ALL
OVER CLEVELAND

"Mother, Daddy took me to the Arcade. He held my hand and we walked a far, far way under this long, long roof, looking up at it, and he went into a tobacco shop for pipe tobacco and took me in a shop that sells children's clothes and bought me this blue tam. See how big? I like the way it flops to the side. And in the ice cream, he asked me whether I wanted fudge or a strawberry soda, so we got to see all the ice creams and sat at a special little marble-top table. And he tried on shoes in three stores and the last one finally had his size, his feet are so little. Wonder how come? And a shop that sells tools of every kind. And oh, there's everything in that place. Daddy told me it's the largest arcade in the world. Oh, and there's four floors of it, and you walk up steps wide as our house from one floor to the next."

Daddy came in blowing on a cup of coffee.

"Charlie, Emily was just telling me you took her all up and down that Arcade you keep promising to take *me* to. I hope you didn't spend too much on this child. You're about to spoil her rotten. How much did you spend on something for me and what is it, where is it, Charlie?"

"And Daddy said he's going to take me up to West Side Market again to-night. I love those beautiful arches with all the beautiful tile patterns in the dome."

"Why, who ever heard of beautiful tiles and arches and domes in a food market?"

VISITING DICKIE IN THE ARMY
WITH JOHN AND JERRY

"Dress warm, boys, it may be even colder in Greenville, South Carolina, than it is in Knoxville."

"Does Dickie get to fly planes?"

"No, honey, it's the Greenville Army Air Base, and he's more with the army part."

"Is he even old enough to join the army?"

"Just barely . . . So, this may be our last chance to see Dickie before his training ends and they send him to Japan or Germany or Italy or some other godforsaken country. Get a move on now, that bus leaves the terminal building at eight o'clock sharp."

The streetcar was passing the stop across from the Methodist church as they reached the curb, but she waved to the conductor, a friend of hers, and he stopped and shooshed open the doors. She got John and Jerry into the Union Bus Terminal and down the stairs to the loading dock just as the driver got in behind the wheel.

While John read a Donald Duck funny book and Jerry gazed soulfully out the window at the landscape and the houses and towns as he always did when Cap and Mother took him with them on drives in Cap's new Lincoln Mercury Zephyr, she went back over Dickie's whole life. His troubles, his travels.

"Momma, they's a soldier at the front door," Jerry called to her one day. Behind the sooty screen door stood Dickie in a khaki uniform and cap, that cocked, wet-lipped grin on his face.

"No, Jerry, I ain't a soldier. This is a merchant seaman's uniform." And him only fourteen going on fifteen.

Jerry was eager to tell him, "I just saw Humphrey Bogart as a merchant seaman in *Passage to Marseille* at the Broadway. But not in a uniform like yours."

With the camera Jenny gave Jerry for his fourteenth birthday, she took a picture of her three boys posing in front of the propeller of a fighter plane. Then Dickie got her in a pose between Jerry and John. Then as Jerry got Dickie by himself in front of a propeller, she just hoped and prayed Dickie could stay out of trouble and make something of himself in the army air force wherever they shipped him.

REMEMBERING ALL HER GIRLFRIENDS

I keep telling Jerry when he calls that I'm doing all right except for my knees, and he keeps urging me to have the operation the doctor recommends before it's inoperable, but I just . . . Well, at least that therapist got me on my feet again. Poor Zoe. Her daughter called to tell me they had to cut off her mother's right leg because the diabetes got out of control. And Zoe's stuck up there on that hill in those retirement apartments, in the same building that was St. John's Orphanage where John and Jerry had to stay that time I was almost dying. When Zoe played the piano—even at church and funerals—she sounded like a honky-tonk.

When I think of my girlfriends and what they have come to. None of them running around anymore, dancing, romancing. All of us the same ol' same ol.'

Of all my many girlfriends, from the old Cleveland years on up to now, Ginny Cover has been my favorite. I love her to death. And yet she's not beautiful like Zoe and Ruth and even that rambunctious buck-toothed Ruby. Ginny's homely, face too fat, so her eyes look oriental. Mother hates to see her coming out on the back porch when we're all out there in the cool of the evening. Jack drops her off. Mother's probably jealous. Only one of *her* old-time friends ever comes to see her. Sarah. "She bores me to death," Mother says. Doesn't even keep a photograph of Sarah, Granny Merritt's favorite niece.

She kept many snapshots of Ginny. Of Ginny and her together, and Ginny and Cliff, and Ginny and Jack before she divorced Cliff.

She let her memory take her to those mornings when they lived on McCalla and Ginny lived upstairs in one room, separated from Cliff.

And she was seeing Jerry off to school after grapefruit or oatmeal, unable to afford both, and Jerry simultaneously was seeing her off to work. She to Miller's Ready-to-Wear on Gay Street, Jerry to Dixie Vim gas station on Henley. Jerry walking to save money, loaded with a chuck roast beef sandwich, she riding the bus, packing a boiled ham and American cheese sandwich. Jerry in a work shirt she ironed for him, she in flattering blue, wearing high heels that hurt her weak ankles.

John out of the reform school came to a house new to him. He got no job. He watched Jerry and her kiss each other good-bye, then going off to work, leaving him to his own devices, for which he usually had no specific plans. Jerry took a picture of him at the kitchen table pouring milk out of a quart bottle, looking him in the eye. Ginny sometimes came down and talked with John, maybe fixed him a scrappy breakfast. Jerry took a photo of Ginny, too, sitting across from John, turning to face Jerry. No photo of Emily there.

She shook her head. When they first moved into half the house on McCalla, their daily lives were simple. Then they got complicated.

Jerry's best friend Ralph must have assumed for some reason that Ginny was promiscuous, because she got it from Ginny that one time when Emily rented a room to her in the house on McCalla, Ralph surprised her when she was taking a whiz in the downstairs bathroom. He used to come in through a window when nobody was home and take a bath and wait for Jerry. He hung around the kitchen until Ginny came out and tried to get her to crawl in bed with him. "I turned him down flat." Emily wasn't totally convinced.

Ralph was so sure of himself in ways that made him charming, it's a wonder he didn't ask Emily for it. But he did get in Betty the nurse's bed upstairs when Ginny moved back in with Cliff and made the room available.

SHE NEVER GOT TO PARIS

Well, I never got to Paris, that Jerry told me I should. Phil did. Jimmy did. Chuck would have loved Paris. Maybe Dickie. I must ask him. Maybe John will get overseas, but I can't imagine which cities would draw him, can't imagine John wandering the streets of Paris. Jerry gave a lecture at a conference in Paris, though, last year. No, in another town, then they all trooped off to Paris. William Faulkner's hundredth birthday, he said.

But she, she never made it to Paris. Not to London. Not Rome. Not to—Well, overseas at all, nowhere. Maybe Jerry will make it to all those cities, the way he has all over America, every point of the compass, and up and down. So has John, out there now, on the move. And so did Dickie, but stuck now in those awful Lonsdale project houses with Gloria and her mother.

She yearned to go. Very, very much. Seeing them on TV. Why never Cleveland? They only mention it, as a jokey place to live. Why? It's not. It wasn't.

It's my true home, I don't care who knows it. Bury me by Lake Erie.

But later. Not now, folks. Not now. I'm here, for sure, and I'm okay, folks.

LETTER FROM RUTH

"Darling Emmie, Received your cute letter today. I've been thinking of you so hard and worried about you getting mad because I can't write to you. I think I still love Dave. I always will, I guess. Just a fool. Jack came in the other week—said he had called me a couple of times. Funny thing, he had all the information about my private life and doings. I denied it all and got a big thrill out of lying to him. We did have a long-long talk (But I didn't stay with him). He said I was being cynical again about our times together. It went on and on—don't think I will see him again—even if he wants to. I think I am in love with Elmer but have a feeling lately that he sees someone else. Altho all of his future plans include me—or so he says. But how can I leave my little Momma? She is so sick all the time.

"I don't want to love. I don't care about being hurt again. Once is enough. However I am going to Greenville with him to meet some of his folks.

"I would give anything to see Jerry's play. Well, hell, I just may do that.

"I wish you could come up this weekend, as I am free. Enjoy Zoe's company very much but she isn't you. Emily I am so unhappy. (Have all the fun you can, honey.) I never hear from the little Captain. Lots of love, Ruth."

LETTER TO DICKIE

"I didn't forget your B-day. I have been grounded for 10 days with the flu. Each day thinking I would go myself and select your card, which I finally did yesterday. Just to the grocery and here I am in the Doc's office writing, waiting. I'm breathing like your Mammy does now. She just came home from the hospital Thurs. I took her one day (Asthma) and 2 days later came down with the flu. So Dot has had to be the one to go to the house and Greg helped a lot until he went on a new job yesterday announcing at another religious station. At the hospital they used the breathing machine & oxygen and Mammy is better now.

"So 46 yrs. ago this past Thurs. the Doc said I wouldn't live to give birth to you but I fooled him, didn't I? I had p-monia and uremic poisoning and was bound for the promised land for sure.

"Wish you you'd send me a picture of Melissa (I love that name). Tell me how much she weighs, etc. etc.—Teeth yet? Have you had your teeth pulled yet?

"I was glad to get Gloria's letter but would like a few lines from you. And also a photograph of that old motel you said you all live in. I can't picture it. Jacksonville seems so far away.

"Kiss Melissa for me and regards to Gloria's folks. Love as always, Mother."

John.

JERRY TAKES HER ON A DRIVE
INTO THE SMOKIES

"Where'd you like to go this time, Momma?"

"Well, we've taken a drive to so many places, Biltmore mansion, my favorite. Oh, honey, I'll never forget that house as long as I live. And to Cumberland Gap, that Abraham Lincoln museum, and Lafollette to try to find some kin to Granny Merritt, and Lone Mountain, that was nice, and, oh, just here, there, and yonder. Well, too long a time since I've seen the Smokies. We could get back before dark, don't you reckon?"

"I think so. I always wanted to go the back way out of South Knoxville on that highway to Sevierville and then cut over to Cosby and hit the Smokies that way and Gatlinburg, then come back through Maryville maybe."

"Oh, honey, those hairpin curves going up and down the back way to Sevierville make me so nervous, scares the living daylights out of me."

"What if I go slow?"

"If you go slow."

He did, and even so, she did enjoy the thrill of the steep climbs and then down, and even some of the curves. WATCH FOR FALLING ROCK.

"Jerry, it sure was nice of you to put John in a rented car again. It was so cute the way he turned around so he could drive back by and blow the horn, that John Madden grin on his face. He needed to get away, taking care of me so long. Only break he gets is he loves driving up to Middlesboro and playing the lottery."

"I hope it doesn't break down on him this time."

"He sure was up the creek without a paddle."

He told her once that he wrote down all her expressions after their drives.

All the way to the Smokies, she told Jerry all her troubles, and they ate dinner in Gatlinburg at that one place that has live trout in a tank of water, and all the way home she couldn't stop herself from dozing off as he told her about *Cassandra Singing*, the novel he was still yet writing.

JOHN IN A WRECK, JERRY
IN THE MERCHANT MARINE

"Dear Momma, I hate to tell you, not to worry you, but I was in a big o' wreck in Texas. A truck driver gave me and my dog a lift, and on a hill, a car was of a sudden in our lane and we crashed. The truck driver pulled me and my dog out of the cab, but my copy of Jerry's *Bijou* got burnt up. When I went to visit the truck driver in the hospital, he was dying. He whispered his dying words in my ear, 'John, I will always be looking out for you.'

"So, Mom, don't never forget, he is watching over me, so you don't ever have to worry.

"Got me a new car. She is a beaut. My Airedale rides with his head out the window and we are happy go lucky wherever we may be. Jacksonville, Florida today, who knows tomorrow? Say hello to Mammy, Cap, and Phil, and here's a big kiss for my best gal. Your loving son, John Kenneth Madden.

"Here's a shot of me, the dog, and my car."

"See?" She passed the picture over to Mother. "Mother, I finally got a letter from Jerry, from Galveston, for crying out loud. He says, 'My ship is *Seatrain Louisiana* that carries boxcars and tank cars full of fuel that blew up Texas City, Texas. That's where we go next.'"

"What's that child doing on a boat?"

"Mother, he's in the merchant marine."

"First I heard of it. Like John?"

"No, not marines. He's a seaman on a merchant ship's how he explained it to me."

"Never breathed a word to me."

"Well, I told you about him working the night shift at the White Tower hamburger joint and sitting all day in the Seafarers Union hiring hall, didn't I?"

"If you did, I don't remember."

"Well, I did, Moth-urrr."

"Well, you needn't act so smart. I can't remember all the things you tell me, Emily."

"All right, I'll hush."

"No, read me the damn letter from start to finish."

"Where was I? Oh, before he signed on that ship, he says he met Marlene Dietrich."

"He did not."

"That's what he says here in black and white. Says he thought you and me would love to know he met Marlene Dietrich. First met her daughter, Maria Riva who's in all those TV dramas. Met her on the set."

"I do like to watch her."

"And he tried out for a part in a Broadway play."

"I hope he got it, the little devil."

"No, they turned him down. But he did meet a famous poet that's not famous anymore. Runs around with a much younger girl and lives in a room furnished only with a naked mattress."

"Will you hush? I don't care nothin''bout sich as that."

"Says he and Raven—"

"Who in the world is Raven?"

"Dave Van Vactor's daughter, you know, calls herself Raven Harwood now. She and Jerry talk to that poet in a bar in Greenwich Village—name's Maxwell Bodenheim—and you can buy one of his poems on a dirty sheet of paper for fifty cents."

"I always thought Jerry wanted to make something of himself."

"Mother, he's a writer. Writers live like that. Look at Jack London."

"Jack who?"

"Now you're just being contrary."

"Well, the queen of contrariness is sitting right across from me, sure as the world."

Emily laughing got Mother to laughing.

Phil came through the front door. "What you all laughing about?"

"Just foolishness. Cap should be pulling in here from Oak Ridge directly."

"He's right behind me."

Emily folded Jerry's letter, stashed it and John's in her pocketbook, snapped it shut.

LETTER CONGRATULATING GREG

"Dear Greg,

"I can't get over your voice being so deep. It isn't squeaky like so many growing boys. Greg, I was pulling for you in my mind the night of your speech. Don't feel too bad that you didn't win. Your time will come some day.

"I talked to Jerry and Robbie and they thought your speech was very good and your diction and delivery very good. So just remember, honey, you can't win them all. We have to take disappointments in this old life that just about kill us at the time and later we can look back and laugh about it.

"Well, I better look in on my patient. My relief laid out on me, so I must be on duty for 24 hours. Bye now. Love, Your grandmother, Mama Emmie."

HUNTING DADDY'S KILLER

ON DECORATION DAY

"Jerry, where in the hell have you been? We had to go off to decorate the graves because we couldn't find you and then when we got back, no Jerry. Where? Where on earth?"

"I was playing the Green Hornet down in the addition and me and Joe got lost in the sewer pipe and when I got home and nobody here, I took my Roy Rogers BB rifle and set off on my Western Flyer to hunt down that man that killed Gran'paw Charlie, but it got a flat, and so I walked down the rayroad tracks, and crossed the river trestle, and it sundown, I was scared to death and hungry and chilled through and through, and couldn't find that lumber yard you all always said was near the rayroad tracks, so I turned around, lit out for home and here I am, plain as day."

"You're asking for a whuppin."

John said, "I didn't hear him ask for no whuppin."

"Shut up or you'll get one too."

Mother said, "Let's not anybody get whupped, Emily. What Jerry needs worse than whuppin' is a NEHI Orange and a grilled cheese sammige."

"You can take him to raise. And John too. Had me worried to death. I'm going to bed and leave you all to your own devices."

HYSTERECTOMY, BUT WHO GIVES A DAMN?

Hysterectomy. The very word's enough to kill you.

"Don't you worry, Mrs. Madden."

If *I* don't, who will? The kids, but we're not telling them. So Jimmy's sister Kathleen will take John and Jerry and his brother Elmo take Dickie in Albuquerque. For how long? Oh, Lord. A day?

"Maybe weeks or months, Mrs. Madden. It all depends."

On the doctor? And on me. On God?

"Emily, just leave it in the hands of God."

I don't really know how. I should have gone to church, I guess. But that was my only time alone in the house. The kids in Sunday school and church. Or wherever they snuck off to. Dickie for sure. But Jerry wanted to see Jonnie Lou, not knowing Iva Lee sitting next to her would be the love of his life, but after Jenny, and then Robbie came along.

Mother, of course. She cares. I know she does. She knows how it is. Nurse's aide at General. Wish she were at St. Mary's. Only just up the hill from good ol' 2722 Henegar Street, sort of our own private hospital over the years.

Jimmy may come home on leave and come see me. If I have to stay in the hospital until I am well. Dangerous. That's what they all say, who survive it. Well, I *am* scared—to death. The kids with no mother.

Mother will mourn me, I know she will. I don't know why she blows up at me so quickly, out of the blue. I know I can be belligerent, but . . .

She always thinks I'm a hypochondriac. Some others do, too. Even my girlfriends. Sometimes. But . . . But what? I don't know. My legs and feet are sure as hell weak. And no teeth of my own, after Baboo. Headaches. Intestinal problems come and go. I can't help it. How could I help it—what I know I feel? Thank God, I love to dance and go with the fellas. And I like dealing with the public. Up to a point.

The doctor strolled in and told her that the hysterectomy went "Very well indeed, very well indeed. But the recovery will be rough."

She thanked God for answering her prayers and made a promise to God that she would get in the habit of going to church. The last time was years ago when she got married in the Madden family's Episcopal church in South Knoxville. But that was not the same thing. She had a sneaky feeling she would break her promise. She hurt. Like hell. She hoped it wouldn't last too long, certain it would. She knew she'd almost died.

"You almost lost your mother," she told Dickie, Jerry, and John in her mind, eager to see them all again and tell them.

"No, my dear, you are in for a very long convalescence, so brace yourself."

John and Jerry could stay with Jimmy's big sister Kathleen and her family, their boy and the girl to play with, over there in South Knoxville on trashy Sevier Avenue. From the window in St. Mary's on the highest hill in North Knoxville, she saw in the distance the highest hill in South Knoxville, across the river, where all the Maddens used to live on the crest. She hated that neighborhood, where she and Jimmy had lived in that damned, dark, dank basement apartment.

Mr. Barbee said no, but Kathleen said, but they're my little brother Jimmy's kids, so he said, oh, hell, all right. But Dickie would have to go stay with Jimmy's big brother Elmo in Albuquerque.

Mother will visit me soon, and maybe Phil. Least I won't ever have to worry about getting pregnant by Bill Williams or somebody. Scared to death every time in high school and in Knoxville before I met Jimmy. Ah, sweet mystery of life, as Nelson Eddy used to sing. When I played it on the piano, Jerry said I sounded real good singing it. Through the open window one time, I heard him singing it by himself in the side yard at Mother's. Maybe that's where his love of classical music got started.

LETTER TO JERRY ASKING FOR MONEY

"You little stinker why don't you write me? No letter in over 2 wks. Just a Mother's Day card. Set yourself down and write me.

"Are you ever going to get a furlough? Honey don't try to surprise me by coming to Nashville because that would just about be the time I went to Knoxville for the weekend. Be sure and let me know so I'll be in town.

"Had a big Military Parade Sat. and all the boys marching. I thought of you and your poor feet. Are they any better? What are you doing now? Still artwork doing training aids and such, I hope—to keep you off your feet.

"Jerry Madden that shaved-head picture looked just like a convict. I almost screamed when I saw it. Please send me a *good* one. Full uniform, if you can.

"Such scratching. Trying to write six letters tonight.

"Jerry I guess John wrote and told you about little David. In the hospital over a wk and died a wk ago. The twins would have been a mo. old this past Thursday. I think he and Eliz are calling it quits. He is to be discharged out of the Marines again in a couple wks. They caught up with him being in before under-age. Don't know whether he will stay there or come home.

"Jerry do you have some extra money? Seems I just live from wk to wk. Now my radio. 6.50 to get it repaired and no music in my room for 2 wks. Sometimes the silence gets unbearable. Anytime you can slip me a five or ten I'd appreciate it. Sitting in this same chair or laying in bed listening to the radio is the story of my life.

"Haven't been home since Easter and no telling when I can again. It is so expensive. $12 with all expenses. 1/3 of a wks salary. I have offers for a ride every week to go over to Knoxville on Fri. Eve and back to Nashville for work Monday. But this Sat. I have to work, so that is out.

"Mammy had a letter from Bob. Last week. Imagine. He ought to know that when I say no it's forever.

"Married Bob one day, he broke his promise the next day never to drink again, so I got the marriage annulled on the third day, and left Terre Haute, Indiana for good.

"Poor guy thought she might tear it up and wrote IMPORTANT PLEASE READ on the outside. He wrote to tell us that Raymond his stepfather had died of cancer and wanted Mammy to let me know, as every time he calls they tell him that I am out of town.

"If you do get to come in the daytime I work at Paul Moore's Drugstore 603 Church. 2 blocks from the Maxwell House hotel where I got fired. Love, Mother."

MAKING JERRY GO SEE DICKIE

IN THE JUVENILE

"Jerry, you want to freeze your fanny off?" She stood in the doorway to Jerry's cramped "sanctuary," as he called it, wearing her quilted housecoat, her hair helmeted down with bobby pins.

"It's not too cold."

"Well, listen, honey, I promised Dickie I'd visit him today at the juvenile, but Louie was on such a rampage last night, and I had to spend my lunch hour begging and pleading with people to help me get Dickie *out* of that fix, I just am too sick and nervous to make it. *You* go, will you, honey, and take him some stuff? Tell him I'm comin' tomorrow anyway for the hearing."

"Okay. I'd like to see him anyway."

She pressed a fresh blue shirt and tan whipcord pants for Jerry, then attacked his forehead and cheeks with her fingernails to squeeze out blackheads and burst pimples, leaving his face a red moonscape, oil slick, while John watched, giggling.

"After I come from seeing Dickie, I'm gonna go to church with Iva Lee."

"You are not. You're going to the A&P and get the groceries, like I told you last night."

"Iva Lee and church are more important. We cannot live by bread alone."

"Jerry, what's got into you lately—sassin' your mother like that? You used to be the *sweetest* boy."

"Skip it, Momma. I'm *going* to the store after church."

"No, forget it, just go on right now and to hell with Dickie. After all, he's *only* your bro-ther. Jerry, if you roll your eyes like that just one more time, I'm going to smack you clean into Kingdom Come."

"Momma, it's time for the streetcar. If I miss it, visiting hours'll be over. I'll tell Dickie . . ."

"Get out! Get out of here and leave me alone. John, stop that silly grinning."

JOHN RESCUES GREG

Greg called her Emmie—not Grandmother. But Blake always called her G'ammie Emmie. Greg very seldom saw his own mother, and when he saw her, Emily reckoned he called her Naomi, not Momma. Maybe he did say Momma before she abandoned him to all those Smiths.

Mother and Cap had taken him to raise, after John took it upon himself to rescue Greg from Naomi's people in Carthage. Late at night, he told Mother and Cap and Phil to come look at the big ol' cardboard box he'd snuck into her living room, said, open it up, Mammy, and she did, and up jumped poor little five-year-old Greg in overalls like a farm boy.

When I told Jerry that about Greg in that box, he told me that the last time he ever saw Chuck was when Chuck in his cavalry uniform opened the flap of a big box Jerry was playing in and looked in at him, grinning. Killed in Sicily within the year.

Greg does do like John, Dickie, and Jerry and call Mother Mammy, but he calls Cap Pappy. But she thought Greg calling her by her nickname Emmie or even Emily sometimes and never Granny was disrespectful, as if the only real grandmother he had was Mother. And that affected Emily's whole attitude toward Greg. Not that she would ever want to be called Granny and to have taken that little stinker to raise herself. She was glad Mother and Cap took him in and treated him as if he were their own. She wondered whether Phil was jealous. It was Phil who accused *her* of being jealous.

Dickie and Naomi had Greg for only a few years and then prison again for Dickie over running marijuana out of Mexico across the border, and Naomi taking up with country music singers who happened to eat at the truck stop where she worked the counter. She fobbed Greg off on her family and Cheryl Ann off on her relative, good-hearted Elmer and his wife, Evelyn, secretary at Kay's Ice Cream.

Cheryl never claimed Dickie as her dad, but it hurt Greg that his own daddy never showed much interest in him, whether from prison or out roaming the forty-eight getting into one kind of trouble after another, mostly con jobs, selling cheap jewelry or passing bad checks.

So she felt the only true grandchild she had was sweet little ol' Blake. If only he lived by her in Knoxville and not eight hundred miles away in the swamps of Louisiana among all those hurricanes and alligators.

"And mosquitoes big enough to carry off chickens."

JIMMY JUST BACK

FROM WAR AND DRINKING

"Jimmy, you want to burn us all up." She stood over the bed, reaching across Jerry for Jimmy's smoked-way-down cigarette. Jimmy surrendered it to her.

"Wasn't setting fire to the coal house that time enough for you? . . . Are the kids asleep?"

"Kids, you asleep?" Jerry kept quiet. "They said, yeah."

"Smart aleck . . . Listen, Jimmy, honey, I just came in to say, you and me got

Jerry and Blake, 1962, at the home place.

to *try*. We got to move out of Mother's house and have our own family life. But only if you quit killing yourself with rotgut whiskey. Will you promise to try, Jimmy? I still love you, honey. Jimmy? Are you *asleep*? . . . You son of a bitch."

As she passed the bathroom she tossed Jimmy's cigarette into the toilet and it hissed back at her.

She heard Jerry praying. "Everybody seems so strange to me, God, even people I know, even my own momma and daddy—even Mammy."

He once told her that for six years, since they'd lived on Cedar Street, he had drifted off to sleep every night having a friendly talk with God.

"SORRY TO HAVE TO TELL YOU, BUT . . ."

"Dear Jerry. Sorry to have to tell you, but Mother and Cap had a fuss and broke up for good. Or probably not, since they've done it twice before. I got a letter from Dickie. He's out of that army prison and has got himself back in Tennessee state prison and John's in the reform school's hospital and I have to catch a bus this morning back to Nashville. While I'm there, I may's well see about a job at the cigar counter in the Sam Davis Hotel, too, so I can stay by and do for them what I can.

"So hold down the fort, honey. And try not to sass your boss, or your teachers, or the principal."

"How about the weatherman?"

"How about I slap you winding?"

Jerry kissed her goodbye, and she went out on the porch and down the cracked steps to the streetcar stop, a spring in her step, in spite of everything.

FRENCHIE'S BETRAYAL

Frenchie knew Emily was in sore need. But Frenchie put in anyway for the job of taking care of the old lady, telling her Emily had accepted another job in north Cincinnati. And that, besides, she was more qualified, had more experience, and was stronger than Emily, so that she could pick the old lady up if she fell, and handle her in bed, wash her, get her into her clothes, take her to the toilet and back. Emily hated some of the things practical nurses had to do, but she knew she could have managed the old lady somehow. Said Emily had too bad a temper, and the old lady insisted on having absolute say so and needed absolute calm.

Frenchie reminded her that she had gotten her many jobs all over Cincinnati, so she shouldn't hold this one thing against her. That they had been best friends too long to break off.

She remembered Ginny doing her dirty a time or two over the years, but they always reconciled. She thought Frenchie was much more compatible, intelligent, and odd in nice ways, and never dreamed she would clash with her over anything. She remembered having more fun with Frenchie than any of her other girlfriends.

They were all still loyal to her—Ruth, Zoe, Madabee, Ginny, too, and Ruby, except that Ruby's new husband kept her no better than a captive, jealous if anybody, man or woman, looked at Ruby cross-eyed. Ha. Ruby herself was a little cross-eyed, not to mention buck-toothed, but pure damn attractive anyhow.

She read for the third time Frenchie's letter of explanation, but was not impressed. Mean. It was mean of her to do her that way. She hoped Frenchie threw her back out, lifting that fat old lady. No, that was no fun. It had happened to her, and she still suffered now and then. She liked working in Cincinnati, but felt she needed to leave, so she wouldn't run into her some Saturday night on a dance floor somewhere out on the town.

But, no, Dickie was on his way to live with her until he got a job. And no telling whether John, too, would show up all of a sudden. Her boys. And Jerry in New Haven, Connecticut, of all places, going to Yale Drama School, and Robbie pregnant. She tried to stop thinking about everybody. But she couldn't. Mother sick. Cap with eczema tormenting his hands, poor fellow, always scratching, puffing away on a King Edward. And Phil slipping deeper into alcoholism along with the rest of the men folk on both sides.

HUNTING WITH JERRY TO BUY A PIANO

She kept her ears open for the sound of Jerry's car, ready to go piano hunting. It's gonna go right there in the same spot where Mother's own piano used to set before she sold it after only a few years, where Cap and Phil knocked down the wall and expanded the living room. No, not the same spot. The same position, east wall, almost touching the south, new, wall. Same thing. Sort of.

On Mother's piano, she had taught Jerry how to pick out the piece he heard her play and came to love throughout his childhood, "Claire de Lune." And on his own, his other favorite, "The Polonaise," that he heard Cornel Wilde—well, really Jose Iturbi—play as Chopin in *A Song to Remember*. Well, he sure did. Then he bought the 78 record, Iturbi playing, and John, of course, just had to break it. Shatter it. Accidentally. On purpose? Made Jerry go into a red-faced rage.

She wondered what came over Mother that she gave in, let her play it when she visited. "I just like seeing it settin' there, Mother." Jerry had wanted to buy another one for her for years, but she never lived in a house or one city long enough.

Jerry told her he used to meet Iva Lee at the Lawson McGhee Library to listen to "Claire de Lune" and "The Polonaise" on the record player with earphones—John mispronounced it "earfoams"—and that it was so beautiful it hurt and made him squeeze her hand so hard she got tears in her eyes. "From the music, I hope, and not me squeezing her hand, sometimes my fingernails digging into her palms."

They looked all over town, for-sale ads in their hands, secondhand stores and people's houses, and found none good enough or cheap enough.

After he dropped her off at her little apartment on Morgan, she wondered whether Jerry could still pick out "Claire de Lune."

MEETING JIMMY IN THE MIDDLE OF GAY STREET

Hanging up her waitress apron and walking out the front door of Kuhlman's Drugstore and Soda Fountain into twilight, balmy air on her face, she sucked in a breath of freedom.

On the curb across the street stood the young man—not so young—who had parked himself on his stool at the soda fountain until she agreed to let him take her to dinner and then to see *The Jazz Singer* at the Tennessee. Seeing her, he waved his hat and smiled triumphantly.

A younger man wearing a hat that sat down on his big ears was about to step off the curb across the street and walked, oblivious of the red light, past her date, a loping, sauntering walk. She sees that he sees her coming out of Kuhlman's Drugstore just off work there, hesitate on the curb, then step into the street, the light green now. As she reached the middle of Gay Street, cars passing left and right, she saw the young man start to smile at her. Watching out for passing cars stalled her long enough for him to reach her, stop in front of her in the middle between the southbound and the northbound streetcar tracks.

"Where you going, pretty girl?"

"To him." She pointed to the older man who waited on the opposite curb.

"Aw, why don't you come go with me?"

He put out his hand, she took it, he turned her, led her back to the curb in front of Kuhlman's.

"Where're we going?"

"Café. Want to see a movie, too?"

"Well, yeah. What's your name?"

"Jimmy."

"Mine's Emily."

"Where you live?"

"In North Knoxville off Broadway on Henegar. Where you live?"

"Up yonder." He pointed to the end of Gay Street where a ridge peaked. "South Knoxville, cross the river on top of that ridge."

She was glad he led her past the Strand and Tom Mix, then past the Riviera and Joan Crawford. Up ahead, the Tennessee or the Bijou.

The red and blue lights of the marquee of the Tennessee shone directly though the café's dull and wide window.

She was eager to see Al Jolson in the all-talking, all-singing *Jazz Singer*. Remembering for no reason at all, Mother saying about Al Jolson in "*The Jazz Singer*," "I can't stand to look at him." Mother turned her head, shaking it, her mouth scrunched up. "A New York Jew in black face. Lord, have mercy." She wouldn't let Phil or Chuck see it, but Emily connived with Chuck to sneak to see it, who later took Phil.

"I'd rather go to Lyle's lunch counter in the Market House, but it's closed this late."

Sanitary Grill, narrow aisle behind the long counter, narrow walk along the wall, all the stools full, men and women.

"Well, if it ain't little ol' Jimmy."

All heads turned toward the door, but that didn't turn shy Jimmy's head, he took it all in stride, loping toward a stool opening up at the end. She watched.

"What you got there, Jimmy?"

"Ah, I got me the 'It' girl of Gay Street, Joe."

She liked that, but she didn't like seeing that one girl, older than the others, fawning, then turning her head, lowered, and Jimmy placing a placating hand on her shoulder as he passed.

"I saw him first."

"You don't see I got a lady with me?"

"Jimmy, you think you can handle that one?"

"Girl, are you kidding? Hel-lo, Jimmy."

He took her hands as she passed.

"Well, she's mine now."

"Didn't you wait on her at the fountain in Kulhman's?"

"Ain't seen you since yesterday."

"Aren't you Greek?"

"Every day."

"I'll have a Greek salad, hold the onions."

"No Greek salad."

"In Cleveland, where I come from, Greek restaurants serve Greek food."

"Jimmy, would you eat Greek food?"

"*Hell* no."

"You and all Knoxville, hell no. What's your drink?"

"I don't take a beverage."

"And buttermilk for Jimmy boy."

Her pearly blouse had turned rainbow—lights from the Tennessee Theatre reflected in the mirror on the wall at the end, shed its colors on her.

Well, after this, *The Jazz Singer*.

Jimmy leaned back on his stool so he could dig into his pocket.

"What do I owe you, Max?"

"He asks me that same question every day. To tease me, Jimmy?"

Jimmy ducked his head shyly, slyly, smiling, looked over at Emily. His laugh was a long breath, ending in a soft sigh.

"His cousin David that runs the meat packing company says to me, give the poor little orphan anything he want."

"My momma and daddy died when I was eleven."

"What he always want is a hot beef sandwich with the gravy on top, the smashed potatoes, the slaw, and the apples pie. Don't you eat apples pie, young lady?"

After her mother's apple pie, nobody, nowhere comes close enough.

Outside, he turned her away from the Tennessee Theatre, left at the corner nearing Market House Square, and its odors gave her stomach a sinking feeling.

There was the Crystal Theatre, a hole in the wall, but they passed it.

"I like the Rialto better."

She had seen and heard about it, too, a worse hole-in-the-wall picture show than the Crystal. But she knew she would go with him, wherever he took her.

Holding Jimmy's hand, she waited for one of the rats to run over her shoe.

One did. When she yelped and jumped up, he gently pulled her down. "Aw, they ain't hurtin' nothing."

Back on Gay Street, Jimmy put a streetcar token in her hand. "Bye honey, see you at Kulhman's."

He loped down Gay Street toward the river bridge and the steep ridge where it was said you could see the remains of a Yankee Civil War fort.

On the streetcar heading north, she imagined Jimmy walking across the Gay Street Bridge over the Tennessee River ("it's no Lake Erie") into South Knoxville and climbing past the East Tennessee Packing House the rich Maddens owned and up the steep ridge.

SEEING JERRY'S FIRST PLAY

Watching "Call Herman in to Supper," she was terrified that the young mother and father would find little Herman drowned, but at the same time she was proud that Jerry had won with two others in UT's statewide playwriting contest. Only sixteen years old and already his first play. Theater-in-the-round, a type new to her. In a large room on the second floor with beveled lead glass windows all across the wall facing Knoxville and a view of city lights from high on what they called "the Hill."

A neighbor man came into the cabin and said he had found little Herman sure enough, drowned. She cried, and looked at Jerry's profile and saw Iva Lee was crying.

When the lights went black, she saw across Knoxville all the way to Sharp's Ridge, the red pulsing light on the radio tower that warned low flying planes, and imagined the railroad tracks somewhere in the dark between UT and the ridge that Jerry said he was walking one cold twilight when he heard a woman's voice calling, "Herman, come in to supper, honey, come to supper," and imagined a play about that woman and Herman, and her husband. And the blind and deaf gran'paw calling little Herman to lead him to the supper table. Jerry always did have a wild imagination, only three when he told stories to Dickie and John and the neighborhood boys and girls on their high front steps.

He was smiling now, holding Iva Lee's hand, as the applause grew louder, and it kept on. She was so proud she couldn't stand it when the young director came out to take a bow with the actors, and he called Jerry down to be among them. Jerry called everybody's attention to Iva Lee, and then the director asked Emily to take a bow as the mother of the playwright. She stood up, her legs shaky, and Ruth put her arm around her waist to brace her. And she presented Mother and Cap. "And my good friend Ruth is here with us." The applause was something she would never forget. But she felt bad that she had left out pointing out Jimmy, who had tagged along, and him stone sober for once.

Iva Lee took a picture of all of them out in the hallway, her, Ruth, Jimmy, Cap, and Mother. Phil couldn't be persuaded to come see his own nephew's play.

Mother told everybody that Jerry had told her the story of the play the day after he heard that woman calling Herman in to supper. And then she had to point out that Aunt Maudie sent in a movie idea back in 1920 or so to Hollywood and that they came within an ace of buying it.

Then Joe Baldwin, who taught a free playwriting class at night at UT that he let Jerry into, took some shots of Jerry and Iva Lee together.

"Call Herman in to Supper. A Mountain Tragedy" by Jerry David Madden won second place out of three other one acts. Too much like Tennessee Williams, some said.

"Never read him," Jerry said.

"Ruth, you should see the stories and poems and plays Jerry's written, a stack a mile high."

THEY COME AND TOOK JOHN
TO THE JUVENILE

She opened the front door and looked around to see who all might be sitting in the living room.

"Where's John, Mother?"

"They come for him, honey."

"Who come for him?"

"Sergeant Lovall of the juvenile department. Claimed John laid out of school all last week and stole some wallets today from the Emporium. And that lummox Edward Dunn trudging right along with him. Bill Williams just called, so don't breathe a word about this when he comes by."

She was always ashamed to let people know, even Cap.

Even though it had always hurt when people made fun of him because of his brothers, Jerry told her that he had never felt ashamed.

"Why, why, why, does John *do* me this way?"

"He likes the way we talk about Dickie."

"I don't know what you're talking about, Jerry."

"He listens to us wondering where Dickie could be now and when he might come home, and whether he's in trouble, and how sorry we feel for him being in the Juvenile, or jail, or prison, and . . ."

"All I know is that poor thing's back in that awful Juvenile. And now John's got the reform school staring him in the face. I think about him locked in and———" She started crying.

"Well, he may be locked up, but he sure runs loose in our heads."

If he hadn't been working at the Bijou, Jerry could have watched over John the way he used to. Now they'd send him to the reform school.

"I feel sorry for him, Momma, and I know what anguish you're suffering."

She knew Jerry experienced her feelings, too, and he'd told her before how he always felt guilty over failing to prevent bad events from happening to members of the family. Yes, he could be hateful at times, but when you come right down to it, he's too sensitive for his own damn good.

MOTHER PROMISES TO TAKE JERRY
TO CADES COVE

While she was turning over the chuck roast and Cap was taking Phil's Dodge
out to tone up the rubber and tune up the engine from being parked too long,
not driven, result of a drunk-driving conviction, she heard Mother promise
Jerry again in a low voice that she'd take him to Cades Cove in the Great
Smokies this summer after she and Cap returned from their honeymoon in
Florida—and that wouldn't be long.

"Well, there's not much to it anymore, with all those tourists overrunning
Gatlinburg." Emily stood in the doorway, holding a dripping stirring spoon.

"Well, I promised Jerry since he was a little feller to show him Cades Cove."

During the war, Mother used to sit on the long concrete bench under the
oak tree, resting in the evening after working her victory garden, and she'd
tell Jerry and John about the Smoky Mountains and how she longed to go
back someday in a fine automobile and she could take along her ancient, blind
mother and her feisty sister, Maudie.

"We gonna climb high up on Rich Mountain and look out over mountain ranges and mountain ranges and mountain ranges, blue, and gray, and
misty—smoky, smoky—and some places where the sun hits, and others in
cold dark shadder, and nothing but mountain wilderness all around for miles
and miles and miles, and then down we'll go into Cades Cove—little farms
scattered all over and two white churches with their little graveyards and that
old mill."

Haunted by her vivid memory of seeing what those mountain folks had left
behind, Mother talked of it as if it were something vague in her own people's
past, maybe the Cherokee part of her, but Jerry talked of it all as if the trees
and wooden fences and log cabins and beehives and even the horses and cows
were things of that past vividly alive today, and he responded to the images as
if they'd come down directly to him, as touchable as the grass and the mimosa
trees and the sticky green stalks of flowers coming up in Mother's backyard
right now. No wonder he said he dreamed of becoming either a detective or
a writer or an artist.

"And coming back, we'll eat us a big meal in this hotel in Sevierville where
the Ku Klux once hanged a man and where Cap put out a fire years back and
ate defiant in the grand dining room in his big muddy boots after they tried

to throw him out. Far back as Cleveland, I promised Chuck I'd take him all through Cades Cove. But now . . ." She smothered back tears.

"I want to take a look again at Chuck's old rusty sled."

Emily watched Jerry go down to the circus-wagon coal house.

When he came back up, he told Mother, "I hope Cap won't paint the old circus-wagon—or throw Chuck's sled out."

During dinner, Mother told a string of anecdotes about "poor little ol' Chuck."

When Mother started a fuss with Emily over nothing, Emily said, crying, "Sometimes, I feel like Chuck's ghost."

JIMMY YELLING FOR HER OUT
ON THE STREET

She listened to Jimmy out under the streetlight yelling until she couldn't stand it another minute.

Flinging the quilt off her, she leapt out of bed and stomped to a front window that was open so she could breathe in the night air that was hot as a furnace.

She yelled in a whispery, suppressed way, "Jimmy! Shut! Up! Get! Away from in front of this house!"

Jimmy stood in the middle of the streetcar tracks, reeling, reeking, she imagined, of the white lightnin' that he got from up in Buzzard's Roost, the rest of it in his rear pocket, bottle flat against his kidneys where it all got to finally, yelling into the numb night, "Emily! Emily! Goddamn it, come out here. Yeah, you know it's me . . . Jimmy. Emily! Goddamn it . . . Come out here . . . I want to talk to you!"

"I'm calling the police on you this time."

"Let 'em come. Hell, who cares?"

He rambled on, repetitiously, mumbling, suddenly bursting louder, a sudden breeze turning the leaves, showing their milk-green underbellies behind him in the streetlight.

She walked sluggishly into Jerry's bedroom and stood beside his cot, knowing he was awake.

"Jerry, get out there and see if *you* can make him shut up."

"Do what?"

"Your daddy's been out there in front of the house yowling since one o'clock. 'E-mi-ly. E-mi-ly.' God. What will the neighbors think? Miss LaRue'll probably ask us to move, if you don't pacify him."

"Jerry! Jerry!"

"See, now he wants *you*. I yelled at him to hush or I'd call the cops, but he won't let up. I don't appreciate even being associated with him. Everybody in Knoxville knows your daddy lives in that trashy L&N Hotel, chockablock with drunks and whores."

"What time is it?"

"Two o'clock in the blamed morning."

"What's the matter with him? He hurt?"

"You needn't sound so worried about your precious daddy. The SOB is weepy drunk. Screaming, 'We got to help Dickie, Emily.' Where was he when Dickie got into trouble in the first place?"

"Overseas in the war, Momma."

"You want me to smack your face?"

"Momma, it's two o'clock in the morning."

But he was getting up. Nothing on but those old undershorts she told him not to wear in public, barefoot, he staggered outside.

She stood in the doorway looking at Jerry go up to Jimmy and heard them talking in the low, soft voices they usually used, and went back to bed, pulling the quilt over her head, reliant on Jerry.

REVIEWING HER LIFE

All in all, taking in all the years, what had she been? In a letter once, Jerry called her "a courageous mother." Well, she reckoned so, especially in the early years, raising all three of them, losing Ronny, and then year after year trying to get John and Dickie out of jail. Jerry had been there, close, during those years.

She wished she had been able to be also something more than a mother. Jerry once asked her what she most wished she had become, said he assumed concert pianist or theatrical dancer or swimming champion, and she'd told him a secretary. She'd taken shorthand and typing during Jerry's years in the army, but she was too nervous to master those two skills and went on being a hostess and a practical nurse, among a raft of other jobs.

Jerry and also John but not Dickie, that she could remember, had stood beside her a time or two, looking left and right at the other graves: Daddy, Phil, Chuck, Granny Merritt, who had bought the ten plots in the 1920s, maybe when she worked at Knoxville Woolen Mill and bought that huge house on Euclid. Around on the other side of the plot, Dickie and John would join Greg's first wife's two plots, needed for an ostentatious monument, leaving a grave for Jerry, which, he told her, neither Robbie nor Blake would ever visit, because they saw no meaning in graves and favored getting turned into ashes in a jar or just pitched into thin air.

RUNNING JIMMY OUT OF THE APARTMENT

In a little while, she called Jerry and Rusty in to a breakfast of cinnamoned fried apples and piping hot biscuits.

John was still asleep on the cot by the kitchen table.

From the kitchen window, she saw Jimmy get off the streetcar. He hadn't been home in three nights.

Jerry seemed to her he was relieved his daddy was home, but when she started screaming at Jimmy, he and Rusty went back outside and into his chicken house sanctuary.

She threw at Jimmy a plate full of last night's supper she'd saved for him. Chicken gravy and mashed potatoes drooled down the walls very slowly and a broken plate and chicken legs and green beans and cornbread lay on the yellow-stained old linoleum floor.

Cringing, Jimmy backed away from her into the hall and turned on a dime and got out of there.

Jerry came back in. "Where's Daddy at?"

"I turned him out into the street."

"What for?"

"Now, you just shut up, Jerry. It's none of your business. He's probably headed straight for Mary's, so you needn't feel sorry for him. Save it till that husband of hers breaks out of Brushy Mountain Prison and catches your Daddy in his half of the bed, and I hope he blows his head off."

She told Jerry that Baboo wouldn't have died if his daddy hadn't spent the money she gave him for medicine to get drunk and waller with Mary.

"You told me that before . . . Well, I reckon I'll go out and write some more." John had slept through the whole short time Daddy was in the house.

That night in the dark, she went out to Jerry's chicken shack sanctuary to tell him that she and his daddy had separated.

Jerry cried and she cried and screamed, "You love him more than you do me!"

John suddenly appeared in the shack doorway. "What's you all talking about?"

"I was just telling Momma about my summary of my new novel 'The Cosgroves of Destiny.'"

Jerry went off to the Bijou to work the night shift. When he came in at midnight, she was still crying, and she cried all night, cussing Jimmy.

TRYING TO GET DICKIE OUT OF PRISON

"Dear Jerry,

"It was wonderful to have you home again for a few days. I get so terribly lonesome by myself so much. My nerve is about to fail me to face this long summer—hot as H-today—100. I slept till 9:30—off & on. Dressed, and went to church. Ate breakfast and lunch—Brunch. Ham and waffles—now back to these dreary 4 walls—probably drag myself to a show and then it will only be 5 bells. Weekdays pass OK but Sundays Roy isn't here for a month long. I worked 12 hr. last Sunday and got my radio. Have it on real low and the big fan awhirl.

"Bill Williams passed through here again Monday. Stood him up again. I think he's thru with me. Don't care too much. Not for him or any other. Get so tired of dating here and there. Maybe someday I'll meet someone to make a home with. Lord, maybe some man from Cleveland, and you know I don't mean little Cleveland, Tennessee, which, remember, your Gran'paw and Gran'maw Madden came from.

"Jerry, I am thinking seriously of going back to Knoxville for 3 mo. and then back over here as I think I can do more for Dick here in Nashville. Only I am so afraid I can't get a job as they are so darn scarce. The lonesomeness at times almost kills me to where I can't carry on an intelligent conversation anymore. Living in Knoxville I'd have 2 mon. to get a minister to vouch for Dick, get him a job and have an apt. for him to come to if they let him out.

"I am going to stand by him this one more time and then if he slips I can't help it. I'll get him a parole if I have to go to the Governor again.

"Let me know what you are going to do now that your training is over and if there is a chance of going overseas. I do wish you wouldn't apply, not even to Paris. They'll send you soon enough. Then over there your feet might go down and then you'll be up the creek without a paddle for sure.

"Just can't believe you'll be 21 next mo. No more little boys do I have. Be sure and tell me if you took care of the insurance payment. Love, your mother."

MOTHER'S VOICE AMONG
THE BLACKBERRY BUSHES

Mother's voice. That one time we went blackberry picking down in the addition before they started building the houses, a wilderness of vines and bushes and briars, and the sound of big, luscious berries hitting her tin bucket and her voice melodious on the other side of the bush between us higher than our heads, "Emily, I wish you could see these wonderful berries, a million of them within reach."

LYING IN BED, READING,
SNOW OUTSIDE

The linoleum floors in the home place were always very cold. But getting the mail, she liked the breath of bracing air.

Snowbound, she reveled in the beauty of it. Her experiences in snow or looking out at snow, coming down or lying, was lifelong, from Cleveland on Lake Erie to Knoxville and many other towns and cities prone to snow. John used to dash out with a saucepan and come in with it full, awed that she could turn it into ice cream with Pet milk from a punctured can. Dickie made fun of John's excitement, Jerry just piddled with it as being not close enough to the real thing, and look, there's specks of coal ash the rising smoke let down.

Mindful of snow all around for miles, she snuggled into her blankets and, propped on her cool pillow, plunged into *The Foxes of Harrow* by Frank Yerby that Jerry curled his lip and raised his eyebrows over. She reached for the last chocolate-covered cherry in the Russell Stover box, knowing she would gently set the box on the pyramid of selfsame boxes next morning.

She sighed. She sighed. Sighed, deeply, as if devoted to sighing, for its own sake. Acid reflux. Too many Russell Stover assorted chocolate-covered creams. She knew better. She just didn't give a rat's ass, as little Clyde the Biltmore bartender used to say. She had to pee, but she couldn't stop reading *The Foxes of Harrow*, this second time around. Due back at George's department store lending library by the end of the week. The bed was toasty warm.

Sleepy, but she still had to write to Dickie, John, and Jerry, all three in far-flung places now. And mail the letters she already wrote to Ruth and that Turkish husband of hers, in Cairo of all places. And maybe Ginny. But she was still mad at her for not writing more often.

Sabu's asleep now, but I hope she doesn't take a great notion to claw the damn curtains. Cats just don't seem to care. Especially Siamese. How exotic, that name. Oh, damn, the cat box. Oh, to hell with it. If she thinks I'm gonna get up and sift it, she's got another think coming.

TALKING ABOUT DADDY

ON A DRIVE WITH JERRY

In from Baton Rouge, driving a secondhand foreign car so low slung she had to struggle to get in it, Jerry was taking her on a Sunday drive into the Smokies via Maryville and Townsend this time. They got to talking about her daddy.

"Momma, what I remember most about Gran'paw before he died when I was only three is him walking down the backyard to his car parked in the alley, short tubby fellow smoking a cigar, lugging an ice cream freezer for a picnic—at Chilhowee Park, was it?"

"Honey, I forget."

"Just a view from the rear, but that sight did it for me. Oh, and I'll never forget us boys lying on the dusty carpet on our bellies looking up at Gran'paw sitting in that wicker rocking chair, listening to *Major Bowe's Talent Hour* on that old-fashioned Westinghouse radio cabinet that had legs so it looked almost as big as he was. Might track one down and buy it sometime."

"Yes, and his belt laying across his lap if one of you made a noise interrupting his pure enjoyment. How about the time you and John and Dickie snuck into Daddy's car, playing like you could drive. And John bellered to get his turn, and somehow he shoved it in neutral and it coasted down to the telephone pole guy wire that stopped it because you left the door open."

"That was Dickie. He jumped out so he wouldn't get killed."

"I forget what Daddy had to say about that."

"Me, too. But I remember him walking us down through the addition, before many houses had gone up, to buy us ice cream cones, and at the curb on Broadway, he told John and me to take hold of his thumbs and hold on and told Dickie to take hold of his belt in the back, and that's when Kay's still had grape ice cream."

"He made everybody keep churning that ice cream freezer we used to have, till it was hard as a rock and we were almost too worn out to eat it, and then he'd take a spoon to it and beat it till it was almost soupy and eat it with a piece of cornbread."

"Hot or cold?"

"Why, honey, I don't know."

MOTHER WORRIED

ABOUT PHIL OUT DRINKING

"Phil ain't come home yet, Emily. What in the world do you think could've happened to him?"

"Don't worry, Mother. Phil made it through the war. He's likely able to make it through Knoxville."

"Well, sometimes he worries me to death. That drinking."

"Frankly, Mother, he worries me, too. Course that boy hitting him in the eye with a rock left him sort of puny ever since."

"What in the world was the army thinking, drafting a boy with one eye half blind?"

"Desperate, I reckon. But he did do well, unless you count the drinking, which may be partly out of the awful experiences he had."

"What?"

"Those awful experiences."

"What awful experiences, Emily?"

"For one thing, helping his buddy stretch out that German girl's arms while his sergeant cut her in half with a machine gun."

"He did no sich of a thing."

"Don't you remember? He told us both that night a year ago when we set him down and asked him what—"

"Emily, hush. Your little brother would never do *that*."

"What about the time he was ordered to blow the bridge before his best friend, that Indian fellow, could make it across, those German tanks right behind him?"

"You makin' this up just to torment me?"

"Mo-therrr, you were sitting right there in that very chair and I was sitting right here on the couch and he was sitting beside me, telling it."

"Crazy drunk, what it was."

"No, he wasn't. Stone sober. He just wanted us to know."

"I don't remember a word of it. Now hush it. Sounds like his footsteps coming up on the porch."

JERRY SEARCHES FOR

THE MEANING OF LIFE

Jerry had propped a note on the kitchen table against the rooster salt shaker.

"Dear Momma, I am going to India to search for the meaning of life, like Tyrone Power as Larry Darrell in *The Razor's Edge*. Even if I have to go to the end of the earth, I will find it. Knoxville is dead to me. Jenny is dead to me. Someday you will understand. Tell Mammy I love her when they get back from visiting Hazel and them in Florida, and I love you and Daddy, and someday when I am a famous writer we will all meet again in New York or Paris or Calcutta. Jenny can tell you why I am going away. And now I belong to the world and God. Your son Jerry."

She got the cops out on a three-state alarm, like the time Jerry stayed gone when he was four in his pink sunsuit and brown tam, playing in a rich boy's enormous toy room, riding his three rocking horses until dark, and the brown and yellow squad car was parked in front of the house on Copeland, its radio crackling, she and Jimmy leaning against the hood, when they caught sight of him sauntering down the hill.

"See, Emmie, I told you he'd come home before dark." To Jimmy nothing really bad ever happened, not even the Depression.

He ran away one other time, to Chattanooga. *Why*, she never got out of him. Lost him his job ushering at the Bijou.

So she went to see *The Razor's Edge* to see what it was that made him act so crazy. Tyrone Power was wonderful, but he didn't make her want to run away to India to search for the meaning of life with some old long-bearded Indian in the mountains of India. If she could just find the right man, one with a good job, one who detested even the smell of whiskey, she could go the rest of her life without needing to know the meaning of life. Even if she knew what it was, where would it get you?

When she stepped out of the Tennessee Theatre, she saw that Crigger boy who was now a traffic cop and asked him if he had heard anything about Jerry from headquarters.

"No. What about him?"

"Well, he's run off to India to search for the meaning of life."

"Well, he should have asked me. I've got it right here in my pocket."

What he showed her was a ten-dollar bill from his billfold.

"I didn't know you were such a card, Herman. How's your Momma?"

"HONEY, DON'T EXPECT TOO MUCH OF JIMMY"

Every shift at Kuhlman's, men, young and old, boys too, asked her out, drawing on fifty-something pick-up lines.

"I suppose you want to drag me to Sanitary Grill and the Crystal Theatre" was her one response.

"What man would do that?"

"The man I'm going to marry. And I'll never see Lake Erie again."

She tried it.

"Jimmy, I want to move back to Cleveland."

If she marries Jimmy, she'll never go. Jimmy Madden or Cleveland?

Jimmy frowned. "What is it about Cleveland?"

"Everything. My friends."

"No friends here?"

"Starting to meet a few. Madabee who works at Miller's."

Jimmy's big brother Elmo sat her down to tell her how Jimmy's always been.

"Jimmy'd go down to the packing house to ask David Madden on the rich side of the Maddens for a dime or two, and after he spent it, it was dark, so he'd just wait at the bottom of the hill for me to go down and get him. Same little Jimmy who you goin' to marry. Kathleen knows."

She asked her.

"Honey, don't expect too much of Jimmy."

"It seems Jimmy is all there is. Not Jimmy and other things that are his."

"Honey, you got him pegged. For all the good that will do you . . ."

"Well, I can't just give him up, can I?"

"We couldn't, because we never wanted to. But sounds like you are giving up everything else."

JERRY, ROBBIE, AND BLAKE

GOING BACK HOME

About to go get in the car and go back to Baton Rouge, Jerry hugged and kissed her, and Robbie hugged her and kissed her, and then Blake, and she kissed them back, one by one.

"And don't forget to bring the home movies next time, especially the one that shows little Blake naked, trying to push the lawn mower."

"I will, Momma. Bye. Bye, Mammy."

She stood beside Mother behind the screen door, tears in her eyes, together watching them go down the three steps from the little concrete porch and along the walk and get in the car.

And she waved and Mother waved and they each waved three times before Jerry's Dodge Dart moved away, up Henegar, Jerry tapping the horn once.

Through the tears in her eyes, she saw tears in Mother's, this moment they shared once, sometimes twice a year, Christmas and summertime.

She remembered Jerry before he married Robbie, going back to sea and later back to the army base, kissing Mother first, as he usually did, and then turning to hug and kiss her. She always stood next to Mother behind the screen door to watch Jerry get in his car and, tears in her eyes, wave good-bye, so damn sorry to see him go. She and Mother standing so close behind the screen, shoulders touching, was one of their most intimate moments. She wished somebody would snap their picture so she could see how they looked.

Then Mother backed away from the screen first and turned back into the living room, then Emily turned, and they went separate ways, Mother to the kitchen usually, she to sit on the davenport and feel sodden sad.

Someday too soon, Mother would be gone, and she would be living alone in the little house, not just visiting or having to live there a short time with Mother and Cap, and sometimes Phil. And she was aware that the frame of the screen door would show only her, remembering, wanting to feel Mother shoulder to shoulder with her.

Well, maybe John will show up in a different car from that last jalopy, and she would hear the screen door whine open.

PORTRAIT: JUST MARRIED

In the photograph they got taken at People's Studio on South Gay Street by the Southern Railroad viaduct, she thought she looked very good. And so did Jimmy. Separate poses. Glamorous even. That hat that framed her face. Her Cleveland friends would love it, like the snapshots she had taken up there a year before that sad day. The piano that came and went, and that day on the train going down, down to Knoxville.

They were married in the Episcopal church on Sevierville Avenue, not his whole family's church, just Kathleen's, where she got married to Mr. Barbee but seldom attended because somebody tossed beer bottles in her front yard and some church ladies passing saw them, swore Kathleen, drunk, tossed them into her own front yard from her porch. Lies like that.

They all were there, Daddy, Mother, Phil, and Chuck, but not Granny Merritt, who was very sick. And Jimmy's brothers and sisters, Kathleen, Elmo, Ed, Frank, and Lois. And a sprinkle of friends on both sides. Not the full church, not the overflowing flowers she always imagined would adorn her wedding while living "up there." But flowers enough.

"I never kissed anybody out in public before."

"This is not the time to be shy, Jimmy. Everybody's waiting for you to kiss me."

He did, but didn't linger. Even when he frowns, he only seems to, just trying to get what it is you mean.

JERRY'S PLAN TO GET JOHN OUT OF PRISON

Hearing from Jerry before he and Robbie left San Francisco driving to Knoxville to spend the summer in the Van Vactors' mansion while they traveled in Spain with Raven and her lover Riva and her little brother Davie made her happy, but the last part upset her.

"Now a more important matter—John's parole, which I asked you to write me about but you didn't. I have been working on a plan for it. The Salvation Army offered to act as adviser (that part is easy) but I can't find a job for him—there is very serious unemployment here. Anyway, we're leaving a few weeks after he would be released, so I don't know what to do. Can you find something there? Let me know what you're doing.

"I have to rush now to mail my novel "Cassandra Singing" to Monica McCall. I hope you have a job now. Did you receive the five bucks? Love, Jerry."

Not too many years ago, it was only the Juvenile Home, Jerry showing up beside her bed. "Momma, I guess I'll go visit John in the Juvenile."

"No, Jerry, there's no point in you or any of the family going to see John today. Let him sit there by himself one day. It'll do him good. You can visit *me* before long at the Lyons View *In*sane Asylum, or maybe in jail, for I just might take a notion to shoot that daddy of yours or that lummox Edward Dunn one—whichever crosses me first."

"Poor ol' John. I'm gonna try to be nicer to him from now on. . . . I feel like strangling Edward Dunn myself, even though I'm never sure whether it's him or John gets them in trouble allatime."

"I feel so helpless. I never really hoped it would be much better when your daddy got back from the war, but I never dreamed it'd get worse than before. . . . Jerry, turn off the radio, honey. It's 'Zip-a-Dee-Doo-Dah,' John's favorite song, 'bout to make me cry."

PHIL SLAPS HER FOR RIDING
HIS BRAND-NEW BICYCLE

Never will forget the time I jumped on Phil's new bike and raced down the street and back up and he yelled bloody murder and came up to me where I was standing in the doorway between the living room and the kitchen and slapped the living shit out of me. Two years later he was in Europe, of all places, blowing up bridges.

That brand-new bicycle parked invitingly on the walkway. Gently setting the bag containing the quart of Kay's cherry ice cream down in the grass, she kicked up the kickstand, pulled up her dress, swung her leg high over the jacked-up leather seat, and pushed off between the high hedges, turning gracefully left onto Henegar Street and sailing down the hill on a loud "wheeeeee," imagining she was feeling the seat of her own Huffy Dream Girl bike up in Cleveland.

In the addition, where two carpenters were knocking together the raw frame of yet another house, she turned around without braking in a wide swirl and pumped back up Henegar and through the hedges onto the cracked walkway, hoping Phil, as temperamental as all the Willises, on Mother's side, had not noticed his bike gone, hoping the cherry ice cream had not melted too much, and tripped up the one step onto the narrow porch and swung open the screen door, and made a beeline for the icebox to put the carton on the block of ice.

Phil rushed at her, met her in the doorway to the kitchen, and without breaking stride, slapped her face, cursing her for taking his "all mine" bike.

"Mother, did you see Phil slap me?"

"Can't say you didn't have it coming, acting so smart. It's his birthday."

"Daddy, you saw it, didn't you?"

"I saw it, and I didn't like it. Phil, apologize to your big sister."

"Mother, do I have to?"

"You most certainly do not. Charlie—"

"Hells bells, Emmie, apologize to Phil for riding his bike without permission, and then Phil, apologize to your big sister for smacking her face, and Jesse, I smell the cornbread a-burnin."

She and then Phil and then Mother did as they were told, and Daddy lit another Lucky Strike.

OFFERING TO TRY TO GET JERRY
OUT OF THE ARMY

"Dear Jerry. Guess you finally received the letter I mailed to Camp Gordon. I was so upset when I received yours saying you were transferred to Fort Jackson and more training. Honey if you really want out, write and tell me all about it. I'll go to the Gov or Senator Kefauver or whoever it takes. I'm so worried about your feet. Tell me if you can get out of that hard training in the ski troops.

"Got John's change of address as he was discharged July 1st. Not a darn word from him. I could paddle his canoe.

"Honey, Vera is a sweet girl but take it easy. I don't believe you are all the way over Iva Lee. And please don't marry until you are out of the Army.

"It has been 97 to 102 degrees here for a couple weeks. Am I ever thankful to have a job where it's air conditioning.

"Don't forget about your stuff. You owe $7.50 now. That one barrel has all your writings and your books and I don't know what all.

"Did you ever pay on your loan? You know Cap stood for it, so you'd better start paying on it. Did you ever get your G.I. Insurance? Please do this and let me know.

"Time to eat my supper. Those ol' Krystal hamburgers I guess. Write me soon. Love, mother.

"Oh, and P.S. Had a terrific gall bladder attack all last week. In bed one whole day. Missing that day's work and $2-$3 for med. made me run awful short. So any contribution to the aged will be appreciated. What are we going to do about that storage? All my worldly goods. It is getting me down. I just can't lose it. So much hard work to pay for it. Sometimes I feel like my real life is in storage."

MOTHER TELLING STORIES
BY THE BOMBER'S MOON

"Bomber's moon." Across the narrow living room, hooking her finger in the shade pull, Mother pulled it down to the sill.

The very sound of "bomber's moon" made Emily shudder. The boys were hugged up by her, Dickie slightly apart, the three that way until the blackout drill horn would blow the all-clear.

Cap was on duty at the Oak Ridge fire station, just outside the gates of that mysterious town they were putting together.

"Mammy, tell us a stor-y." John wiggled deep into the couch cushion.

"Well, way up in the Cataloochee mountains where my people, part Cherokee, come from, the shadow of a panther was seen, and one dark night . . ."

"I dreamed last night a Japanese airplane, a Zero, Kamikaze pilot, came shooting right over our backyard, and it low enough to see his face and it set the curtains on the stretchers fluttering."

"Jerry, who's the storyteller in this family?"

"Oh, Mother, the mood of us all sitting in the dark made him want to tell it so much, he . . ."

". . . The folks in this log cabin heard a scratching on the wood shingle roof like we got now, and . . ."

"And it was a—"

"John, why was you whining to hear a story if you gonna bust in on it like that?"

"I know ever' word, but I want to hear it again, Mammy."

"And I don't mind telling it again for the hundredth time, either, honey."

"Tell it, Mammy, with all the different voices."

In John's eyes and Jerry's, Mother was so wonderful and they all loved her, Dickie, too, the way they loved Jimmy. But who slaved early and late to keep them all together, clothed and fed?

"Ah, shoot fire, I wish you'd tell a new one." Dickie was the one who exposed Mother one Halloween as the witch that rode a broomstick through the dead corn stalks and jumped over the neighborhood bonfire screeching.

"Mother, tell the boys about the time Daddy beat up the principal."

"He didn't beat that poor man up, Emily."

"Tell it, tell it," said John, sitting on the magic carpet in front of Mother.

"Well, children, the way it was, the principal sent little Chuck one day with this note to Gran'paw Charlie, sayin', 'Mr. Merritt, it has been brought to my attention that your son has poured library paste all over Miss Miller's erasers. I must insist that you accompany your child to school in the morning. Bring a switch with you, as I want you to be present when I give Chuck a whipping.'" Mother bent her head and rubbed her nose the better to see the scene. "Boys, I tell you, when Gran'paw Charlie read that note, he hit the ceiling." John looked up at the ceiling, causing Jerry to look up. "He stormed and he stormed and he raged from room to room of this little ol' house, yelling, 'That g.d—.'"

Emily sat forward on the couch, looking at Jerry. "He may a been just a little feller, no taller'n you, Jerry, but if you set him off he could turn his mellow voice into a bullhorn. Used to go out and stand in the backyard and holler for Chuck to come on in for supper and Chuck, curb-hopping over at Sharp's Drugstore, would hear him all the way through the woods, across Second Creek to Broadway, and Chuck'd come running lickety-split."

"Emily, *I'm* telling this."

"Well, pardon me for living."

"So, next morning, Charlie says to Chuck, 'Son, go cut me two switches.' 'Two?'

'Don't wrangle with me. I said, "two," now git 'em.'

"So little ol' Chuck drags hisself over to the hedge outsyonder and breaks off two switches—I was watching from the kitchen winder, wondering what Charlie was up to myself—when all of a sudden, Chuck threw them switches down, and broke off a littler one and a bigger one, and come back in the house just a-smiling to beat the band. Looked like he'd figured something out, but I didn't know what it was till Chuck come home from school that afternoon and told me."

Emily saw that knowing what was coming increased Jerry's fascination, anticipating the way Mother transformed each part with her voice, her gestures, her embellishments. She felt the rhythm of response in the room, noticed Mother's ways of capturing, holding, playing with their interests, even hers, in spite of her hostility at being told to hush.

"Way it turned out, was this. Your Gran'paw Charlie marched hisself up to Lincoln Park Elementary, little ol' Chuck trottin' behind—and he was almost by then as tall as his daddy—but Charlie was just like a buzz saw when he got wound up. So he struts into the principal's office, and this old man looks across his desk at this sawed-off little feller. 'Wait outside, sir, until I'm ready to see you,' says the principal.

"Well, he ort'n a done that. Shoulda kept his mouth shut and let Charlie talk. Charlie raises up on his toes—wore a size six shoe that's even too small for *you* now, Jerry—and in that deep, cocky voice of his, says, 'Mr. Turner, you will see me *now*, for I have come just like your note says, and I have brung two switches.'

'Two switches?' asked Mr. Turner . . . and a hatefuller man you never met. Wore *out* a switch on Dickie the second year *he* went.

"Dead now, ain't he, Emily?"

"I don't know *nothin'*."

"So, anyway, Charlie says, 'Yes, sir. This little'n for you to use on my boy, and when you g'done, I'm a-gonna use this biggest'n on *you*.'"

"Then did he whup him, Mammy?" John was drooling a little.

"Don't know, honey. That's the end of the story."

As they basked in the luminous silence, Emily wished they all loved her half as much as they loved Chuck.

LETTER TO MOTHER FROM JERRY'S HOUSE

"Dear Mother,

"I am writing this in the big brass bed that Jerry told me Blake was conceived in.

"Jerry and Robbie showed me the lovely home where they lived on Grand Boulevard in Boone while he was teaching at Appalachian State Teachers College, leased for 9 months to them by the art teacher. It sets down off the street a little and a lush, large flower garden to the right of it. Boone is over 3,000 feet up in the mountains of Western North Carolina.

"They want you to come visit, too, some time, maybe next summer. I'll come with you.

"Poor lil'ol Robbie has to wrap meat at the Winn Dixie because they need money over the summer before Jerry starts Yale Drama School on a fellowship, and he is nighttime announcer on the local radio. They wanted to live in the country, so the house is east of Boone out a rocky country road on a steep hill above the river, wilderness on each side and above, and they have an old timey barn. And, Lord have mercy, the stone siding of the house goes only about half way up, and then it's tar paper. Dimitri the black cat and Tiger the momma cat come and go as they please and love hunting in the barn. And you'll be sitting in a room and a cow will stick its nose in the open window at you.

"Jerry has a nice little room for a study but he loves to read under a big tree across the dusty road from the river. Thinks it's romantic, I reckon.

"Getting the bus Tuesday, hope Cap can meet me at the Trailways. Love to you and Cap, and Phil when you see him.

"Your daughter, Emily."

CHRISTMAS, THINKING OF EVERYBODY

She thoroughly enjoyed watching Dickie's little boy Greg playing with Jerry's little boy Blake in the living room at Mother's by the light of the colored Christmas tree bulbs that blink off and on and the glitter of the shiny ornaments.

She saw Greg often because Dickie was in prison again and Naomi running loose all around West Tennessee. And now with Jerry teaching at the University of Louisville and Robbie working hard as editor of that weekly union newspaper, they made fewer and fewer trips to Knoxville.

I told him, "Don't you dare leave home without bringing the old home movies, Jerry."

Poor little Blake was just getting over getting his tonsils out, looking a little wan, but had fun, jumping around and yelling, just like John, Jerry, and Dickie used to do.

She was eager to see the kids' faces when they opened their presents in the morning. And she was eager to see what Jerry and Robbie brought her.

She just hoped Jerry and Phil didn't get into another one of their arguments over politics and religion, Phil throwing in "educated fools" about intellectuals and liberals, insinuating Jerry's one of them.

When the holiday atmosphere was cordial, Mother always said, "I look for John to come through that front door d'reckly."

And sometimes he did. Or Dickie. Never Chuck, buried in France, but it's taking your own life into your hands to try telling Mother that.

Everybody felt sad because John and Dickie were missing.

Jimmy had talked Uncle Elmo into letting Dickie stay with him in Albuquerque to help him in his radio repair business and learn a trade. She'd persuaded the judge to say okay.

Uncle Elmo called Jimmy at the factory to tell him the hell Dickie had put him through. Jimmy came by the mayor's house where Emily was a practical nurse to the mayor's invalid wife and her new baby and tried to tell her, as she gave him the bum's rush, for the judge had forbidden him to contact her.

At Mother's, she called Elmo, and Mother and Cap and Phil and Jerry all talked with Dickie. He didn't like the Christmas presents they sent him, which he opened three days before Christmas. Rather have the money.

She screamed bloody murder when Jerry asked could his daddy come for Christmas dinner.

But Jimmy didn't even call.

"No telephones under the Gay Street viaduct, I guess."

Jerry got sick on too much mincemeat pie.

John was missing because he'd walked away from John Tarleton Home one time too many, so she had to send him to a place near Lone Mountain, a twenty-mile bus ride from Knoxville, called Tate Springs in Bean Station that had been a summer resort hotel for wealthy people from the Gay Nineties until before World War I.

WORKING FOR OLAN MILLS STUDIOS
ON THE ROAD

Whenever she heard and smelled creek or river or ocean, it was Cleveland and Lake Erie, she heard voices and smells, sounds and smells of machines, everything, even come in the palm of her hand. Outside the ocean was uproaring. She was so delighted working on the road for Olan Mills, getting to visit Kitty Hawk and such, she couldn't sleep.

She liked traveling to and fro with the people who worked with her, doing special jobs, church members' portraits, private schools, even weddings. Always on the go, pack it up and go, unpack it all and do it again, laughing together, and now and then at night, dancing, and wading in the Atlantic Ocean.

She wrote to everybody to tell them all about it. Jerry stuck in the army. John in Tennessee State reform school and Dickie in federal penitentiary. Mother and Cap, and sometimes Betty and Phil. And each of her girlfriends in Knoxville and the ones she was still in touch with in Cleveland.

Working was never so much fun and frolic. And men. An array of them, and if they drank, it didn't matter so much because she knew she would never see them again, much less get involved, fall in love, and have to cope with that goddamn drinking madness, and their lies to boot. Beer. Whiskey. Wine. She couldn't stand the taste of them. Not even coffee. A Coke now and then, but not a habit.

Somebody came knocking at her door.

LITTLE JERRY WANDERS OFF
NAKED AS A JAYBIRD

Hanging panties and slips on the clothesline, propping it higher up with a pole, sheets and the kids' pants whopping around her in the breeze, she tied a rope to the galluses of little Jerry's overalls and the other end to the clothesline to keep him from chasing after the ice wagon again while she did the washing in a galvanized tub with a washboard in the kitchen. She remembered doing that to Dickie, and in a few years, she'd have to do it to John, who now sat on the floor playing cars with his imagination, in and out of the legs of the chair she'd put the tub on. Dickie was off somewhere with Richard, into some kind of trouble, no doubt. Ruby and Ernest were fussing in the next-door apartment.

Washing and rinsing was a long, long process that having a handle ringer would cut short some, easier on her red hands and arms, sore already and only Jimmy's shirts done. Would life be much different if she had married one of the boys up in Cleveland? Maybe yes, maybe no. Oh, well, the exercise is good for me, unless I develop forearms like Popeye the Sailor Man.

Through the kitchen window, she saw Jerry running along the clothesline, tethered to the line, swaying and flashing in the sun. Is he singing or playing like he's Roy Rogers out West?

Next time she looked out the window to check on him, Jerry's overalls swayed in the breeze at the end of that hairy rope. She scooped John up off the floor and dashed out into the hallway and was about to open the door when there came a knock, knock.

One of the Cooper boys, the one who taught Jerry how to spell hippopotamus, stood at the door, holding naked Jerry by the hand.

"Good morning, Mrs. Madden. I found this little feller five blocks down the street at the railroad crossing walking along as if he wasn't really naked as a jaybird. He finally told me his name, so I knew where he lived. This little feller didn't want to face his mother."

It had turned so chilly his little do-do-pee-pee-so-so stood out ahead of him.

"Well, Earl, you can just turn around and take this little feller back where you found him."

LIVING WITH JOHN IN THE HOME PLACE

"John, honey, why don't you sleep in the back room on the bed?"

"It's creepy sleeping on the bed where Cap died . . . and Phil did, too."

"Mother bought that poor little bed from me for five dollars. Jerry loves to sleep on it when he comes. And you and him and Dickie all slept in that big bed that used to sit there that time we had to live here between Cedar Street and the first house on Atlantic before the war. Remember?"

"Yeah. 'Sides, I like this old davenport."

"We called them couches in Cleveland."

"Well . . . 'Night, Momma."

She lay in Mother's old bed. Lord, Lord, poor ol' Granny Merritt bought this little house to live alone in peace and quiet. And Daddy and us appeared and dug in, and after Granny died Mother ruled the roost, and me and Jimmy moved in a while, and now just me and my brood have come and gone, and in come Cap after his wife died, and he let Dot move in, then Betty and Phil, then just Phil, and now Mother's gone, and John comes and goes.

And it such a little house back then, three rooms, and now two more, plus that addition to the living room Cap and Phil built, and they actually got along from start to finish, but still a little house, these low ceilings and a bathroom so small you can hardly turn around in it, and these linoleum floors cold as icebergs. I wonder who lives in our big house in Cleveland now.

Her restless legs syndrome kept her awake, until she turned on the light and reached for Michener's latest blockbuster. *Texas* was the best. Jerry sneers every time I tell him I'm reading a Michener novel, but I can't help it. He's good. Jerry's just *different*.

Inhaling John's secondhand smoke as he chain-smoked all day and evening ten feet across the narrow living room from her chair, she was glad she'd never had the slightest desire to smoke or drink. Without even trying, she had been one of the most popular teenagers in high school in Cleveland, in the classroom where she was a C student, on the dance floor, on the Lake Erie beach, and without smoking to be regarded as stylish and naughty, and without drinking beer, whiskey, or wine. Her memories were so vivid the loss made her feel starkly sad again.

Would John's cigarette smoke kill her before it killed him? She begged him to cut it down. He tried. Often. She begged him to step outside. He did. Often. Look at what it did to Mother. Cap sitting in this very chair, smoking all those King Edward cigars. Mother's emphysema. Never a smoker herself, like me, suffering Cap's cigar or Phil's or John's or Dickie's secondhand cigarette smoke. She figured her own lungs must be black as that specimen in a jar they showed on TV to scare the daylights out of kids who smoke.

And yet when John went out and stayed out a long time or made one of his two or three-day trips in those broken-down cars that come and go in his life—and hers—she was lonesome for his company. Even though that TV was running day and night, all night sometimes, loud, if not football, any old thing, and he hardly said a word for hours on end to her. Oh, he loves me. I know he loves me. And every time he dreams up a new project, like gathering clothes for kids in Eastern Kentucky that the floods made homeless, he tells me all about it at first, and I take all the calls for him. Newspapers. TV stations. They just love John "Sunshine" Madden. A colorful character if ever there was one. It's a wonder somebody doesn't send a story about him to *Reader's Digest* as "The Most Unforgettable Character I Ever Knew."

I just hope he makes it home before my head hits the pillow.

THE FAMILY ON THE BACK PORCH

She went out and sat on the back porch across from Cap. Wishing Jerry had not forgotten to bring along the movie projector and screen and the three-minute 8mm movies, Blake as a little kid on the farm up Hot Holler Road in Deep Gap outside Boone, and especially—she saw so clearly—herself pulling Blake on his sled down the slope at the farmhouse on Covered Bridge Road off River Road outside Louisville, making her see clearly the snapshot Daddy took of Mother pulling Chuck on his sled in the street in front of their house in Cleveland. Chuck buried under snow in France, among thousands who invaded Italy. Flowers on the graves now, yes, but two decades of snows over there, overseas, over yonder.

"Cap, is Chuck's old sled still hanging in the little coal house down there?" Jerry sounded as if he thought it might not be.

"You mean, Phil's? No, I remember, Chuck's, then it passed on to Phil."

"I pushed Chuck and Phil both many times down that steep, steep hill, Kenyon Street, before he went to war." Even as she spoke, she remembered vividly. "And Dickie and Jerry and John. So does it still hang on the wall down there?"

"Yes, and if I have anything to do with it, it'll hang there till doom's day." Cap took a draw on his King Edward as if to seal his vow.

ARGUING WITH JERRY
OVER *FOXES OF HARROW*

"Jerry, will you return this book to George's and get me *The Foxes of Harrow* by Frank Yerby, so I can finish reading that blamed thing?"

"Did you know he's a Negro?"

"Without getting smart about it."

"Well, I never thought you'd read anything a Negro wrote."

"I don't care. It's not true. All the girls at work've read it and none of them said a word about him being a Negro."

"Few people do know. He just writes for the money."

"Don't they all?"

"*I* don't."

"Honey, you are not a writer. Yet. One play. I'm proud as fire of you, but . . . Just don't get your hopes up. Honey, we just don't come from that kind of people."

"I want to be in with James Joyce and Ernest Hemingway and them."

"But not with Yerby the Negro?"

"Okay. Okay. Okay."

"See. It's only natural. Stick with your own kind and you'll be okay."

"Unless you're Japanese, living in Hiroshima."

"Oh, Lord. Not that again. I don't want to argue. Just return the damned book to George's and bring your dumb momma Blondie and Dagwood."

LETTER FROM LOVER RAY

Emily read Ray's latest letter. Ray signed all his many letters to her "me." Sometimes "You Know Who." Letters on very fancy hotel stationery, impressive hotels everywhere on his sales route. Hotel Phoenix, Taylor Hotel, Hotel Llewellyn, Hotel Patten. Why "me." Why not his name? As Phil said to Jerry, "Never put nothing in writing," because he got stung badly one time because he had done that very thing.

All her lovers came to her from their wives, most of them sick, like Cap's wife, who actually did die. She believed Bill Boles, who did sign as "Bill," but Bill seldom wrote to her. Bill Williams probably didn't give a rat's ass, happy-go-lucky fellow that he always was, Jerry's favorite.

She reread Ray's letter from the Hotel Phoenix in Lexington, Kentucky, July 14, 1954.

"Hi-Sugar: There is much speculation as to what I will do in the near future, all of which I wish to discuss with you very thoro'ly.

"Sunshine Baby, will you be my ol' ray of beautiful light and understanding when I see you Friday eve'n, because I want to see my Sugar as I have always known her, full of life, pep and loveliness, beautiful as a flower which you so gorgeously depict and so lovely a portrait either in my arms or by yourself in any reasonable setting. Now that your health has improved, I am looking forward to this much-needed reunion between you and I with the utmost of speculation.

"Oh yes. Here's a little ol' question for you. Would you rather be a marble or an Egg? Really I know you would be like me. Rather be an Egg, because both rather be layed than played with.

"I have found a far better room for us than the sorry ones you and I have put up in. It would cost about $15 a day in Nashville or most small cities (titties) and up to $50 in big (titties). It is truly gorgeous and I wish & wish you was here. I'd love the socks off of you and put you in this big fourposter bed with a $27.50 Early American spread (Martha Washington) and make real love to you, the kind we both need most.

"How I have missed that sweet, tender understanding kiss, a smile and tear that only you can give with the expression, kindness and loveliness of a Madonna. Darling, I truly miss you so much, but how to change the picture,

I don't know. Marie has changed very much since a year ago. She too has become so much more loveable, considerate and co-operative. God bless her, she is trying to be so divine, but you know me, I don't want to be too divine, I need a little devilishment and a little devil like you to keep me in balance. Love like you and you alone can give to me is the balance staff, because you are not the angel Marie wants to be, but the angel I need and want most, because you and I understand life differently than she and want to live our lives according to the way we feel.

"Well, I have to try to sell a whole new line of ties, so I am off to Paintersville, then Hazard in Kentucky, then Chattanooga and Nashville, and my goal is to be with you in Knoxville for as long as I can manage it. A million hugs and kisses to my Babe.

'Me.'"

SITTING IN THE SPECIAL CHAIR, REMEMBERING

Sitting in the special chair Jerry bought for her, across from mother's chair that has a view of what's outside the front door and beside the antique table mother bought on that visit the two of them made to Jerry's farm in Boone, she feels an intuitive rush of all her eighty-five years, her family, her friends, her bosses, her lovers.

Here I sit, folks, chair-bound, legs hurting, unable.

There sits the piano Jerry finally bought for her—$318 at Cox's Piano Company over on Dameron Avenue, out of what Warner Brothers paid him for *Cassandra Singing*—lid down, greeting cards along the sheet music shelf, the piano bench chocked full of sheet music she used to play and play. Even if she lets John push her over there in the wheelchair, she cannot position herself properly before the keyboard to play. The piano is a daily reproach, sunlight pouring over it in the morning and dimly seen in the evening, and a stimulant to memories of many people, places, many times. Sometimes the sight of it makes her cry, sometimes it makes her laugh nostalgically. Staring at it, she feels her own stillness absorbed into the piano. Sometimes it seems like a tomb waiting for an inhabitant.

When John gets back from Kroger's with the groceries, she thinks she might ask him to raise the lid to expose the black and white keys to the morning sunlight.

"DEAR JERRY, KEEP YOUR VIEWS TO YOURSELF"

"Dearest Jerry. No answer to my letter yet. Have they finished you off? I am anxious to hear how your feet are standing up and if you want me to appeal to get you out before I leave Nashville for home—2 wks I hope. This is the time. Election is coming up and favors are easier to get. Write pronto and tell me.

"Honey I do hope it isn't as hot in South Carolina as it is here. We are all dehydrated.—105 Tues. 107 Wed. Colder in winter and hotter in summer—that's Nashville.

"John came Sun. Looked so healthy. Was so sorry he missed you. I look for him to hitchhike over to Fort Jackson to see you. Doesn't know yet what he is going to do. He bought me a watch with a flip lid and a set of rhinestone jewelry. I look like Miss Astor. Poor kid was so proud and it is so beautiful. But I would so much rather had the money for the storage. Which is slowly driving me insane. Don't you ever breathe to him I said that. The present was a humdinger and they probably charged him twice the price. Will be wonderful to wear in the eve. I expect him to go out into the wild blue yonder again any day now.

"Have 4 letters to write tonight, so will cut it short. Just anxious to hear if you wanted me to go to the Gov. for you. Write us soon and if you think you are going to be there a while longer I will send you a cake. Spice or Angel Food. Orange icing, your favorite? Bye now, Love and a big kiss, Mother.
"P.S. Please keep your views to *yourself*. You might land in the stockade if they get it in their heads you're a communist or something.

"Sure wish I could see you on your 21st birthday. 'Today I am a man.' Anyway I will be thinking of you.

"Love, your mother."

THE DEATH OF BABOO
FROM LOCKED BOWELS

On Decoration Day, Emily showed Jerry, John, and Dickie where their baby brother Baboo—John's name for him—Ronald Dennis Madden, was buried, in Babyland, a plot Lynnhurst had set apart in 1939, the same year he died. They stood around her, looking down at the marker. Only two other little babies so far. Jimmy'd said he would go another time. Mother stood in the road by Cap's car. Phil didn't want to come. Chuck and Ruth were on their honeymoon. Across the road, men were digging another grave.

Ronny lay in his grave, but she saw him as she had last seen him alive, dying, lying on the ironing board in the kitchen on Dempster, the doctor shaking his head, "If only your husband had brought the medicine, this child may have had a better chance."

Locked bowels. But the money for the medicine had gone into goddamn Jimmy's bowels—goddamn whiskey.

Baboo lay convulsing, screaming, on the makeshift ironing board, a padded plank stretched between a rickety chairback and the kitchen table.

She ran into the boys' bedroom and woke Jerry. "Get up. I need you, honey. Don't wake John and Dickie. Jerk your shorts on and come in the kitchen quick as you can. Your good-for-nothing daddy still hasn't come home with the medicine."

As she stroked Baboo, Jerry came out staggering, half asleep.

"Run quick to Mrs. Cabbage's house and ask her can you call the doctor. Here's his number. Beg him to come quick. Baboo's getting worse."

John and Dickie tight asleep, Jerry standing by, she waited for the doctor to come.

Jimmy had come in the door after midnight as if nothing had happened or was going to happen.

"Where's Baboo?"

"Gone."

"Gone? Gone where?"

"They took him to the hospital, you drunken son of a bitch. Where's the goddamn medicine I sent you for?"

"Honey, I thought he'd come out of it. I didn't think it was serious. He was just crying the way babies cry. So I used the money to get me a little snort, calm my nerves from listening to all that crying."

"I will nev-er for-give you, Jim-my."

Mrs. Cabbage woke them at dawn with the message telephoned from the hospital. Ronny was gone. Mrs. Cabbage cried too. And Jimmy.

Hearing the creak of the door, they looked up, and the early morning light from the many small high windows in the room where Dickie, Jerry, and John slept made the tears on Jimmy's face glisten.

Jerry must have heard Jimmy and her crying, sitting on the edge of their bed, Jimmy's arm around her shoulder. "What's the matter, Momma? Why are you crying like that?"

"Your little brother's gone, Jerry."

"Gone where?"

Looking up, red-eyed. "Baboo's dead, honey. Lockjaw. He died in the night in the hospital, honey."

Jerry cried, wracking sobs that made her cry harder. She reached out and took his hand while Jimmy kept patting her shoulder. Jerry sat on the bed, hugged her, and she hugged him.

John staggered in, half asleep. "Why for you all cryin'?"

"You wouldn't understand, honey." She hugged him, kissing his mouth.

"Tastes like salt." John licked his lips.

"Dickie still asleep?"

"No, he's just laying there, listening." John jumped in the bed, wedged between Jimmy and Emily.

"LORDY, LORD, LORD, WHAT A CLAN"

Seeing images of New York from newsreels, magazine photos, and movies, she imagined Jerry in all those places, standing or walking, with Raven or whoever he had met, girls, young men his age, some famous maybe.

She had seen enough pictures, some of them Jerry sent home, and movies to be able to see Jerry in the wool, green turtleneck sweater he bought in Antofagasta, Chile, working on the deck of a ship, or up on the bow, watching the ocean parting below. But not the engine room going through the Panama Canal. She had no idea what that looked like, but she almost felt the intense heat as Jerry painted the engine room the way he wrote to her describing it.

Jerry told her that one of his students from Centre College, doing summer work in the wheat fields of Regina, Saskatchewan, Canada, was drinking beer when he asked the name of a talkative fellow at the bar who was trying to sell him some jewelry, cheap, for Mother's Day. "John Madden." Then asked where he was from. "Knoxville, Tennessee."

"My teacher is a Madden. David Madden, the writer."

"Yeah, well, he's my brother."

Another time Jerry told me about a professor friend at Jacksonville University where he was going to give a dramatic reading from *The Suicide's Wife* telling him about a con man he met in a bar who said his name was James Madden originally from Knoxville. "You wouldn't by any chance know a David Madden who writes novels."

"He's my brother. I can't get him to write a bestseller."

She felt guilty being unable to picture John in the places he wrote about on postcards, Los Angeles, Pacific Palisades, Albuquerque, San Antonio.

John by his lonesome she saw more clearly, his face, those eyes full of dreams, that slightly buck-toothed grin.

Dickie was hard to feature, moving so fast, or stuck in military prison in Germany or harvesting corn under the gun in east Texas.

Thinking of them, seeing them, hearing about them, listening to their fine voices now and then on the phone too, made her see Jimmy, fleetingly, that time she was on the streetcar homeward and looked out the barred window at him loping along, hat pushed down on his ears, not staggering, as if he was fixed upon a destination, while she knew he was merely walking, wandering, or setting off from that slummy L&N Hotel to the Old Gray Cemetery to reach behind that hateful Governor Brownlow's monument for whiskey a bootlegger stashed there for him.

Lordy, Lord, Lord. What a clan.

JERRY BUYS HER A BEDSIDE WATER FOUNTAIN

She lay abed, *We Were the Mulvaneys* by Joyce Carol Oates propped up heavily on her lap, Russell Stover chocolate assortment box at her side, and glanced over at the huge Mountain Valley Spring Water jug, too close to her bed, on top of its dispenser. She tried to concentrate on the Mulvaneys and console herself with candy, hoping to bite into raspberry filling next, but that damned water jug squatting on top of the dispenser kept distracting her, a huge glass eye peeking over her shoulder.

No, Jerry was right. There it is when John is gone late or overnight and you need or just want good pure water. But it stood between brothers—John and Jerry. John because it was a reproach for going off sometimes leaving her with no water by her bedside. Jerry because she didn't want to hurt his feelings after such a surprise gift, that man in a uniform suddenly showing up at the door, knocking until she could struggle into the wheelchair by herself and get to the front door.

She only told Jerry that John had gone off without putting some water on her nightstand, and Jerry asked whether he had done that before, and she reckoned she made it sound as if he was in the habit of neglecting her that way, going off into the night on his mysterious excursions or his various missions of mercy, the month-long March of Dimes marathon his latest.

And it didn't do any good to call Greg, working late anyway at that religious station, disc jockey.

When John came in this morning saying he was sorry before he even shut the front door behind him, and he saw that water monster, he hit the roof. He called Jerry and told him they didn't need a water fountain. She felt bad knowing she would have to call Jerry tomorrow morning and explain without offending him. Compared with that, Jesus and the woman at the well was easy.

FLYING TO BATON ROUGE FOR BLAKE'S GRADUATION

She wouldn't have missed Blake's high school graduation for the world. Nor her first plane ride. High in the clouds. So many clouds.

Even though pictures of it had impressed her and she could willfully recall images of Jerry, Robbie, and Blake standing behind the curving porch railing and long to be in the picture with them, when Jerry pulled up in front of the house on Park Boulevard, she almost squealed in delight, like a teenage girl.

Blake carried her bags from the car up the wide steps to the double front door of beveled glass.

Those Doberman Pinschers scare the daylights out of me, barking at my heels every step I take. I wish I could live in that big house with them, even with those dogs, one of them wearing a spiked leather collar.

Like a mansion inside and out with all those columns out front, and when you go in and into the living room and the dining room, a stained-glass window in the dining room and two more as Blake carried her suitcases up the lovely staircase. Born in a three-room primitive cottage across from where Granny Merritt died of cancer of the anus, and here he is almost a thousand miles from home in a house people slow down to get a glimpse of. Not rich. But money's not everything. That's what they say. I didn't want to hear it when I was raising three kids on my own on little more than twenty dollars a week.

Climbing the stairs was hard for her, and she must lie down a while after her first-ever plane ride up into pink clouds, and that shooshing suddenly down and up again.

Robbie and Jerry insisted she take their room, no columns but two tall windows and art prints on the walls, and look at that old fashioned claw-footed tub. If she ever looped her leg over the side and settled into it, how would she climb out again without the fire department rescue team as that time Mother fell and couldn't get up?

The Doberman Pinschers, mother and daughter, were exploding up the staircase as Blake yelled at them to get back down. One of them jumped on the bed as she was about to drop off and the other stood in the doorway barking. She backed into the bathroom and shut the door just as the first one hit it with its forepaws. She heard Blake chase them back down the stairs.

"You okay, Emily?" Robbie opened the door a little and looked in at her.

"Yes, honey. Don't worry about me. I'm just thrilled to pieces to be finally in you all's house. Let me rest a little and I'll come down. But do, please, put the dogs out."

"I know how it is. I can't even relax in my old home place in Ames because my mother's German police dog is so scary."

She lay down on the big brass bed where Blake had been conceived eighteen years ago in Boone, North Carolina, in that hillside farmhouse. She could see it now, all the rooms, the old-timey refrigerator Robbie painted mauve, and the mint profusely growing by the back steps.

Blake doesn't take after Jerry. More the outdoors type. Kung Fu, acrobatics, dirt biking, hiking, and girls, but there's where he does take after Jerry. That Chinese girl, and now that Japanese girl. Who would have thought it would turn out like that. After all they did in the war, and then what we did to them. Hiroshima. Nagasaki. Well, why not? And be getting married before you know it. Painted his room black. If I ever dropped down on that waterbed, I'd never be able to get up again. Embarrassing, all those naked *Playboy* photos and Jimi Hendrix and that famous Kung Fu guy, whatshisname.

Watching Blake graduate from Baton Rouge Magnet High School was one of her most thrilling moments as a grandmother. If it wasn't for that long blond hair, hippie-style lolling along his shoulders and down his back ... But on Blake it did look good. Jerry says the school declared he must cut it. The school board must have been shocked to see this hippie kid come before them and teach them about freedom. Just like Jerry. Says he might become a vet. Yes, he looked very handsome, and brown eyes, and when he strode confidently across the stage with the grace of his acrobatic and Kung Fu training, his classmates roared for him more than for the others. Robbie and Jerry must be tickled pink, watching Blake walk down off that stage. Hope he doesn't smoke that marijuana. A little beer now and then when you're a kid among other kids. How well I remember, even if I never took more than that first gaggy swallow. Wonder whether he dances or not.

"Oh, Blake, let me give you a big hug."

JOHN DOLES OUT FOOD STAMPS

She hated to bring it up at the start of his visit, but she wanted to go get food stamps. "Jerry, I hate to admit it, but your poor ol' mother's on food stamps. I feel so ashamed."

"John called and told me he was working at the food stamp office, at the window giving them out."

"I still have to sit out there and wait like the rest of them until my own son calls my name."

"I'll try to send you all more money than I have been."

"Honey, we appreciate all you do for us. But since we qualify, we may's well take advantage of it."

"I hate to think of you sitting among all those godforsaken people."

"Honey, you have no idea. You just have no idea. They're so pitiful, most of them. But then I'm glad Uncle Sam takes care of them. Lord, if Mother were alive, she'd be so ashamed that we have come to this. It's a good thing she left the house to me. I was always afraid she'd leave it to Greg."

"Mammy loved you, Mama. I hope you finally know that."

"Oh, honey, I do, I do, I do. It was just something deep down in her that lit the fuse sometimes, more than once, actually."

"What time's John get off?"

"'Bout now."

"Let's go get him. And get the food stamps. Surprise him."

"Let's do. This family's just one surprise after another anyway."

VISITING THE LAWYER

WITH JERRY TO DO A WILL

Jerry drove Emily across the river into South Knoxville to Robert J. Bird's office on Sevier Avenue, at the bottom of the steep hill where Jimmy's folks lived when he was a kid and a couple of blocks from that dismal basement room he took her into as his bride.

Recommended by Phil who had needed his services in the divorce from Frances and other matters, Bird had helped Emily with problems involving Dickie and John over the years. Now she wanted to make a will.

"I couldn't help but notice that you have a canoe lashed to the top of your new BMW."

"Jerry, you never can tell when you might need a boat."

"And, Bob, I want to sell the house to Jerry for one dollar to keep it in the family because he is the most responsible of my boys. If I left it to all three, Dickie would sell his share quick as a wink, and John might too. It means the most to Jerry. But I want him to promise he will let John live there as long as he wants to, rent free."

"What about Dickie?"

"He and Gloria would trash the place in no time. You should see their apartment in Fountain City."

Bob heaved a loud shy. "Spare me. I can imagine. Dickie Madden is something else in my book. Is this what you want, Jerry?"

"Yes, and if John were to move in and later on move out, maybe Greg and his family might want to live there. Which is okay by me. Keeping it in the family is the main objective."

"Poor Greg probably will expect me to will it to him because Mother and Cap raised him in that house. But his kids think it's dark and spooky, that Daddy's and Granny Merritt's ghosts roam from room to room."

"Didn't Rachel ask one night what that sound at the front door was?"

"Oh, Lord, yes, and Mother said, 'It's nothing, honey. Just Gran'paw Charlie, trying to get in.'"

"And him dead, right?"

"So it would be John."

"Well, Emily, it's going to be a long time, healthy and young looking as you are. What, 70?"

"Seventy-five this coming April."

"And if you pass after your mother passes, what, Jerry?"

Emily answered, "My grandchild Blake would inherit it from Jerry because with that dollar, he owns it. Give me a dollar, Jerry."

JOHN SAYS HE LIKES
TO DRIVE LATE AT NIGHT

"Who is it?"

"Guess who."

"It's Dickie?"

"Hell, no, it ain't Dickie. It's John."

"Well, honey, it's after midnight." Emily opened the door wide.

"I like to drive in the dark."

"Where you coming in from?"

"Been to see the world premiere of Jerry's play *Cassandra Singing* in Albuquerque."

"You drove here all the way from there?"

"Freak snow almost shut it down. No, I also visited Uncle Elmo and Aunt Kate."

"I should have known it would be you. Jerry's in Albuquerque and Dickie says he and Gloria were coming up from Florida. Well, get in here."

"Okay. Don't worry. She's on a lease."

"Who?"

"Killer. German Shepherd. But she behaves."

Emily backed way back into the living room as Killer came in, leaping and barking.

"That means she likes you."

"Can't prove it by me."

"Sit, Killer . . . See?"

"What happened to Runt?"

"Had to sell her off. Got stir crazy, cooped up in the car so much."

"What're you driving this time?"

"Nothing. The transmission thew a rod at the city limits and we had to walk it. Didn't we, Killer?"

Killer whined and ducked her head.

"Is the old fence still closed off good?"

"Yeah. Greg filled in the holes where Runt dug under it."

"Let's go, Killer. Git in the yard."

"Does she bark bad?"

"Not in the car."

"Shut the door, honey. It's going to get down to below zero tonight."

"She'll hush in a little bit."

"The neighbors'll think Runt's back and raise holy hell all over again."

REMINDING JERRY

OF PAST EASTER SUNDAYS

As she reached for the flowery stationery Jerry sent her, the thought startled her that she may well have written over the decades as many as ten thousand pages, at ten or eleven a week, from her twenties to this old seventy-year-old lady.

Aware as she wrote this one to Jerry that Easter was coming on soon, she turned over the page where she had ended the letter and added, "You know there are three Easters I'll never forget. Easter that it snowed 8 or 10 inches when we were living on Dempster. Next morning you kids got up to find your Easter baskets, and Dick'd cut his boots down to make house shoes. He sure couldn't go out to play in the snow.

"The next Easter, our first on Cedar, I bought you kids Easter outfits. Slack suits, sweaters and shoes. I felt so proud seeing my boys the first time all of you had a whole outfit at the same time. Then on McCalla when you slept in that closed-in back porch with the refrigerator. I'll never forget—a little box of Easter eggs and a green and brown bow tie. You were 15. I was about flat broke that Easter.

"Had a letter from Dick and he is getting so anxious as the time draws nearer.

"Hope Naomi as his wife who needs him for Greg and Cheryl's sakes can do something for him in Nashville as I would hate to go live there again and have to hunt a job, altho this time I know so many people I don't think I would have too much trouble. Not as much as stuck in Knoxville anyway.

"This letter sounds screwy, but that is the way I feel—so what?

"Hope you write me soon again and let me know if you are sick or something.

"Bye now, Love, Mother."

STARING AT THESE FOUR WALLS

She stares at these four walls, dozes, dreams, awakes, daydreams of herself among her girlfriends in Cleveland, sees that map of all the Great Lakes, felt her lake was all the more important for being among the six others, felt possessive, all seven hers somehow.

The first night back in Knoxville, she'd looked over at Phil, sleeping snugged over against Mother, his face between her breasts. Daddy on the other side of her, wide awake, talking to her, witty, charming. Chuck wedged in at the foot of the bed, twitching. All four sleeping in that one big bed in Granny's bedroom, she trying to curl up enough to sleep in the old wicker rocking chair across the little room from the cot Granny had set up, too close to the heat of the red embers in the fireplace.

Her legs about to cramp, she got up out of Cap's old chair where she'd gotten in the habit of sitting, walked past poor Mother's chair that she never sits in, respecting that it used to be Mother's favorite chair, pushed back against the wall where the old fireplace used to be, that jutted out into the living room, twin to the one in the bedroom, it, too, plugged up, covered over in plywood and wallpaper.

She crawled into Mother's bed, exactly where Granny Merritt's bed once stood before they all descended upon her out of Cleveland.

They've all passed away now, every one of them. And her three boys gone out of Knoxville. Her Knoxville girlfriends dead or not getting out much anymore. She felt too lonesome even to cry.

Changes in her life, children, parents, jobs, girlfriends, encounters with strangers, lovers, illnesses that came and went and returned, her fluctuations from smiling and laughing elation to sad or sulking silence—all part of who she knows herself to be. She talked about those aspects of her long life with girlfriends, sometimes with Jerry, but fitfully and never fully, one aspect or another. Those nights she did not sleep well, in letters, glancingly, she contemplated aspects of her life, past, mostly present, and immediate, but never long-range, future.

"You almost lost your mother." She knew what "near death" was, but did not far project a vision of the future before death. Speaking to Mother and others, sometimes pure strangers, about illnesses that could well end in death made her feel very much alive herself, alive.

NAOMI SLIPS DICKIE A FILE
IN A CAKE IN THE JAIL

When she opened the front door, there was Jerry, lying in wait.

"Momma, I was so eager to show you the picture of Naomi in the paper arrested for trying to slip a file in a coconut-icinged cake so Dickie could file through the bars and escape, I ran up McCalla and rushed into the house and there was this note on the table." He showed it to her, like a cop presenting a suspect to the chief, "Written on the back of 'The White Horse of Fear,' ripped out of my notebook that I left on my cot in the sanctuary."

"'Dear Jerry, Gone dancing with Clyde and Zoe. See clipping. What next? Love, Momma.'"

"I was in a rush and couldn't find a scrap of paper."

He shifted into his radio announcer voice. "It's my sto-ry, Momma, my stor-ry."

GOING LIKE A WHIRLWIND ALL WEEK

"Dear Jerry, at last an answer to your letter. Been going like a whirlwind all week. Thanks so much for the money order. I will pay your storage and save all I can hold back to apply on mine. I will have to use some of it, as I was flat on my can. It will be a month since I worked, you know, and I had been so saving with my last pay and had paid $15 insurance out of it too. If any's left, I will keep it in cold storage.

"I answered an ad last Mon. and glory I was called into work on Tues. Southern Sewing Machine Co. as office clerk. Secretary they call it, minus the shorthand, and salary too I may add. Only $30 per wk. But I can sit down most all the time and the work isn't too hard, only kind of confusing at first. Some bookkeeping and contracts and typing a couple times per wk. I think I can swing it, as the boss seems to be very nice. He hired me once before when he first opened, the time I went instead to the car wash to work. Anyway keep your fingers crossed that I can put my poor tired brain to it.

"I sure wish you could have been here tonight. David Van Vactor was on TV with the Knox symphony orchestra. He was wonderful, as always. So handsome and debonair. Just made me feel close to you somehow. His mustache is getting a little too heavy tho.

"John has started at Fulton Hi for a refresher course. I think he is going to have to whip the principal before it's all over, they clash so often. But he is so interested, and I am sure happy for it. He is taking radio speech and is narrator on Station WKCS, the voice of Fulton High. 15,000 watts on FM. This week he narrated the Galveston Tidal Wave of 1900 and each week some different disaster. He has his own program like you did at WKGN and U.T. Next week he is going to learn to operate the console and have a crack at news commentator.

"Watch to your laurels, old boy, as your little brother seems to have a flair too. He will draw $26 per week for the time he goes, which I hope will be a long time so he can get some education.

"Haven't been able to stir up a job for Dickie yet for when he gets out. It is like finding a needle in a haystack. I am getting more nervous as the time goes on and no luck. I promised, and now I can't seem to get to first base.

"I don't guess I will be going to the hospital soon as my arm isn't hurting too bad since I have taken the medicine he gave me. I seem to have a touch of arthritis in my arms and hands and legs and back. Just crops up at the oddest times. Getting old I guess.

"Snuffy is so lonesome with Skippy gone. We pet her till she is rotten. She misses having her face washed every day and Skippy to tell on her when she does something she shouldn't.

"The folks all have their nose in the television and it's getting on my nerves. Just one crime story after another. Or a shoot'em up cowboy.

"Honey I hope you can come home soon as your trouble is straightened out. Why didn't you just sign their damn loyalty oath? Well, let me know, as I am so worried about it.

"Do you ever write David V.V.? I thought he was going to London. Your loving mother."

DELVING INTO THE PAST
IN DRESSER DRAWERS

She bent over the foot of the mattress Jerry and John slept on in the kitchen, picking bedbugs out of the seams and batting, fingernails cracking, clicking as she mashed them, and the light, really not so bright, since she couldn't afford more than forty watts, seemed part of the movements, the sounds, the smell of bug blood. She woke Jerry, his eyes bright in the light, making her feel discovered.

In her bedroom, she bent over the dresser drawers, sorting—scratch, rattle, clink—late at night. She kept everything. Christmas ribbons, bows, cards, price tags, colored and decorated paper bags, candy boxes, bill receipts, picture negatives. When Jerry or John happened to find a corner of a hidden bargain towel sticking out of a drawer and took it out to use, she'd scream, "That's my good towel." Wanting to save it for the time when they'd have a "decent" home.

And when Jerry begged her to throw some of that stuff away or bring it more into the mainstream of their lives, she, irritated, reminded him that these pitiful rags were all she had to her name, and, more practically, someday they might really need them—don't forget how sudden the Depression came down upon us—and be glad she'd saved them. The outgrown baby and kid clothes, including every stitch that had been her dead baby's, things John wore that Baboo was expected later to grow into, were kept because she could bear neither to look upon them, except when she had to "clean out her things," nor part with them. She could tell that Jerry was more fascinated than repelled by her epic struggles with her stuff, more impressed by the very action of delving and sorting and repacking than by the objects themselves.

Evicted by circumstances from Mother's circus wagon coal house, Jerry sat on the front steps in the evening and looked through his own boxes.

"I'll pay you," she said, through the dirty window screen in her room, the landlady's swing obscuring her face, "if you'll throw that junk in the trash and give us a little more room to breathe."

"I'll take a million dollars as a down payment."

She slammed the window, trapping herself in the hot air of the room.

Jerry came into her and Jimmy's bedroom and talked her into giving him the bottom drawer of her dresser for his writings. Digging through his writings, he found a letter he'd mailed to her from Boys' Club Camp at Big Ridge State Park when he was nine.

"Read it to me."

Almost asleep, she remembered standing shivering on a corner in crisp night air, waiting for the last streetcar, John in her arms, Jerry and Dickie trying to yell like Tarzan in *Tarzan and the Apes* that they'd just seen at the State Theatre, Jimmy laughing, she embarrassed, aware of the gigantic swarm of electric wires looming above and behind them in generator towers across the railroad tracks, next to the three-story, red-brick Standard Knitting Mill, and a vast pond across the street, infested with lily pads, cattails, weeds, and deep green water, showing through a vine-crawly fence.

This, God knows, is not the life I dreamed of in my bedroom in Cleveland.

THE SHATTERING OF HER DOLL'S HEAD

Rummaging around in one of the industrial cardboard drums almost as tall as herself, she found again the severed head of her childhood doll. As she set it aside until she could think of a safe place, it wobbled, fell, shattered.

She lovingly picked up the cranium, blond curly hair intact, the blue eyes in two flesh-colored shards, the parted lips, the chin, the ears. That night, she dreamed the Cleveland house collapsed, shattered, dust rising and falling and settling.

SUSPENDED, JERRY SHACKS UP WITH WAUNITA

And that old Waunita that worked the soda fountain with Phil at Sharp's Drugstore on Broadway and rented that upstairs room after Doreen moved to Asheville lured Jerry into *her* bed, and Emily caught them smoking and drinking beer and this, that, and the other, both bare-assed naked. Made Phil laugh to learn he and Jerry both had done it with her.

Turned out the principal had punished Jerry by making him stay home three days for sassing his feisty typing teacher, knowing he couldn't stand to be away from Iva Lee.

"Ginny just told me that you've been spending the whole day in bed with my son. He's only fifteen, woman, and you look thirty if you're a day. Get up out of that bed and get your rags together and get your boney butt the hell out of my house. I knew the day I rented this room you were no count. First my brother Phil and now my son. And you a married woman. Don't you dare say a word to me, woman. I'm not through telling you what I think of you, you hussy. What if you were to have a baby by Jerry? He loves Iva Lee. And look at all these beer bottles and cigarette butts. Who's gonna clean it up, and how in the world am I gonna get rid of the smell, not just of beer and cigarettes either, so I can rent this room. Who wants to walk into this slummy room and rancid odors? Are you gonna lie there all night? Get up! Get up!

"Jerry, you get yourself back down those stairs before I kick you down, you hear, you hear me? Waunita, I am not going to tell you again. Up. Hiding under that blanket won't shut me up. Want me to come over there and jerk a knot in your tail. Bitch.

"That's more like it. Now get some clothes on your skinny ass. What Jerry saw in you is beyond me, with him having that sweet, lovely Iva Lee, how he could—no, just leave those bottles laying there. I can't wait for you to get out of my sight. Seducing a child. Have you got no shame, woman?

"Jerry, I said get on down those stairs. Don't make me come down there. She's getting dressed and throwing her rags in a suitcase. You owe me two weeks' rent, Waunita Bowers. If I don't get it in the mail, I'm coming after you at Sharp's. Doc Sharp would be shocked to know what you've been up to. As for Philip telling Jerry you thought he was cute, I don't believe a word of it. Shut that suitcase and get a move on."

She threw her out of the house and tossed her suitcase to the curb just as her ex-husband came to pick her up, dressed in his handsome Greyhound bus driver's uniform.

MOTHER BUYS A CAFÉ

"Children, I have bought me a café."

"What in the world, Mother?"

"Emily, I took your daddy's insurance money that was left after we buried him and put it down on a little café at the top of the hill next to that old YMCA, 'longside the fire station."

Chuck just sat on the couch grinning. Phil bounced up and down beside him, nonplussed.

"What's become of your job at JFG?"

"Quit it. And you can smell the coffee, my café is so near JFG, which is what we serve at the counter. It's all counter, 'cause even skinny tables won't fit in. I call it Merritt's Café, and on my card—take one—it says, see, "Quick lunch. Regular meals 25 and 30 cents, sandwiches and short orders." And guess who works for me, Emily?"

"Who?"

"Why, you, of course. That little drawing of the girl carrying a tray is the very image of you, except we don't have no trays."

"I have a good job at Breezy's."

"You'd rather work a sewing machine in that racket than help your widow of a mother?"

Emily parked John, Jerry, and Dickie at the Strand where Phil was an usher, where they dished out horse operas.

A one-story, shotgun construction at the top of ten wooden steps with a rusty, wobbly iron railing, Merritt's Café hugged up against what was once the YMCA and had become the Avon Arms. Resembled a castle, painted cheaply, white and orange, UT's colors. It sat across the street from the side of Knoxville's main fire hall. No bigger under the mulberry tree than a good place to play marbles, Mother's place was not much wider inside than a fireman's arm spread. A long counter with stools. And the smell from JFG coffee factory nearby, where she and Mother worked before Daddy's dying put insurance money in Mother's hands.

By noon Emily was pouring coffee for two firemen. The smells of turnip greens, salt pork, cornbread, pinto beans, onions, Idaho potatoes, hot lard grease, pork chops, liver, dirty dishwater, clogged drains were all one aromatic swim that filled the café with an aura of possibilities, when in strode a big fireman who instantly took a liking to Mother.

"THEY COME AND GOT DICKIE"

"Well," said Mother, as Emily stepped through the front door of good ol' 2722 Henegar, Jerry, then John behind her, "they come and got Dickie," in that mountain tone of fate.

"When?" She came to a full stop just over the threshold, Jerry still holding open the screen, John pushing at him from behind, scenting catastrophe, asking, "What's the matter?"

Mother sat in her favorite chair across from the front door, her face contorted into mock crying, her voice a high whine, simulating a wail. "They just come right through my front door—didn't knock or nothin'," and she beat her palms on the arms of her chair.

"*Who*, Mother?" She knew the answer.

"The *po*-lice. And stromped through the house without a word to me, and me trying to ask 'em what it was they wanted, and on out the back door, and straight down to the coal house, and yanked him out and drug him through my tomato vines up to the house again, and right *through* the house, tracking mud, and *out* the front door, and drove away just as my neighbors showed up on their front porches and Cap drove up in front of the hedge." Mother bent and shook her head, pinching the bridge of her nose. "You just don't know, Emily, what I been *through* this mornin'. It's nothing but hell and damnation."

"Oh, Lord, Lord, I thought we'd have a peaceful Sunday dinner for a change."

"They *ain't* no peace in *this* family, Emily. I thought when you all moved out,

I'd be left alone awhile to get my strength back, and now this. Why couldn't they come for him at *your* house?"

"Moth-er." Emily stood on the exact spot where she'd stopped, holding the lemon meringue pie she'd carried in the mile walk from her apartment on Atlantic. "Dickie has not *been* to my house."

Jerry squeezed around her into the living room. "Last *I* seen him was when he did me a somerset over his head through the kitchen window."

"What happened?" John held a full bag of bargains Emily had bought for Mother at Watson's in Market Square, his slightly buck teeth exaggerating the look of awe in his big brown eyes.

"Well, for God's sake, Emily, come in and shut the door before I die of the pneumonia." Mother pulled her quilted bathrobe tighter about her neck.

She went on in. "Didn't you ask to see a search warrant?"

"Emily, they come and went so fast, I didn't have time to notice I was *being* searched. *I* have to *live* in this neighborhood. You can move in and out as you damn please."

"Mother, you *told* me to move—in fact, you said for us to get the hell out."

"Well, I can't have *po*-lice cars roaring up to my door on Sunday mornings. Now that's all they is *to* it."

"Mother, *I* can't help it. Will you just calm down and tell me what happened?"

Mother reared up in her flowered-print chair, lips pleated like crimped piecrust, her finger pointing at Emily, who sat on the edge of the davenport. "Now don't you sass me one time, young lady, after what I've been through—for *your* young'un."

"Mother, let me catch my breath before you start."

"Start? I'm finished. Start? I'm finished takin' care of other people's young'uns."

"Other *people*. Mother, I *am* your daughter, you know."

"We never had a lick of trouble with the law in this family until Dickie—"

"You don't have to worry, you don't have to worry any *more*, Mother. This time, they'll put him *under* the jail and he won't see daylight for ten years." She veered off anger onto the verge of tears.

"And the sight of them dragging Dickie out of the coal house had me on the verge of hysterics anyhow. That poor young'un had nothin' on but his undershorts."

"You mean they wouldn't even let him put *clothes* on?"

"Emily, they was draggin' that young'un through the house, and he kept saying, 'Least let me put my pants on, mister, least let me put my pants on,' and this big ol' fat one says, 'You shut your g.d. mouth.'"

"Oh, Lord, you don't reckon Dickie's done something else since he run off from State Training School."

Mother's breasts shook, as her head, bowed, nodded rapidly, but when she raised it, her eyes were bright, and she was trying to keep from smiling, "Euuuuuuuu, law. I'll never forget the sight of Dickie—just as the po-lice car scattered gravel all over the hedge taking off—Dickie tosses his undershorts out the back winder."

WITH JERRY, ROBBIE,
AND BLAKE IN CLEVELAND

Making her bed, she came across a letter from Jerry from a year or so ago, tucked between the mattress and the headboard.

"Momma, Robbie and I sought your house in Cleveland on 47th St., and maybe saw it. We imagine you walking where we drove, Lake Erie, on 5 or 6 blocks from Lorain and Fulton, but blocked off by factories and other industrial sites. Crossing the bridge to the Ohio City area, over to the rest of Cleveland, we imagined you at 12 or so seeing those very high, very impressive bridge statues, 2 at each end, for the first time in about 1922, and you comparing them and the bridge with Gay Street Bridge in Knoxville, White Store, Chisholm Tavern, and both ends, great Gran'paw Willis' car and buggy repair shop on the South end near where Daddy was raised and where you and he got married in about 1919, and also the two halves of Cleveland too. And how the City Center building must have impressed you, and the West Side Arcade building, the Mau and the Rose buildings. I imagined you walking with Mammy and Gran'paw Charlie and Chuck on those uptown streets, Prospect Avenue. We are about to go home, having spent 7 days up in Michigan, all the lakes but Ontario, on vacation. I love you."

She wondered where her piano was now, seventy-five years later. Still somewhere in Cleveland, somewhere else in Ohio? More far-flung?

She often revisited that trip Jerry, Robbie, and Blake took her on to see the old house in Cleveland—Forty-Seventh Street. The lady next door, sitting with her husband in their front porch swing, said, "There's nobody home. They're on vacation." Emily'd told her why they were all standing fixed on the sidewalk.

"Why, Emily, is that you, honey?"

Her old self as a kid and as a teenager remembered by the folks next door. She wondered whether they remembered hearing her play her new piano that one time.

No, but she remembered Mr. Merritt standing on the porch, watching the movers bring it in and again the same man bringing it back out, loading it on this dirty rattle-trap truck.

Emily's heart beat faster every time she saw that scene in memory.

Then Jerry drove down the street to where at the dead end was the public swimming pool, and Blake wished he could go in. Then the drive up to Lake Erie and Euclid Park Beach, and Blake riding the little cars.

While Jerry and Robbie rode the skyline, she and Blake stood on the ground looking up, waving.

A tour of Cleveland with her son and grandchild. Something special.

"JIMMY, NO DRINKING OR I'LL DIVORCE YOU"

"Where's the milk I sent you for?"

"They ran out."

"Like hell. You blew it on beer."

"No, not really."

She dug into the silence. "Jimmy, honey, I know you been through hell these past three years—"

"Well, I really didn't pay it too much mind, Emmie."

"I mean the war and everything."

"It was just—well—no, honey, I just did what they told me, except when General Patton ordered me to 'Get that goddamn ambulance out of my way,' so he could get by, and I said, I sure will, sir, soon's I unload these wounded fellas. He cussed me up one side and down the other, but—Well, no, that wasn't hell either, Emmie, to be honest, it was just one of those things."

"You're just lucky General Patton didn't court martial you. Slapped that sick soldier that time, you know."

"Oh, well, it was just one of those things. . . ."

"Well, what I was about to say was, it's just that after all this time—I'm not the same person to put up with your drinking."

"I'll try to quit it."

"No, you *got* to quit, Jimmy, because I can't stand it anymore, not even for the kids' sake."

"What's the kids got to do with me drinking?"

"Not just drinking. It's us living together. You got to quit—quit or we can't stay together. Promise me you'll never take another drop."

"Okay. I promise. Can I sleep on that side of the bed? Kathleen's house, when I was a kid, I always was by the winda."

"Oh, you and your sister Kathleen."

"You hush about Kathleen, Emmie."

She watched Jimmy walk around the room once and a half and fade out the door, closing it softly.

There he goes again, off to see big sister Kathleen. She's always saying, "Poor lil' ol' Jimmy." What about poor lil' ol' Emily?

BORROWING A FEW BUCKS FROM BOB

"Bob, I hate to ask you again so soon, but I'm so desperate to pay the damned rent, I—would you lend me twenty dollars and sixty cents?"

"Sure, Emily. You know I'm always glad to help you and Jerry when I can."

"Jerry forks over most of his paper route collection. John does his part by eating us all out of house and home."

"What about Dickie?"

"Dickie just goes on being Dickie. He tries to bum cash off me or filches it from my purse."

"Phil? Cap? Your mother?"

"Bob, just forget it."

"No, I'm just asking you, what's your general situation when you're between jobs. Here, take half my wad."

"Looks hardly a wad. Thanks, Bob, a million. You're an angel."

"Aren't angels female?"

"Don't forget Gabriel."

"And don't leave out Michael."

"Which one is he?"

"Emily, don't you ever go to church?"

"Did the day I got married."

"I was just about to raise that subject."

"Well, please don't. I don't know whether I'm coming or going these days."

THINKING OF GROWING OLD

When she told anyone that she was sixty, she almost wept. She had done that when she hit fifty, too. All the men in her life were out of her life now, and she was steadily in touch only with Ginny, but not in person, mainly in letters, and she called her, and she talked with her other friends on the phone now and then, especially Ruth, but also Zoe, about their families, and TV shows now, more than movies, and grocery sales.

When John was on one of his jaunts, she took a cab to Kroger's in Broadway Shopping Center and talked with each clerk she encountered and customers looking at the same tomatoes, corn, and lemons and such, and every once in a while someone she had known for years or met recently, and they asked each other what their kids were doing nowadays. What about lovers? She never asked.

She moved slowly down the aisles, looking at almost the entire inventory, which drove Greg half-crazy those times when he made time to take her. Her own grandson wouldn't stop most times at the Dairy Queen for the soft ice cream she had loved ever since she used to date George Upchurch, who introduced East Tennessee to what was then the new thing—Dairy Queen. Greg always in a rush. And Cheryl Ann visited only once a month or so to give her one of the pies she made at Ramsey's Cafeteria over by UT campus. She usually shared them with the folks next door or across the street who did a thing or two for her now and then.

What would she do if she didn't have Sabu, even though she had ripped wallpaper and curtains and drapes and scratched her without cause or warning like Elmer did?

If only her best friend from her teenage years, sweet Helen, would break away from her obligations in Cleveland and come see her again, as she did during the war on the Greyhound and again about ten years ago in a new Cadillac. She always wanted to go up and visit Helen and go to the old places with her one more time. But, but now, now she reckoned it was too late.

BIRTH OF JERRY

She had a distinct feeling that Jerry could wait no longer for that doctor to get his fat ass across Knoxville to good ol' 2722 Henegar Street.

Sure enough, Mother screamed, "He's crowning."

Quick as a wink, Emily's own screaming was no longer necessary. Mother had the baby in her arms, minus the umbilical cord, and stood ready to put him in Emily's embrace.

Holding Gerald David Madden in her arms, Emily laughed and everybody else laughed.

They called Jimmy in from the front room where he sat surrounded by Phil, Chuck, and Daddy, as if for protection.

As she swung very slowly over to the edge of the bed, Mother said, "Emily, where do you think you're going?"

"Mother, take the baby till I can stand steady on my feet. Jimmy, I want to walk. Take hold of me."

Jimmy helped her down the one high wooden step into the backyard, and they took little steps down past the garden, the chicken yard, and the coal house, and past Dewey Camel's grape arbor, and up the alley a ways and back.

"Guess we better get me back in bed, Jimmy."

Mother stood in the back room doorway. "That doctor finally showed his face. He asked where's my patient, Mrs. Merritt, and I says, cool as a cucumber, why she's down in the alley with her husband, strolling up and down in her nightie."

STILL PRETTY AND CHARMING

She was proud that at almost ninety, older than Mother when she died, her hair was mostly the same auburn as when she was a girl in Cleveland. A hard life had not turned her hair gray as it had her girlfriends', who took to dyeing it black or at least color-rinsed it, like Ginny. And she knew she was still pretty and that her smile was still luminous, that even when having

Baboo had caused so many of her teeth to go, the dentist convinced her taking them all out ought to be done to enable using dentures. Her smile in the old photographs was somewhat different. If only her body had not turned so plump and her ankles swollen, she might still be a beauty, like Hedy Lamarr is at age eighty-five. Vain? Yes, vain, excuse me for living.

But for the past thirty years what good had it done her? No men in her life. But that was really her, not her looks. She knew she was often hard to take. "To be loved," Mother told her more than once, "you have to be lovable." She could, she knew, be hateful without enough reason for it. Fly off the handle. Bitch. Be a bitch.

But when she consciously turned on the charm, she was charming, her voice lilting high and melodious, her head thrown back. And she never, like some women, had to practice in front of a mirror. People said she was a natural. Naturally charming, naturally bitchy.

Embarrassment was hardly the word for what she felt when she heard John tell Jerry on the phone one afternoon in a panic, "Jerry, Momma's gone geriatric on me."

MOTHER AS GOLD STAR MOTHER

GIVES SPEECH

She was proud to be sitting in the Lyric Theatre beside her mother, dressed up to the nines. Well, so was she, so as not to embarrass her mother. Mother wore a stylish black hat on her new permanent curls and her repaired gray fur around her shoulders, the same fur that got caught in the door handle of a passing car as she crossed Broadway against the light. She hung the ripped fur in an open closet as a conversation piece. She seldom went out, except fishing with Cap and Phil sometimes went along and Jerry a time or two, but when she went where she would be seen, she dressed to be seen.

Many snapshots display Emily and Mother equally dressed for an audience with the queen of England, standing usually by a bush in bloom higher than the top of a nearby window of the small house or by Cap's new lime-colored Lincoln Mercury Zephyr, the most perfect prop.

As a clerk in Miller's Ready-to-Wear, Emily, too, was always ready to wear the dress that set her off most attractively, and her self-image inspired a gliding glamorous walk, exuding a Joan Crawford confidence that got a proud-of-her response from Jerry when he showed up to go with her down the elevator to the basement lunch counter.

This tribute to the fallen—flags on both sides of the podium, flowers decking the stage—was in the old theater where stinky wrestling matches were thrown every Friday that Jerry loved to go to, mainly to see Dynamite Lay pin down the Green Shadow, and where the Knoxville Symphony Orchestra conducted its concerts four times a year across the street from the Bijou, next door to Louie's Greek restaurant. And here comes Jerry, still in his cute usher uniform, because he had to sneak off duty to hear his grandmother.

A soldier came up the aisle to escort Mother down and take her black-gloved hand as she ascended the steps onto the stage. Seeing her up there representing all the gold star mothers of Knoxville, Emily saw the star in the window of good ol' 2722 Henegar.

A WNOX announcer stepped up to the microphone. "And now . . . Mrs. Jesse Jane Merritt."

"I speak to all mothers who have had loved ones in this great struggle that is at an end—but particularly to those with the star of gold to symbolize that a son has paid the price of victory with his life.

"We must resolve that our sons, whose blood hallows the soil of the far-flung battlefields, shall not have died in vain.

"We must try to instill in the hearts of all Americans the resolution that we cannot afford *ever to* let it happen again.

"We must look at the problem of peace with a probing eye and keep our thoughts centered on our sons who paid the price.

"All war is frightful . . . all wars cost lives, *precious* lives. We must endeavor to keep America awake. It is up to us, the Gold Star Mothers of Americans, to make America remember always the sacrifices of our sons—brought about by the world's cruelest gamble—*war.*"

Mother's delivery was impressive to Emily's ears and Jerry's. Her grammar, style, and pronunciation were almost British. Emily always spoke good English, retaining her training and her experiences talking and writing in Cleveland, so she'd helped Mother smooth off the rough edges of the wording of her speech. She spoke the small-town East Tennessee dialect that Emily had to listen to most of her life. Mother often seemed aware she was saying "arsh potato" instead of "Irish" and "maters" instead of "tomatoes," playing it for effect, tasting, relishing each countrified word and phrase. Emily was happy to know that Mother had it in her to deliver a speech with the grammar and in the voice of the queen of England, inspired by the spirit of President Roosevelt himself.

She and Jerry stood up and applauded wildly, and she had to make him stop whistling as if Dynamite Lay had floored the Green Shadow.

JERRY INTERROGATES HER
ABOUT THE FAMILY

"Momma, where did Daddy go to school? Young High?"

"I reckon so. But he never actually told me, honey."

"Who took care of him after his momma and daddy died? The Madden gran'paw and gran'maw that I never set eyes on."

"His sister Kathleen was the one who raised him."

"Was she or Uncle Elmo the oldest?"

"Elmo. Elmo is so tall and homely and the others are such good lookers, I wonder sometimes."

"And what about the other Maddens?"

"Every time I walk over the Gay Street Bridge, I can look down on the East Tennessee Packing House and know that the poor Madden branch is working for the rich Madden branch that won't turn loose of a single dime for mothers like me."

"You all named me after the rich David Madden, but tell me again who you named Dickie after."

"Your daddy was the one who chose the James from ol' J. B. Madden."

"It's James Richard, so Dickie is named Richard after who?"

"Don't tell your daddy but I named him Richard after one of my boyfriends in Cleveland."

"And John after Gran'paw John Luther Madden, right? But where did Luther come from? Martin Luther maybe?"

"I never asked, and if you want something out of your daddy, you have to ask more than once, even if he's stone sober."

"Where was daddy working when you all got married?"

"The East Tennessee Meat Packing House, like the rest of the poor Maddens."

"And you all moved into a basement room near the home place?"

"Seems like Jimmy has lived most of his life in a single room."

"So you were born on the north side of the Tennessee River and he was born on the south side."

"The Tennessee River is no Lake Erie."

"Tell me, Momma, were you pregnant with Dickie before you married daddy?"

Jimmy seemed to assume he could, so he just did one smooth swipe and her dress was up above her knees.

"His big sister Kathleen came right out and asked me, 'Emily, have you gone and got yourself in trouble?' like poor, sweet little ol' Jimmy had nothing to do with it. I told her, 'I'm not sure,' and she said, 'Poor little ol' Jimmy.' Makes me sick to my stomach."

"Why poor little ol' Jimmy?"

"'What will the poor thing do?' Kathleen said."

"After I squalled and squalled about being cooped up in that one room he married me into, your daddy said, 'You reckon your mother would let us move in with them?' as if that wouldn't be just another, smaller, more crowded one room, me pregnant with Dickie. I said, 'Well, let's see, Jimmy. There's Granny Merritt dying in that terrible stinking one room. There's Phil and Chuck and Mother and Daddy and if you and me move in with baby Dickie, two rooms and a kitchen ought to be plenty enough room for the seven of us, with an inch or two left over up close to the ceiling.' Even sarcasm he always takes sheepishly. 'Why not we go up on the ridge and move in with your folks or in with Kathleen?'"

CASHIERING AT KNOXVILLE'S

FIRST CAR WASH

She got a job as cashier in a new type of automated car wash where machines do all the dirty work. Just a block away from Knox High, where Jerry was in the eleventh grade, where Chuck and Phil went before they went off to war.

Jerry came by almost every day after school. He liked talking to her boss. So did she. But don't tell anybody.

Jerry asked him to buy him a bottle of wine, his first, and he did. White wine. But Jerry said it upset his stomach and made him too sleepy to write his stories.

The car wash was four blocks from their house on McCalla, but she couldn't walk it, she had to call a cab when she missed the streetcar, which stopped on Magnolia only a block from the car wash.

She liked meeting all the car owners, and a few asked to take her out. She asked, do you dance? If yes, she went. She was happy in her job. She knew dancing made her look healthier, but sometimes she still had to take a day off to get well.

She kept expecting the boss to make a pass and imagined ways of fending him off. She liked his wife, who was a looker. But he never got more than just very friendly in a chesty, manly but not sexual way. And she was glad. She wanted to keep this job, and sex or romance could ruin it. She had had too many different kinds of jobs in her time, getting on buses back to Nashville or Chattanooga or Cincinnati or Columbus or Strawberry Plains to do practical nurse duty, her favorite work.

Somehow, oddly, she liked this one where, except when it rained, all the activity kept her interested. Handling money was okay except for the fear of coming up short and not knowing how it happened.

One time Jerry took her place for a few hours while she went to see Dr. Christenberry about her feet. Jacked up on that stool kept her off her feet, thank goodness for that. She could dance all night but jobs that kept her on her feet were killers.

And now here was Jerry having to wear braces and a metatarsal bar to correct incipient claw-foot deformity. The surgery, bone transplants in both feet two years ago, made a difference, but Dr. Inge and that severe German therapist said braces were also necessary.

She had to wear special shoes herself. No more high heels for her.

THAT WOMAN ACROSS THE STREET
STOLE HER DRESS

"Momma, I love to hear you tell the story about that woman across the street on Dempster and how you knew she broke in the house while you and Daddy were at work and Dickie and me were at school, and wherever John was that time?"

"Well, honey, what happened was, I saw her uptown wearing a dress I couldn't find in my closet, and it had that one button missing and showed her cleavage which was why I was looking so hard for it so I could sew on a button so I could wear it, my own cleavage being more noticeable than hers, come to think of it.

"So when I saw her leave her house in one of her own tacky dresses, I got me a kitchen chair and carried it across the street to her back porch, and climbed up on the door knob to get my footing, and slipped in through the transom, and rummaged through her own closet. And there hung my dress, brazen as hell. So I took it, and got out the way I came.

"That's why she gave me so many peculiar looks at the streetcar stop and all the way uptown, and I see her now and then even these years later, and do you think she even says hi? Oh, no, just that same peculiar look."

"You remember her little girl?"

"Yes, why?"

"She's the one with Barbara that came up to the fence in her backyard when I was playing cowboy in the WPA ditch and asked me to show them me peeing."

"Oh, Jerry, hush that kinda talk."

PHIL AND EMILY FUSSING
AT MOTHER'S HOUSE

"You have always played sick to get Mother's sympathy."

"I have not. How about you, little brother?"

"That boy hit me in the eye with a rock."

"No, I'm sorry about that, but you've always looked a little sickly, hoping Mother will treat you like her baby boy."

"I'm just shy. Always been."

"Well . . ."

"But you, well, maybe you don't just play like you're sick every time, but the world knows you're certainly a hypochondriac. Admit it."

"Phil, when I am sick, I am sick, so stop saying that."

"Nobody is sick off and on as often as you get, without dying."

"The doctors—"

"Tell you what you want to hear."

"What are you two squabbling about?"

"Oh, nothing, Mother."

"Philip?"

"I was just telling her to stop acting sick so often."

"Are you sick again, Emily?"

"No, Mother. I mean, well, I can't shake this virus."

"The one you had last week or is this a new one?"

"Oh, you can both go jump in the lake."

"Don't you sass *me*, young lady."

"She's got to sass somebody."

"She's your big sister, Phil."

"That's right, take her side against me."

Mother turned her back on them. "I've got to go lay down."

LOOKING AT PHOTOS WITH JERRY

"Get out the pictures, Momma."

"Well, you go sit on the davenport and I'll see if I can find the box of pictures in the cedar chest."

"You used to put me to bed in that cedar chest when I was little and we stayed all night here, and I was always afraid the lid would fall and bury me in the pitch dark."

"Why, honey, I didn't know . . ."

She brought the dress box from Miller's full of photos to the davenport and lifted the lid.

After an hour of showing and telling what she or Mother had often shown or told Jerry and sometimes John, although seldom Dickie, for lack of interest, she came across pictures of the inside of the house in Cleveland.

"Will you just look at how ritzy our house looked in Cleveland compared with this shack we're sitting in? Daddy took them just before we came back down here. Look at that fireplace and mantel. Recognize that picture above the mantel?"

"Yeah, there it is hanging on the wall above our heads. That's not a real painting. Right?"

"Just a country scene, a print, in the frame when Daddy took a photograph of the room."

"Who's the girl in the picture?"

"Don't remember."

"Is that the wicker rocker Gran'paw used to rock in?"

"Sure as the world is. One of the few sticks of furniture we brought with us. That chair by that window and that pretty vase we had to let go. Isn't that a nice breakfast nook? And see its fancy light fixture above the table? I sometimes had my girlfriends over all night and we ate breakfast there. Especially Helen. And there's our nice kitchen, all tile floor."

"Looks like a back staircase that comes down into the kitchen."

"Well, that's what it was, honey, what it was. Oh, and see the beautiful, beautiful Victrola cabinet? Gone. Gone with the wind, honey. Like my new piano. See. The light's too dark. But see? And can't see that tall lamp so well, but it was very costly, I tell you. And just look at how lovely the dining room was, that curved frame around the two tall windows. And the five-legged table. We kept the lace tablecloth. But Mother never let us spread it on the round table that Granny had when we came. Have any idea what this is?"

"That's the dresser Phil's got in the back room."

"The very one. The very one I catch you standing in front of the mirror flexing your muscles in the mirror."

"I'm doing the Charles Atlas exercises."

"That beveled mirror weighed a ton, still kept up by those two spindle posts."

"Don't cry, Momma. I love every one of those pictures. Who's this pretty woman?"

"That's me at only thirteen, all dolled up for Easter."

WARTIME LETTERS FROM PHIL

AND CHUCK'S RUTH

"You take it, Emily. Anything to do with Chuck hurts me. I can't bear it."

When Mother handed her a long, single-spaced typewritten letter from Ruth, Emily's feelings about Chuck's loss of Ruth flooded over her. It was dated only a few days before Chuck was killed in action in Sicily, August first. He may never have gotten her letter to him. In his letters to Mother and to Emily, he always asked them to urge Ruth to write to him, and yet Ruth said Chuck hadn't written in six months. Emily's sadness grew more intense.

Whiskey. Damn whiskey. Ruth stood it as long as she could. She and Emily had that in common. Whiskey husbands. Otherwise, Ruth was different. Beautiful in an unusual way, maybe odd, a little. Pretty eyes and lips and those firm full cheeks, like the singer Ginny Simms, in that picture of her in a WAC uniform, her breasts grade-A movie star. Well, Chuck may be short like all the Merritts, but he was handsome like a movie star, too.

Ruth wrote from an air base in Florida. She still called Mother Mrs. Merritt. "I've been meaning to write since I've been here but I am just now getting settled. My work is very demanding of time but I love it very much. I've been working day and night for the past two weeks but it doesn't bother me in the least, nor do I mind it, knowing that it is important and directly affects the progress of our country. It is such a satisfying feeling, knowing that you are really doing something worth while and you just don't tire as easily as you might in civilian life." Emily liked the way Ruth expressed herself. "This being a P.O.E., I mean, Point of Embarkation, there are numbers upon numbers of men here. Soldiers, sailors, coast guardsmen, Canadian Crews and what not. The planes are beautiful too, and they have become part of my life. I think I would be lost without hearing the roar of planes taking off during the night. The days are just a constant roar, some coming in, others taking off. All the latest planes, the B-29 you probably have been reading about is really a dream."

She was envious of Ruth's adventures and her attitude. She probably knew the women who trained pilots and ferried planes overseas—the WASPS, who were on the cover of *LIFE*.

Ruth was sent to Alaska ten years before they sent Jerry there as punishment for maybe being a Communist.

Mother and I, and Jerry, too, put away, store, keep everything, especially every scrap of paper, even notes, grocery lists, so that having reread all Chuck's and Phil's letters to Mother, far more from Phil than from Chuck, I'm much more mindful than ever of Mother reading them just as the postman delivered them, twice a day he came in those days, how concerned we all are for each other, how much love, simply stated, binds us all together over years full of turmoil, conflict, but more often, daily, affection.

She read that Chuck suffered Ruth divorcing him, in love for ten years. He wrote that he cared about Phil, who'd replaced him as curb hop at Sharp's Drugstore on Broadway, who stayed out all night too often for a nineteen-year-old kid, and then concerned that he might go AWOL once he was in the army. Only a few days before he was killed in France, both Mother and Ruth wrote long loving letters to him that he never got to read. Phil got in, despite his eye injury from that kid hitting it with a rock when he was seven or so, and he suffered the loss of Maxine Cooper whom he called Mac, who after a slew of intense love letters in bad grammar took up with a 4F close to home. Ruth and Mac, the loves of her brothers' lives.

Phil wrote over a hundred letters to his mother, loving, caring letters, full of news, using "swell" often, signed "your loving son," that Emily got tired of reading after a long while. But she felt close to him when he wrote to her, saying, "Emmie, I had a *real*, fresh orange yesterday. Maybe it sounds silly to get excited about an orange but after eating them out of a can for months in the form of watered-down juices, it's quite a novelty to eat one the old-fashioned way by cutting a hole in it and squeezing the juice straight into your mouth."

He told her that he got a letter from Jimmy who asked him to meet him in Paris.

"Well, Sis, it looks like the war is just about over, doesn't it? Things are moving fast now. Today was the kind of day I'd like to take John and Dickie and Jerry up on Sharp's Ridge. Maybe I'll get home in time to take them fishing before it gets too cold. Tell Jerry to keep an eye on things until I get back and tell John to keep out of trouble. Tell Dickie that he is the man of the house while Jimmy is away and he must take care of things. Well, I must close for now. Write soon and often. Lots of Love, Phil."

She remembered the very day, coming into the bedroom where Mother was sitting at the sewing machine, trembling.

"Why, Mother, why are you crying, Mother?"

Mother handed her the telegram. It told her that Chuck was missing in action in France.

"What are you all crying about, Momma?"

"Jerry, go on back outside and play, honey."

"Jerry, I'm sorry to tell you your Uncle Chuck is never going to come home."

"Emily, he's just a child."

"Mother, he has to know sometime."

"Why, Momma?"

"This telegram came telling us he is missing in action, honey."

"The last time I saw him, I was playing inside an old cardboard box on the sidewalk beside Rose's drugstore, and he lifted the flaps and looked in at me. The sun was so bright behind him I could hardly see his face."

"Don't cry, Jerry honey."

"Let him cry, Mother. He loved Chuck."

"We *all* loved Chuck."

"Except Ruth, and it nearly killed him."

"We all still yet love Ruth, too."

"I don't blame her. It could happen to Jimmy."

"Or—"

"Don't say it, Emily."

"I love Phil, too."

"We all love poor little Phil, Jerry."

"Hush, Emily. I can't bear to think of telling Phil. He looked up to Chuck."

"Both of them always asked about each other. Worried about them."

"Missing in action. That means he's not really dead."

"Well . . ."

"I bet you a million dollars he'll come walking in that front door, one of these days."

Strange, strange as hell to think of my skinny little brother blowing up bridges in France, just turned nineteen, only eighteen when he went into the army.

And wandering around Paris, chasing girls and drinking champagne, dashing off to Holland to smell the tulips, praying in the Reims Cathedral, which Jimmy saw, too, and arranging to meet Jimmy in Paris as if it's only a roadhouse on the highway somewhere in Knoxville, and planning to visit Chuck's grave soon's he can locate it in France somewhere, and in charge of eight German prisoners in a sign shop where he's made over a thousand road signs pointing to towns and cities here and there in Europe, and taking courses in drafting, American history, and such, sending home German lugers and bayonets and caps and helmets, and soon the little dog he rescued, Snuffy, and paintings and drawings German soldiers in his shop did of him and of Maxine from a photograph and that horse in the snow. And look at all those photographs he sent home. Cute shot of those two French girls. My little brother, almost blind in one eye from that boy throwing a rock when he was a kid, and every letter asking about Maxine and whether she still loves him, if only he could control his Merritt temper, and those, oh, God, those awful sappy things he says to Mother, "My best girl and sweetheart and your loving son," and so on and so forth, and asking about Cap, whether he still comes to see Mother, and about John and his antics, and whether Dickie is back home from Germany and settling down, and Jerry about the clarinet he sent money to buy for him, and about the ladies, as he calls them, whether Jerry is still chasing them, and he's only twelve, and, well, yes, he is, Phil. Little brother far, far from home.

Happy twentieth birthday, honey. Almost a man.

JONNIE LOU GILMER, JERRY'S OLD FLAME

"Maybe I will have some new news for you this time besides just family stuff. Ran into your old grammar school flame, Jonnie Lou Gilmer, in the bank the other day and had been seeing her around for some time and so just up and asked her if that was her. She seemed glad to hear about you and said tell you hello. She is getting married next mo. I think she said, and I didn't think to ask her if it was any one you knew. She sure is a cute little trick. Must work in a beauty shop as she was making a deposit and had on a white uniform. Or a nurse.

"David Van Vactor's mug is spread all over town for the symphony and I sure wish you could be here to go. Did you know your dad's boss ol' Breezy Wynn is business mgr. for the Symphony? O Brother. He and David had their pictures real chummy like in Sun. paper and I meant to send it to you and it got away from me.

"Had something else kind of nice to tell you but for the moment it has slipped my mind. I did mail you a cake, and I sure hope you get it for Sun. I tried to make it extra good and got it a little rich and crumbly and had to cut it in two because I had no large box large enough. Anyhow, my heart was in the right place.

"John is still enthused in school, and I wish you would write and tell him how glad you are, and that you wish him all the luck in the world as a radio announcer, and he is going to have the leading part in 'Mr. Roberts' if they can tone the language down fit for childish ears. He was so thrilled last night.

"I think he is soaking up some math too. Wish I had had a Math brain, as this bookwork is driving me nuts. I didn't know about the bookkeeping and so much detail. This guy sure gets all he can for his money. $30 per wk. I get 2% on all sales and sold one this morning and made $2 and have another coming up tomorrow. We do more on Sat. and I am sure going to come in with my selling britches on, as I need some kale.

"No luck with getting Dick a job yet. I ran my legs off Wed. afternoon. My afternoon off and no soap, only Coca Cola bott. co. said he would give him one in Mar. when business picked up.

"I could take your old man and beat his ears off. He carried Dickie's official papers for two wks and not a thing did he do. Honestly if he lives another year I'll be surprised. I met him to get the papers back and he looked 55 yrs. old and I'll bet he doesn't weigh 130. I feel sorry for him and again I could wring his neck. So there will be no help there.

"Mammy and Cap are still fishing and Cap caught a 5# bass and it gets bigger every time he tells it. But they enjoy going to Douglas Dam and Mother wouldn't ever get out if she didn't go, so I guess it is good for them.

"I am just about ready to get off and so will maybe add a little when I get home. May go to see Marlon Brando in *On the Waterfront* across the street. It is supposed to be very good. Did you see Jimmy Stewart in *Rear Window*? It was the best I have seen in many a day.

"I got such a screwy card from you. About a house off post & no blankets or sheets. The 1st word I knew of a house. Honey I am having to use all my bedding here at Mammies as she is short and we are keeping up 4 beds in this teeny house. Let me know more. Maybe I can send some.

"Later.

"Did see Marlon Brando and it was very good. My stomach is still jumping.

"I'll say goodnight, and let me know all about your situation and if it has improved. You had Abrn. on your new address. Does that mean Airborn? or what?

"Hope you get a few days off soon. Tell me all you are doing.

"Love, Mother.

"P.S. When payday comes around don't forget me and your storage fee too. I also paid Cap $3 out of the other for your phone call."

CHARM GETS HER JOBS, TEMPER GETS HER FIRED

She knew how well her charm worked on possible employers, but the only understanding she had about the fact that she had won but then too soon lost many jobs in her life was that she was also too gifted in the sass department.

Had she gotten that characteristic from Daddy? No. From Mother? Very likely. But Mother had no reputation for sassing any of her employers—JFG Coffee, Breezy Wynn Sporting Goods, Knoxville Woolen Mill, or General Hospital or the patients she took care of as a practical nurse in homes. Philip had her inclination to sass, but mostly within the family.

She hadn't passed it on to Dickie, maybe to John; both used reproaches based on idealistic principles and to con people. But now you take Jerry, who could be so sweet and charming, but who could sass with the best of them, she herself, his teachers, and even hoodlums who taunted him while he worked at the White Tower hamburger joints all over Manhattan and he said Boston, too, and maybe on ships as a merchant seaman, but certainly in the army. Why? Always asking why when they gave an order. She could also be arrogant and superior acting, which she knew she was not really guilty of.

So there she sat, jobless, in goddamn Knoxville, jobless, penniless, still sassing her boss in the safety of her mind. What next then? Well, John did say he might be coming through, and she might persuade him to stay with her, get a job, and share expenses. Meanwhile, Jerry was due to get paid, maybe could shell out a few dollars. Mother and Cap. She hated to ask them again. But didn't she always pay them back?

"Hello, Mother. What's you all doing?"

"Not much of anything."

"Well, me, I'm just sitting around studying the classifieds."

"WHO SAYS GINNY'S HOUSE
IS LIKE A WHOREHOUSE?"

"Momma, somebody told me that people in Ginny's neighborhood think her house on Riverside Drive has become a whorehouse."

"What—are you—talking—about? Who—said so?"

"Just somebody who heard about it from somebody else. A woman came up to me like she knew me and blurted it out."

"I'd like to get my hands on that bitch for spreading rumors about my best friend."

"She said men in cars are always coming and going all night long at Ginny's."

"We both have friends who are men and they do come see us. Women, too. Ruth and Madabee and Zoe and Katie Lee, girlfriends we have known for years, and sometimes women come with men, and it's a party."

"They say the landlord's about to kick her out."

"They, who?"

"That woman just said 'they.'"

"She and her kind are just like that woman that told you I danced in the burlesque show at the Roxy. Damned lies. Why? Why would anyone tell a child such a tale?"

"Not exactly a child, Momma."

"Young enough for such lies to hurt your feelings."

"It scalded my scalp just to hear it, but I didn't believe it. Maybe you ought not to stay all night with her so often."

"See. There you go. You sound like you believe it of your own mother."

"No, I mean—Well, Phil yelled at you that time because he said his friends down at the watering hole told him stories about you and your girlfriends that make him look bad and taunted him. So, to keep people from dreaming stuff up . . ."

"They are all my friends, Jerry, and I will do as I damn please, and to hell with everybody else. Sorry 'bout you and Phil though."

HER COOKING

Like Mother, she was well-known to be an excellent cook, except for eggs, which she refused to fry, because the very sight of them turned her stomach.

Cornbread, the best. Cakes, coconut, devil's food, especially applesauce cake with orange icing, sometimes sliced bananas between layers, always for Jerry's birthdays, his favorite. Green beans, with shelly beans that folks up in Cleveland never even heard of. Baked macaroni and cheese. Bread pudding. Fried chicken. Fried pies, tart apricot her favorite.

Every summer she suffered whatever kitchen and outdoor heat came indoors, needing to cook and preserve, put up chow-chow and sauerkraut and peaches, before they rotted right there in the bushel basket, and blackberry jam, tomatoes preserves, and apple jelly. Shelves chocked full.

Stuff that went out of her hands into boiling water and then into Mason jars large and small that she loved to reach for all winter long and feel in her hands as she twisted off the lids. Much of it got too old or she couldn't find enough people to give it away, so some rotted. And oh, yeah, seafoam candy, but mainly fudge with black walnuts. The ingredients of the home-churned ice cream, peaches, strawberries, maraschino cherries were always perfect even when, during the war, she had to call on Pet condensed milk. She went from wood stoves, hotter'n hell, to electric, but never really had a kitchen up to the quality of the things she cooked.

Being nervous, volatile, she often got flustered and couldn't coordinate all the dishes in a meal, so that she often yelled and cursed and mock-cried, making Jerry feel guilty that she was cooking for him on his visits, so that he told her he was sorry, and not to cook for him.

"Why, honey, what are you talking about?"

CAP IN OAK RIDGE, "THE ATOMIC CITY"

Rummaging through and reading Mother's letters to Chuck and Phil and to herself made Emily feel sadly nostalgic but elated too, having doors and windows opening to Mother's life. Here was one from Cap to Mammy on the stationery of the Army Service Force, United States Engineer Office, Manhattan District, Oak Ridge, Tennessee. July 6, 1944. Strange he almost always capitalizes the words and never uses punctuation. He was Dutch, not German.

"Hello Honey I received your Letter and Card and Sure was Glad to hear from You and that You are Ok and enjoying yourself Honey the same day you left I answered a Call to a Troop train wrecked 7 miles outside of La Follette. Killed 33 injured 2000 I made a run of 50 miles to this Wreck, Helped take out the Dead and Wounded also held Light while they gave Blood Transfusion and operated. Honey that was one of the Horriblest ever I seen. If that had been that evening earlier than it was I would have went Nuts I stayed there all Night I was thinking about you all night while I was Driving that 50 miles at 1 AM Honey I still Love You better than my self Honey I pass right over this spot that evening this Train jumped over a Cliff 1000 feet High, Lit in the river Honey don't Forget me honey write Me Soon I feel so lonesome without you. So good Bye darling with many Kisses."

Why was Cap's name torn off the bottom? Maybe to keep their love affair secret, he being married. In those days, the strong advice was "never put it in writing."

She remembered the time she woke up bitching about this, that, and the other, making John itch to get out.

"I'm going to Mammy's," he said, defiantly, damn well aware she would refuse to let him.

"No, you are not. Cap's over there, and they need to be alone."

"What do they do?" John leered.

"Wipe that look off your face." Suppressing a smile made her bust out laughing.

John laughed with her.

"You're beggin' for a whuppin.'"

"Well, what do they—?"

They laughed as if on cue.

"I'm gonna go see."

"But don't expect her to let you in."

GOING DANCING

Jerry was at his birthday desk writing another story, she reckoned, sitting in that one-armed old chair that survived the years since Daddy moved them out of Cleveland all of a sudden and back to the little house where she was born. Jerry called it his sanctuary although it was on the open stairway landing by the window.

"I'm off, Jerry. Going dancing with Ginny and a couple of the other girls somewhere out Maryville Pike."

"Honky-tonking like Kitty Wells?"

"Don't get smart."

"So, I guess you're going off with that ol' George Upchurch again."

"He's still trying to get those ice cream stands started." She loved the hell out of frozen custard, and he was very nice, a big man, smoked Dutch Master cigars, and drove a shiny new Packard. "I can't wait to get out of this g.d. town—even if it's just for a few hours."

"I don't need to go honky-tonking myself 'cause I already wrote a story about it."

"Jerry, Zoe wants me to spend the night with her after we go dancing, so you take John to Mother's and spend the night there. I don't want you all sleeping here alone in this bad neighborhood 'round Happy Holler and find your throats cut. Then Zoe'll drive me over for Sunday dinner. Here's some streetcar checks. Don't wait till dark." Going down the stairwell, she paused, her head floor level, to say, "And if you forget to empty the icebox pan again, I will beat the living fire out of you." She knew he knew she didn't mean it, just talking mean.

Jerry knows I love to dance, and I stay out dancing all night sometimes. Sometimes he watches while I put on rouge and powder and do my lipstick to go out, but he never sees me dancing.

She went down the steps, deliberately flouncing, feeling the wavy motion of her silk dress along her thighs. She was eager to feel the stroking of George's hand, wishing now (and she would wish again when he actually did it) that it was Bob's hand. But no, not since she told him to go to hell and stay there had she gotten a letter from Terre Haute.

"A MERRY XMAS WITH AN INFECTED LEG"

"Dear Jerry, Well, here we are, Christmas time.

"Cap was in the hospital and not a single one of his adorable six children, no, five, plus all their kids, too, would come and sit with him, only Dorothy. And me. They didn't write or call. They can't seem to get over Mother and Cap being in love while their mother was dying of cancer. But they're a tacky bunch anyway.

"Honey, don't forget to save the S&H green stamps for your poor mother. I reckon I will have a merry Xmas—with an infected leg.

"Electric bill sure boomed up—up. Love, Your Mother."

DICKIE AND THE COLLIE DOG
IN THE SNOW

The first morning after they moved into the house on Dempster, Jerry ran into the bedroom and screamed to Momma that he was looking out the kitchen window and saw Dickie running in the snow under the trees, his wrist in a huge collie dog's wet mouth. She laughed and told him, "That's a collie dog's way of playing, and Dickie just enjoys making you think he's being attacked."

After Jimmy went to work at Breezy's, she took Jerry and Dickie with her to the A&P.

"Momma, why is your belly so big?"

"Ask me no questions, Jerry, and I'll tell you no lies."

"Why don't you tell me?"

"Because I am going to have a baby."

"What's being fatter got to do with it?"

"Honey, that's just part of it. I'll tell you the rest when we get back home."

She figured out later that while she was in the A&P and let Dickie and Jerry wander, they snuck out into the alley and Jerry stood watch while Dickie crawled through a secret entrance he had made and ransacked the grocery store next door, abandoned since the Depression. As they were carrying the groceries, she saw Hershey bars and Dentyne chewing gum sticking out of the pockets of their Mackinaws. She knew what they had done, but pretended not to have caught them red-handed.

JERRY CALLS FROM SAN FRANCISCO

"Oh, Jerry, why do you all have to go to San Francisco when you could stay in Knoxville and go to UT? San Francisco seems like the end of the world, and it'd cost an arm and leg to call you way over there. And what about their earthquakes? I'll never know whether you are alive or dead."

"Momma, Robbie and I want to live in an interesting city, and San Francisco is a great place. I'll be studying creative writing with Walter Van Tilburg Clark, the man who wrote *The Ox-Bow Incident*. Remember that movie, starring Henry Fonda? And a lot of poets and novelists and artists live there, what they call the San Francisco Renaissance."

"I know, honey, I know. Well, I love new places myself, so I know. And it's only for a year?"

"Yeah. Then we may come back. Hell, we may send for you to come live there."

"You can leave me out of it. Those earthquakes. And isn't it always locked in with fog? And Alcatraz? Promise your mother you'll stay out of Alcatraz."

"I will, but I don't know about Robbie."

"Oh, yeah, well, Robbie is the best thing that ever happened to you. Just be glad you didn't marry Iva Lee. Where would you be without Robbie?"

WASHING JOHN'S DO-DO-PEE-PEE-SO-SO

After he took a bath in the big metal wash tub in the kitchen, she made John stand up, whining, on one of the round-backed kitchen chairs she'd painted green, as she washed his "do-do-pee-pee-so-so," the foreskin pushed back, a weekly ritual.

Jerry came in from ushering at the Bijou, the bright kitchen light overhead falling directly between them. "I'm so glad I was circumcised when I was a baby."

"Jerry, I found us a wonderful little house. John. *Hold still.*" She slapped his leg and John started bellering. "Shut up. Shut up!"

"Well, I hate to leave my ol' chicken shack sanctuary."

"If I never see Atlantic Avenue again, it won't be too soon. There's too many sad memories here. And no more g.d. apartments for me. I'm sick of living in a rat's nest."

Jerry got up Thanksgiving morning to start packing. John snuck off before noon. She screamed at Jerry forty-'leven times, and he went out to the run-down chicken house, his sanctuary. She heard him shattering lumps of coal at the wall. "Get back in here, Jerry, and take down my bed."

At two o'clock, Cap came by in his old 1941 Packard and drove them over to Mother's for Thanksgiving dinner. When they went in, John was reading a Donald Duck funny book by the Warm Morning heater.

"You *better* hide behind that funny book. And wipe that silly grin off your face."

After dinner, Cap drove Jerry and John to the Broadway Theatre. Jerry told her it was unjust that she had to work even on Thanksgiving.

Next day, Mother and Cap wanted to see the new house, so they drove on over to Eleanor Street in East Knoxville. She had forgotten to give Jerry the key, so they stood on the front and back porches and in the dead grass at the sides, peering in windows, and then Jerry found one of them unlocked and crawled in, and they tiptoed like housebreakers through the rooms. Jerry staked out one for his sanctuary and asked Momma which one she intended for the roomer who would help with the rent.

But she got in a rage listening to the landlady announcing a long list of dos and don'ts, so she found another new place to live.

She stuck a note to the sooty screen with a safety pin. "We have moved to 216 East Oklahoma Street. God help us. Key in the mailbox."

TALKING ABOUT THE DEPRESSION DAYS

She told Jerry and John that the brown and yellow police car pulled up to the house, and the cops took Dickie away because he and some other boys had stolen stuff out of R. T. Lyons's boarded-up grocery store. "The Depression did it, caused R. T. Lyons to close."

"Why do you and Mammy and them refer to the Depression so often?'It's the Depression, it's because of the Depression,' as if it's something before I came along. Sometimes it hits me that I was there, from 1933 to now, anyway. I remember the picture in the paper in about 1938 that you all keep with the family photos of Roosevelt speaking at the L&N rayroad depot."

"I suppose you remember the Depression too, John."

"The who done what?"

And then a few months later, Jerry came home and told her that it was Al Jolson talent night at the Bijou, and guess who suddenly showed up on the stage and won it? Dickie, the fugitive.

"We know, he's here in the house right now, just got up from sitting on the edge of the bed with me and your daddy, telling us all about it."

"Next show at the Bijou is *A Night in Casablanca* with the Marx Brothers. That's us, me and Dickie and John."

"Why, Jerry, sometimes . . . the way you talk . . ."

Dickie showed up suddenly in the doorway.

"John, you get in bed with me and your daddy, and Dickie you sleep on the cot in the kitchen with Jerry."

NEEDING HELP, ALWAYS NEEDING HELP

She loved Blake for himself alone, not because he did anything for her. He never had occasion to, not around her often enough or for long spans of time, not allowing for times when she needed anything, not even a cone of Dairy Queen. Yes, maybe he did that for her once or twice. It was just wonderful visiting little Blake in Louisville and then teenage Blake for his high school graduation. Pictures of her with him and standing between Jerry and Robbie. And visits with Blake's half-Japanese wife Monica, whose mother had watched from a cave as the atom bomb hit Nagasaki, and visiting little Kunico-Nicole. She looked over often at the framed photo of Nicole hugging her neck, sitting in this same chair.

Neither John nor Greg could ever do enough for her, and she knew it, but she couldn't keep herself from reproaching them often for the things they didn't do, even things, sometimes, that she knew they simply couldn't do for her. She needed help. She always needed help, almost ever since she and John moved down to good ol' 2722 Henegar Street after Mother died.

And Jerry. Oh, Jerry, when he visited, immediately, compulsively, went to work around the house, helping her, cleaning up, mostly, when she would rather he just sat and talked to her. Well, he did talk with her when he took her for rides into the country, to Cumberland Gap and the Lincoln Museum at Lincoln Memorial University, Lone Mountain Park, the Smokies, and that time to the Biltmore House. Wonderful, wonderful. And sending money. He had always sent her money. From his merchant seaman days, the army years, and ever since. But starting with his paper route at nine, then ushering at the Bijou.

Dickie on his rare visits, just passing through, would help, but without feeling. Just do it, and that's that. John whining, reluctant, and Greg a lot like John that way, but Jerry with a "oh, glad-to-help" attitude.

LETTERS IN BOXES ON THE BACK PORCH

"Momma, how could you put all these letters out on the back porch in old cardboard boxes. They're all damp and squashed."

"I was poring over them last month. Honey, I had to do something about all that stuff running me out of my bedroom."

"But they'll get rained on out there."

"John keeps promising to take them back down to the garage."

"But there's holes in the roof of it."

"I can't help it."

"Okay, I'll put them in the garage back in a dry corner."

"If the rain's got to the big drums full of my other things, please move them, too. John."

"What?"

"Jerry's putting that box back in the garage for me, so you don't have to worry about it."

John didn't say anything. Glued to that TV, eating a TV dinner from a folding tray table, watching UT lose to Alabama again.

"John."

"What?"

"I said—"

"I heard you the first time."

Jerry held the box in his arms, ready to set off to the garage. "Momma, this is our history."

"I know, I know. Letters from everybody, everywhere." Especially from her best friend Ginny, maybe a few thousand pages and envelopes from the forties to yesterday's, so many she had not been able to answer all of them.

When Jerry came up from Baton Rouge to visit, he always plunged right into whatever mess or problem about the house he found. The roaches were terrible, so he brought some special Bengal spray from Baton Rouge. And the rats and mice, and John was not good at dealing with them. The crude, earthen half-basement took in water and the dampness attracted the bugs. Jerry had pulled out the old dining room sideboard and found that rat hole in the wall and nailed a scrap of plywood over it. He's used to living in that mansion of a house in Baton Rouge. He throws out all kinds of stuff, some of it she wanted to keep a while longer in case some need arose, or just because. Her favorite pot John scorched and tossed out in the yard, smoking up a storm.

"Jerry, please sit down. All you do the whole time you're here is fix things. Let's us just sit and talk."

"It's hot as hell in here, Momma. Let's go out on the back porch."

"No, honey, I never go out there anymore."

"How come?"

"Too many memories. It hurts me."

"Anywhere you go in this house are memories of Mammy."

Sitting on the back porch had been pure pleasure and solace to all the family. The view of the long backyard down to the alley, Dewey Camel's white-painted, wooden grape arbor, and his garage on the left, and the old circus wagon Daddy towed here across Knoxville, first used as a coal house and now for storage. The flowers galore.

Picking apples off the huge tree that the lightning split, struck down, but that every spring gave forth a profusion of apples. Mother never let her pick even one solitary apple. That pink flamingo Mother and Cap brought back from their visit to Uncle Ed and cousin Hazel in Florida. The ornate concrete bench. The old vegetable garden, the mimosa trees, the great oak that had to come down, else crash into the wood-shingle roof. Cap and Phil had trucked in scrap marble from Tennessee Marble Quarry and created a porch of it and a low terrace and covered the grass, too, a little way out into the backyard.

Sitting out there in the old metal lawn chairs, Cap in his porch lounge, somebody out in the yard in the hammock, the talk in the twilight, then the dark, soothed nerves, knitted everybody all together delicately, even as they fussed, but mainly as they told memories as stories. The voices and the crickets and dogs barking in the distance, the sound of traffic carried over creek water from busy Broadway, and planes going over, and cars passing "like sixty" out on Henegar, and neighbors' voices coming and going, and suddenly behind them the rusty cry of the screen door opening, and there was Phil come home from work at the city tax office or Dorothy come to see her daddy, or God knows who else, always expecting John or Dickie, and Mother never gave up on Chuck showing up from missing in action.

"But never me?" Jerry played like it hurt him, mock crying, but it really did, she knew it.

That one time, after Jerry went off to visit the Van Vactors, Raven just in from Los Angeles where she still tried to get into the movies, Emily hankered to see the old letters. Three big boxes full. When she dumped the first box in her lap, she realized that over the years, she must have written thousands of letters, to members of her family, Mother, Jerry, John, Dickie, Robbie, Blake, Greg, to her many men friends, especially Bob Price, John, Bill Williams, Bill Boles, Russell, and women friends, especially Ginny, Ruby, Madabee,

Ruth, Betty, Frenchie, and saved every single solitary one they sent to her, food-stained, cat-stained, smelling of all the cigar, pipe, and cigarette smokers around her, and she kept every letter they wrote to her, along with grocery lists and "to do notes." Pretty stationery lured her to write.

And she wouldn't take anything for that letter from John from Mobile. "Dear Momma, From now on, and tell Jerry and Mammy, my name is Sunshine Madden because I was passing through Cornelia, Georgia where I was in jail that time and Jerry got me off the damned chain gang by getting the people I passed bad checks on to accept restitution, and I saw these six black kids playing basketball without no shoes on, and I took them all trailing behind me into one of the stores and conned the owner to put tennis shoes on those kids for nothing, and when they thanked me, one of them must have heard me say to the owner, 'Bring a little sunshine into their lives,' because he piped up with, 'Thank you, Sunshine,' and that got all of them, the store owner, too, to yelling, 'Thank you, Sunshine.'

"When I was back on the highway, it started to rain something awful all around me but not much of it hit the car somehow, so when this highway patrolman that I noticed was following me turned on his red light and I pulled over, I asked him, 'Sir, what was it I was doing?'

"'Nothing, but I just wanted you to know that I been following you for three miles in this rainstorm, so how come you ain't got no rain on your car? You must be the Sunshine man they was all talking about back in Cornelia when I was having my coffee.'"

John's handwriting was hard to read. She made her own handwriting clear and distinctive. Her letters were vibrant with sayings, more general than southern, full of energy, even when she was simply laying out details of her work, her illnesses, of family and friends. Very little talk about the movies she saw or the many books she lay abed until after midnight reading, a time or two all night long to the finish. Books rented from department stores or on loan from libraries, which Jerry when he visited returned for her, and then John after he began living with her. Letters from many places—Chattanooga, Nashville, Cincinnati, Columbus, and on the road working with Olan Mills. Many, many letters. Lord, have mercy.

TALKING WITH JIMMY'S BIG SISTER
ABOUT JIMMY

While Jimmy was in the living room with Kathleen's husband, listening to *The Lone Ranger*, his favorite radio show, Emily slipped into the kitchen, eager to tell Kathleen first, as the sister who raised Jimmy after his mother died when he was only eleven, that she wanted to marry Jimmy.

Kathleen shook her head. "Why, Emily, I don't think Jimmy's ready for that. He may never be ready. People've always done for Jimmy. He don't know how to do for others. If you can get him to marry you, you'll just have to *do* for him, like all the rest of us. Women and men, too, *like* to do for Jimmy."

"So do I, but of course . . ."

"Good luck, honey. *I* sure needed it. Jimmy and his ways."

"Maybe he will change, if we get married."

"Well, honey, the Jimmy you see is the Jimmy he always was and always will be."

COFFEE SHOP HOSTESS
IN SAM DAVIS HOTEL

"Hi, Jerry: I guess you thought I was never going to write. Honey I just can't tell you what a pace I've been going for a wk.

"Changed jobs. Hostess in the coffee shop at the Sam Davis Hotel.

"Didn't you tell me they named it to honor—like that statue on the Capitol lawn—the Boy Hero of the Confederacy, that the Yankees executed as a spy? I love that photograph you took of John leaning against the cannon that time Jimmy and you drove to Nashville and the reform school let him go into town for a day, even though he had escaped a few weeks before and was brought back from Florida. Made him wear coveralls too big for him with RUNAWAY on the back.

"Had to take about $25 a month less. But not so hard on me. Your old lady is now a boss and hires and fires and supervises. You know I like that and I miss bossing you boys.

"Have been going to see Dick 3 or 4 times a wk and this official and that official about the trial till I am a nervous wreck. The trial is in the morning and I feel like I'll fall apart before then. I am so afraid Dick is going to get a sentence instead of a parole. They checked and found out about him being in that Colorado prison in Canon City that year and his army air force prison time in Hamburg and the dishonorable discharge goes against him. Tomorrow will tell.

"Had a letter from John. He's been sick with intestinal flu but is up now. He wrote you, he said, so take time out to ans. It is shameful how you all have drifted away from each other.

"Well, I guess I'd better turn in, have to pull out at 6 bells. Work 7 to 2— 5:50 to 8:00 for all of $100 per mo. and lousy meals. We have to wait until the guests eat.

"Well, I'll be saying night-night and write me soon. Love, Mother."

BLOODY TAPESTRY JIMMY BROUGHT FROM THE WAR

"Oh, Jerry, why did you nail that bloody tablecloth to the wall of your dining room, of all places?"

"You don't think it's beautiful?"

"If it didn't have that blood stain, I might. I carried it from house to house ever since your daddy spread it out on our bed his first day back from Europe like he thought it'd give me a thrill."

"That's why you let me have it. You said it made you sick even just packing it away and unpacking it."

"I'd forget it, and then there it was. I don't know what possessed your daddy to bring it back with him, of all the things he could have picked. And Phil opening that package in the living room at Mother's and showing that German luger and that knife and that German helmet."

"When I first saw it, I thought the word Christian on the lining inside meant he was a Christian, but Phil said, hell, no, that's his own name."

"And that officer's cap."

"No telling what Dickie brought back from Hanover—"

"Hamburg, Momma, Hamburg."

"—because he'd sell it all soon's he could."

"He's fond of the profit motive."

"I bet he got far more than they were worth. And little John playing German with that awful stuff and Phil yelling at him to keep his mitts off his souvenirs. I do like the painting of that horse in the snow among the village rooftops that that German prisoner that worked for Phil in the sign shop painted, and the one of Maxine he painted. She broke his heart though."

"I've got to ask Daddy to tell me the story behind that—I call it a tapestry."

"Don't raise your hopes. He'll probably just give you that shrug of his."

ASKING FOR MONEY
FROM THE RICH MADDENS

On her lunch hour, Emily visited John at the Juvenile Detention Center. She came back late, and Louie threatened to fire her again.

Jimmy staggered into Louie's and bummed some money off Jerry while he was eating his favorite hot roast beef and gravy sandwich at the counter.

Emily ducked into the ladies' room and stayed in there until she thought Jimmy had left. But he was talking to Louie on the way out.

"Jerry, I hate to tell you, but we got to move again. Mrs. Easterly's kicking us out. Too far behind on the rent."

Desperate, she got Herbert Madden to come to the phone and cried a commitment out of him.

"Jerry, jerk your clothes on, honey, you got to get moving. Go to the Packing House for me and pick up a check I finally talked Herbert Madden into giving me to help carry us over the end of the month. No use bugging your eyes, honey, that man's not giving us but $10. David Madden isn't working there these days, or he might have come across with more, you being named after him. If you hurry you can catch the streetcar. It just passed the house and's about to turn around by now. You can get an egg and toast at the Blue Circle, then hotfoot it across Gay Street Bridge to the Packing House. The rent's way overdue. Jerry, did you hear your mother? Get up from there and go. Git!"

LETTER TO GINNY

"Well, Ginny, that's John 'Sunshine' Madden for you every time. Like the time Jerry came rolling into town from Lynchburg College, where they made him writer-in-residence for five months, ahead of a trail of black smoke from that big Buick, and John had just got a settlement check for that wreck by Target in Fountain City and needed to buy himself another used car and so he took Jerry with him and did buy a car but bought Jerry one too, on the spot.

"So this morning John hit the road early for Eastern Kentucky with his car crammed full of clothes for the victims of that flood you saw on the news last night. Look at all the trouble he got into from age 11, in and out of correction facilities, and now he's a sort of celebrity around Knoxville and on over into Hazard and Harlan. And years ago, rescued little Greg from those Smiths. Persuaded President Johnson's personal aide to send Cap a special commendation for his years as a fireman.

"Never comes back without some present for his mother. How can you keep from loving the little dickens? And that grin that tells you he's just worked a con for the good of the poor or orphans and that mouth when he goes on the war path to correct some kind of injustice or pester the city council until they name Gay Street Bridge for Greg's Phyllis because the icy pavement sent her car over the bridge. That's one he lost.

"That's all for now. Will write more in the morning before I stagger off to work."

RAY IN THE MAXWELL HOUSE HOTEL

After standing on her feet eight hours at the Maxwell House Hotel's cigar counter, she didn't mind sitting down in Ray's room, helping him sort ties to show buyers when he hit the road again, for Lexington, Kentucky, this time around. Sorting with Ray was one of the nicest feelings of intimacy she ever experienced with a man. Not greater than making love on the bed they sat on to sort, of course. The best kisser, and he declared often that she was *his* best kisser. Best dancer of them all, even over Bill Williams and Bill Boles. Poor Jimmy. Kissed okay, but it was his shyness that made it good. One of the best at just doing it. But not at lovemaking as such. But if I still love him, I don't really know.

Whereas Ray now, he's good at all of it. And at taking her places she never imagined doing with other men, to concerts, plays, the Ice Capades, the war memorial that's like a great palace. And that Parthenon. Who needs Greece?

Lord have mercy, he was, when he was in Nashville, too seldom, the one who ranked highest in her esteem. When she looked up from arranging the cigar boxes in the case and saw him crossing the lobby toward her, her knees went weak a little. But another married man. At least he wasn't a drunk, like all those others.

READING ALOUD TO JERRY

A PASSAGE FROM *BIJOU*

Because John slept on the twin bed in the back room now, first Cap gone, then Phil gone, Jerry slept on the davenport in the living room when he visited.

When he looked in on her, she sat up straighter in bed, holding *Bijou* cracked wide open.

"I just love this part here, Jerry. Let me see, where is—Oh, yes, I turned the page down. I always put in our real names, just for my own sake.

"'Going back home through the WPA ditch in the steamy moonlight, leaving the Green Hornet and Kato in a fix until next week, Dickie stops, puts his hand on Jerry's head. "Quiet . . . I hear Momma cryin.'" Jerry hears nothing. He follows Dickie home, running. The doors are closed, the shades down. Red-faced, gray-haired Miss Teddie, that takes care of them when Momma's working, leads them into the bedroom. Jerry can barely see the tiny red face peeking out of the covers in the crook of Momma's arm. It wiggles and explodes into crying, and Jerry sees the mobster's car crash again and explode in the Green Hornet chapter play and the baby is born in Momma's bed in the same moment. . . . Momma catches John trying to feed the baby a banana. . . . They all stand around the kitchen table between the cook stove and the sink, watching Momma bathe the baby, and John keeps calling it Baboo, but its name is Ronald Dennis Madden.'"

"I'm glad you like it, Momma."

"My favorite part. Of course, you know, honey, that wasn't quite the way it was. Was it?"

"What's added is from my imagination."

"Well, I certainly hope this passage is mostly made up. Let me see, where . . . ? This one. 'He crawled back in bed. He remembered how it was during the war. Momma and Daddy had separated even before he joined the army and he woke up several times at night and found some man sitting in the living room, the lamplight casting a strange aura over everything in his sleepy vision. "He's a good friend, honey," she would say. "He wants to help me."

"'One night, when he was about nine, he couldn't sleep, feeling guilty about accidentally knocking a bird's nest down out of a slender tree he was climbing. The blue eggs broke and the sight of the yolk was like the spilled guts of a baby he'd murdered. Momma and the man assured him he couldn't help it, and she told him to go back to sleep. Then he dreamed that his mother was dying and the only way she could get well would be for her to take a magic serum or for him to 'do it' to her.'"

"Jerry, I love reading *Bijou*, and this is my third time, but did you have to describe me that way for all the world to read?"

JOHN HOME FROM REFORM SCHOOL

John coming home disrupted her routine severely. The officials stressed to her that she was legally responsible for keeping him out of trouble. Home? Not really home for him, because he so seldom lived with her and Jerry since he started going in and out of homes for problem kids and Juvenile Detention Center and State Reform School. Will it be prison next, like with Dickie?

She and Jerry had a good life in the apartment on Hill Street, a routine. And now Iva Lee was coming back into Jerry's life after the breakup that nearly killed him and he was going to UT, acting in plays and writing them. She hated feeling this way, but John being there was an intrusion. She was glad to see him, sure. But every day she dreaded what he might get into next. The fact he took the girl down across the alley on a date, was that a good sign? A pretty girl, but odd, like her one-armed mother. That old house across the alley on the cliff that always looked like one more drop of rain and it'd slide down into the Tennessee River, and two Negro women living in the lower level below the sidewalk level. The mother ought to draw the shade. Not naked, but almost. Caught Jerry at the window one time. "Just looking at the moon, Momma."

Jerry was used to having his bed to himself, but he was glad John was out.

Not so glad when he brought to the house a puppy and put it in the basement by the furnace in the dark and never went down to see it, and Jerry had to feed it, until it got sick, and he had to put it out of its misery. No fair to Jerry, who came back up in a crying fit.

John sentimental about having a dog, but not about taking responsibility. Having it, just having it, his own dog, is what mattered most.

She lay awake imagining and worrying about what John might do because of the troubles he had gotten into over the past seven or so years.

PIANO AND THE BRONZE STAR

She hadn't written yet to tell Jimmy that she hoped to put money down on a used upright piano she had her eye on from the check that he enclosed in his letter from France. Said he received extra moolah as a winner of the Bronze Star for volunteering to dash across a valley into the mountains under fire, his medic truck turning over several times, to bring wounded back out of the hills. General Patton had come roaring up in his Jeep and screamed to him to move his goddamn ambulance off the road so he could roar on past, but Jimmy refused, and Patton praised his guts. Or that's how Jimmy told it anyway.

She knew Jimmy wouldn't give a damn how she spent that money, but Mother accused her of thriving on secrecy, even though in her own mind she was convinced she deserved the piano for all the suffering that being married to James Helvy Madden had inflicted upon her fun-loving nature.

The piano would take up much of the bedroom-living room of her two-room apartment. But having the piano would make the already cramped living space, Jimmy's and her bed in the front room where the piano might sit and Jerry's and John's cot in the kitchen right by the wood stove.

What depressed her was the overflow into the two rooms and the hallway of her stuff in boxes and industrial drums that she had hauled like a nomad from house to house, from one end of Knoxville to another ten times or more, out of the past and into the future. Even after they'd crammed a good deal of her stuff in the old chicken shack by the alley, she'd had to stack drums and boxes full of stuff too precious to risk roof leaks and prowlers in corners of the two rooms, scraps of cloth draped over them, and along the wall in the hall, despite the landlady, who lived across the hall in the other half of the house, raising Cain every day or so.

All she needed now was for Dickie to show up, still running from the cops.

Peeking into one of the boxes, Jerry asked, "Momma, you ain't gonna save these old sugar ration books, are you?"

"You just hush. You never know. You were too young to remember how it was."

Once each spring, summer, and fall, she sorted through her possessions, some of it accumulated before Dickie's birth—stored in a garage, a coal house, an attic, a hallway, a basement, sometimes half of it stored at Mother's—to shake out the mice crap and dead bugs, cluck her tongue over lacey evidence of moths, and rearrange, repack, restack. She knew Jerry just hated the days when she lit into the drums and boxes, screaming, crying, cursing because he did everything wrong helping her.

After the stuff had been repacked, and the boxes and drums stacked again, she threw away or gave to the Salvation Army very little. These worn, rain-streaked, soot-stained, mildewed boxes and drums seemed mute testimony of the troubled times she'd endured married to Jimmy, raising three kids, losing one baby, missing that better life elsewhere.

MISS LARUE AND HER MAID "BLUE"

"I found out that Blue grew up with Miss LaRue in a big fancy house upriver."

"They seem slightly sinister."

"Why, Jerry, Blue wouldn't hurt a flea."

"Maybe not, but I'm still a little scared of them, don't know why."

"They're just odd."

"The two of them living the way they do, and Blue being a black lady bossing poor old Miss LaRue the way she does. Not that I don't like them. I do."

"I know, I know, but—well . . ."

She carried the pork chops from the kitchen out onto the screened back porch where the air was cooler but not much and called Jerry and John to come to the table.

Blue was hanging up an item of clothing on the line in the screened-in porch. "Somebody is going to have something good smelling for dinner."

"Yes, my little boy is with us now and he loves pork chops and cornbread."

John came out onto the porch licking his lips and grinning that big-toothed grin.

"Jerry, where are you?"

"I was under the house. Found a book. *The Face of a Nation* by Thomas Wolfe, just lying there on the dirt, all by itself."

"Well, come and get it before John wolfs it all down."

John had finished his chop before she or Jerry were half through.

"Is that all there is?"

"There isn't any more, honey."

"But I want another one. Can't you fry another one?"

"All out, honey."

John whimpered pitifully. "All the time I was in the reform school I dreamed of coming home and eating my fill of pork chops. I can't help it if I'm still hungry."

"Well, if you'll just stop that whining, you can have mine."

"Momma, don't give him yours. You worked all day and came home and fixed dinner and—"

"I can't stand that whining."

John cut into the chop and took a huge bite and grinned at Jerry and chewed, his mouth wide open.

"You'd take the food right out of your momma's mouth?"

"Well, she give it to me."

"It's okay, Jerry. Don't raise a fuss. I can't stand to listen to you all fussing after working all day." She stared into space.

READING OLD MAGAZINES
FROM THE LIBRARY

She flipped through the trove of magazines John checked out of the Edgewood Neighborhood Library for her. Nothing good compared with the old issues of *Redbook* before it got so it was mainly for young mothers, but she was so proud last year they abridged Jerry's novel *The Suicide's Wife*. Those were good times when she and Jerry used to walk down to Gay Street Bridge after eating at the S&W Cafeteria and pore over the used magazines in the Knoxville magazine exchange store next to the White Store, and sometimes she would plan to meet him there after his shift ushering at the Bijou, and he'd already be there, going through the old paperbacks. He liked the covers, but she didn't know whether he actually read the books all the way through or at all, not even *God's Little Acre*, which shocked the nation. He liked the pictures, too, especially in *Cosmopolitan*. And she heard him whisper the names of the authors and the titles in a radio or movie preview voice. When he went into the army, he left about a hundred of them stored in one of her big, thick cardboard drums. Now four of his books are published. He liked the illustrations in *Redbook*, *Liberty*, and the *Saturday Evening Post*, too. Carrying what they chose, they'd step next door to the White Store and get the groceries and walk up to the car barn by the Bijou and ride the Lincoln Park streetcar to Atlantic Avenue.

BILLS TO PAY, THINGS TO DO

She didn't know whether she was coming or going, and it being only Wednesday. By Saturday night, she wouldn't be worth two cents. But everything had to get done, and the list was long. Where's that envelope she was using to make a list? Right under her nose. On the back of one of John's letters, she poised the pencil to add to the list. Let me see now.

Pay Mother back ten dollars.

Call Frenchie, but don't tell her off until I know for sure.

Call Ginny to see if she's coming to Nashville this weekend.

Wonder how Cliff is doing? Hope Ginny's still seeing Jack on the sly. Wish I could see Bill.

Oh, yes, write to Ray. Check my work schedule.

Find that book of Jerry's he asked me to send him. Probably on at the bottom of the damn barrel.

Pay KUB to keep them from cutting off my electricity.

Return *Leave Her to Heaven* to Miller's lending library.

Feed the stray cat after I get Sabu back in the house, flying and crying like she does.

Call Mother to tell her about bacon on sale at Krogers.

Ask Sharp's to deliver cough medicine.

Make up a Christmas gift list.

Hunt for Dickie's new address.

Too sleepy. Finish in the morning.

Oh, yes. Keep up burial insurance on John, Jerry, and Dickie.

DADDY AND MOTHER FUSS OVER HER

"Emily, don't pay no attention to her. Jesse, why do you talk so mean to your own daughter?"

"Why do you keep taking up for her, when you know she's not doing right."

"Don't she wash the dishes? Don't she help keep the floors spick and span? Don't she offer allatime to *do* for you?"

"What?"

"You know what. I can hear from the next room how she's always trying to please you."

"I wish you all would hush arguing."

"We're not arguing, honey, just trying to set a few things straight."

"Yeah, she does things after she wears me out arguing about it."

"I never hear it."

"It's that pouting and shrugging and eye rolling that aggravates me till I have to yell or I'll explode."

"Well, just try, that's all I'm asking, to give a little."

"You pay her more attention than you do your own wife, Charlie."

"I'm trying to read the newspaper in peace."

"Yeah, just let it drop. Your momma warned me about the way you act when things get hot."

ILLNESS AND OTHER WORRIES

She sat behind the cash register at Howard Johnson's worrying about Jerry being investigated by the army for refusing to sign a paper saying he was not a member of or sympathized with the Communist Party or any other such outfit. She remembered what she told him after those meetings with the Christenberry Junior High principal and the one at Knox High: "Jerry, keep your mouth shut. I can't keep being late to work going to see the principal. And quit writing those ol' stories in class and sassing the teacher when she tears them up."

When she got home she would write to him and tell him again to keep his trap shut, especially it being the Army, for God's sake. But she had to laugh when Raven came into the restaurant and told her what Vera told the FBI when they asked her if Jerry liked girls. "He gets his share."

"Dear Jerry, Your Momma almost kicked the bucket. The doctor said to give it time, the healing, and I will be good as new. Sorry, seems like all I write you is bad news, if not Dickie, John, so, honey, keep your trap shut or that devil Senator McCarthy will shut it for you. He looks like Murder Inc. It was almost as bad as that time when Jimmy was in the army and I had to let them put you and John in the Juvenile Detention Center until room opened up at St. John's Orphanage, because your aunt Kathleen's husband, hateful thing, got sick of John's antics. You'd think your Daddy's sister would keep you. And Mother got that practical nurse job, so she couldn't take you in. And after they let me out of the hospital, I had to have peace and quiet for a long recovery. Mother did all she could for me, and Phil was still there, but useless at nursing, and Cap looked in on me. Then these last few weeks living in fear all over again. Mother and even my friends and maybe you do, too, think I put on being sick. Well, if you could have visited me, honey, you would know how it really was, because I really did almost leave the world of the living for good.

"I can tell you now about this latest sickness, because I am better enough to see the end of the tunnel. So like I say, keep a lid on your opinions, and try to be a little more like Phil when he was in the army. His letters told how he loved knowing he was serving his country. I was surprised at how patriotic he was, and proud of Chuck, too, though, even after he was shot in Palermo. For all I know about it, Sicily is the end of the world.

"Personally, I would a whole lot rather they sent Chuck home in one piece and let him lie next to Daddy, instead of just sticking him in a hole among thousands of others far-away France. Night, night.

"Mother."

GENERAL PATTON LOVED JIMMY

In the mailbox with all the bills and a postcard from John from Pacific Palisades and a letter from Jerry from Baton Rouge was a letter from General Patton's son, of all people. Using her fingernail, she slit it open and in shivering anticipation worked it out of the envelope and unfolded it. He told her that when he learned of Jimmy's death, he was eager to write to her and tell her that his father loved Jimmy, that Jimmy had defied him on the road to Rheims, refusing to move his ambulance from blocking the General's jeep until he had loaded all the wounded he could. "Do you know who you are talking to, soldier?" Jimmy said he did, but he would have to wait. And he did. And he never forgot Jimmy, and he told his son about the time this ambulance driver by the name of Jimmy Madden refused to clear the road for him. She remembered that Jimmy loved General Patton and always thought his death in his Jeep years later was not accidental the way it was claimed.

After she read the letter to Mother and Cap and Jerry and Robbie and Phil and Betty at the dining room table, she put the one from General Patton's son back in its envelope and tucked it away for safekeeping.

REMEMBERING JERRY'S SECOND BIRTHDAY PARTY

My God, where did all the years go? Tomorrow, Jerry will be sixty-six. I've got that snapshot of him at age two sitting on a table out in the back yard on Cornell Street, stacks of presents all around him. "Is this all there is?"

Then by the time we were living on Cedar Street in Lincoln Park, I had to throw a birthday party for all three boys at the same time on Jerry's birthday because John and Dickie were born in February, too cold to have a party with only a Warm Morning heater to keep kids warm. John's is on Valentine's Day.

So one year I hit on the best all-around present for all three. A desk with three drawers down the right side, one for each, and a long drawer to the left above the knee space for such stuff as pencils, scissors, a ruler, and rubber glue. Dickie at the top, John in the middle, but when Jerry said he wanted the bottom one, that made John whine to have it for himself. But Jerry won out. A few years later, Dickie hit the road, so John and Jerry fought over the top drawer. So I made it my drawer. But John would pilfer around in Jerry's, making him hit on John, mad as a lion like he can be if you cross him.

Then John started his coming and going, and in and out of homes for wayward kids and reform school. So when Jerry was in Knox High, he had all four drawers, crammed full of his stories, his movie stills and magazines, I don't know what all. Then when he, too, started wandering, New York, the merchant marine, the army, teaching, I didn't want to let it go. So it's out there now on the back porch, loaded with my junk, this, that, and the other, and on top of it, bulging cardboard boxes stacked to the ceiling.

Time flies. I just can't throw it out. When Jerry comes, he always peeks in the drawers like that old desk is sacred.

SHE AND JOHN TALK
ABOUT MOTHER AS WITCH

She and John sat in the old squeaky metal lawn chairs on the small, marble-topped front porch under the little porch roof out of the sprinkling rain and waited for the children to come up and down Henegar Street and come up to them for trick or treat.

"It ain't what it used to be." John tossed his cigarette butt into the rhododendron bush. "Scary as hell in them days. Might get beat up or really get hurt, but we went out anyway, me and Dickie and Jerry, and if you didn't treat us, we really damn did trick you. We heard garbage cans turned over all up and down the street. Not this one. Houses too few here, so we'd go over to Emerald Avenue where they got some fancy houses, and one of them's a real ghost house. What ever happened to soaping up the car windows? Hell, the parents go out with them these days, holding their hands. *You* never did that."

"Never occurred to me, but I was still yet worried to death. Remember when we and all the neighbors built a bonfire every year in the back yard and roasted weenies and marshmallows?"

"Yeah, and Mammy'd say she was going in the house to get mustard or something and while we thought she was still in there, what do you know but here come a witch in a black dress on a broomstick galloping around the bonfire all of a sudden and veering off over into Mrs. Atchly's garden among the dead, rattlely corn stalks."

"Yes, and wouldn't you know that one year, Dickie had to spoil it all by exposing Mammy as the witch, followed her into the bedroom and caught her changing into the witch outfit, and then telling *you*, just to ruin the mystery for you."

"Oh, me. Wish Mammy was here with us. And here comes the kids from all around. Where did I put my werewolf mask?"

TALKING TO MOTHER ON THE PHONE

"Mother, are you listening?"

"What?"

"Are you listening to me?"

"Yes."

"You seem far away."

"Who?"

"You. Mother, listen."

"Well, say what you have to say. Did you get the Kleenex?"

"Yes. Buy two, get one free."

"I only need one, honey, I already got three."

"Then, why tell me to get more?"

"What did you want to tell me?"

"I said—"

"I was listening. I was just wondering if them bushes outside the winder survived the frost."

"Everybody seems not to listen."

"What? Who?"

"Us. Us Merritts. And Maddens. We sit around and talk to each other, but everybody seems lost in their own little world. Oblivious."

"Not me. I hear every word."

"But you seem lost in thought."

"Emily, you know what your trouble is?"

"No, Mother, please tell me what my trouble is?"

"You don't think of nobody but your own self."

"What, Mother, pray tell, have I been doing for the last hour, instead of drifting off to sleep?"

THE DISGUSTING WAY
JIMMY EATS BELLY EGGS

She always had a slight aversion to fried eggs, but what turned her against them for good was watching Jimmy at breakfast their first morning together take a fork and mash his fried egg into tiny bits of white and stir the yellow

207

thoroughly all over them. Two eggs sickened her even more, watching the process all over again. When she asked him not to do that, he laughed, and kept at it every morning.

Then when Dickie was old enough to imitate Jimmy mashing the eggs, he did it, then Jerry followed up on the habit, but John turned the scene all the more disgusting when he called fried eggs "belly eggs."

Knowing Jimmy stabbed his fork into the belly eggs just to provoke her to beg him not to, she wondered whether he had always done that, and whether he did it when he ate alone or out in public. Once the kids took it up, they always stabbed their belly eggs and smashed the living daylights out of them for their wives to endure the sight of it, especially Jerry because Dickie often had no wife, being in prison, and John, being gay, would have had to keep it up alone most of his life.

REMEMBERING DOING THINGS WITH JERRY

She heard Jerry pull out his cot to unblock the back door, squeeze through to keep from waking her, and go down the steps out of his "sanctuary" into the backyard, letting in a blast of cold air that reached her in bed.

"Jerry. Shut—the—damn—door!"

It banged shut. Jerry was probably going to meet Ralph and them in Cecil's daddy's four-door, fancy model Chevrolet. Hunting for girls and beer. She bet he first finished working on that play, "Call Herman in to Supper." Mother told her what it was. He told Mother while she was cooking green beans. He didn't tell his own mother. He likes to tell everybody Mother taught him how to tell stories. Wonder what he can tell people *I* taught him. Well, we have always been close. Especially with Dickie and John on the road or locked up. Almost like making a date. Meet you at S&W or the Market House for lunch. Meet you after work at the Riviera. Meet you at the Knoxville Book Store. Meet you at the White Store. Goodness. It's really like having dates. Kids don't usually show up with their Momma in public. Not that he's a Momma's boy. Nobody could ever say that about him, the way he chases after girls. And they chase after him. Calling all the time. Well, hope they don't luck out getting beer. Girls is something else. And that Ralph is not that handsome but sure is charming, not cute and lovable in the way Jerry's fast friend Billy Tindall was in Lincoln Park Elementary.

DADDY TAKES HER ALL OVER TOWN

Daddy took her into the heart of town for a surprise. When they got off the streetcar, Daddy took her by the hand. At eighteen, that made her uneasy, afraid her schoolmates might see her and not know he was her daddy. Where is he leading me to, she wondered, not asking, because Daddy enjoyed surprising her.

A store full of shiny black pianos of all kinds, grands and uprights. "One of these days your daddy's gonna buy you one of these pianos, so you can dream about the day you come home and there it sits in your very own living room."

Then he led her on a tour of the heart of Cleveland. Seeing the newly finished Tower Building, the tallest in the country outside New York City, thrilled her.

Suddenly, he stopped and turned her around, facing the grand entrance of the Tower Building and the train station just inside. "I know a fellow high up who has some pull." He led her through the doors inside and turned her aside and into one of the elevators. The elevator doors opened onto a view of the sky, the moon, some stars. She couldn't speak. Not talking, he led her to a view of the city, and told her they were on the fifty-second floor, the top. He pointed out Lake Erie, even though it was as obvious as the sky. "There's Luna Park and the Ferris wheel, and there is Edgewater Park, there's the Public Market where we will go later. Looks like a palace. There's our favorite movie theater, the Hippodrome. See the public library? Our neighborhood."

He pointed out about fifty sights, to most of which they had often gone over the years, some that were new to her. Her stomach throbbed at each thrilling view, differently than when she was going up in the elevator. An hour later they were in Otto's Restaurant.

Only a few days later, they were inside the tower again, boarding a train back to Knoxville, leaving behind her new piano, sold, the crate stuffed with their worldly goods, Daddy and Mother and Phil and Chuck never to return, Emily only that one time she visited Helen, and that time with Jerry,

Robbie, and Blake when she was fifty and she showed them her old house and neighborhood and swimming pool and high school. And the tower, but not inside.

BECOMING INVISIBLE

She sometimes felt she was becoming invisible to John. They'd lived together in the old homestead for over a decade now, and John had held various jobs, plumber's helper, warehouse worker, clerk at filling station stores, food stamp office clerk, drugstore delivery man, making seat covers, ripping up carpets in rental units, junk barn worker, and pursued various money-making endeavors on his own, selling rare baseball cards and costume jewelry at major flea markets all around, and doing humanitarian projects, responding quickly to needs that came up, floods, or fires, or the ravages of storms, mostly over in Eastern Kentucky, going to city council meetings to speak out against government mismanagement, causing some people to urge him to run for mayor, while she sat at home alone, and he rushed home and ate, sometimes cooking something fast himself, then rushed out again, often to run down one of the young boys he was befriending in various ways. Smoking up a storm always, sitting across from her on the couch, watching television, always too loud, without ceasing, and always asking her to repeat what she'd said or asked him three times already, and when he slept on the couch, he'd leave the TV on, and she was scared to death he would fall asleep with a live cigarette in his hand and set the house afire. When she asked him where he was going, he was short or mean to her, and she blew up at him or cried, and he stormed out of the house. He used to plant and tend and harvest a garden, and they had sat on the back porch together and talked more. But not now. No, now she felt she was becoming invisible to him.

"I MISS YOU BOYS"

"Dearest Jerry,

"I was so disappointed that I couldn't come home the weekend that you were in Knoxville.

"Financially I just couldn't make the bus fare. If you hadn't sent me that money I just couldn't even have eaten, as I only drew $21 that first pay, having missed a day, and hours was lousy and not much commission. Still no radio. This makes 6 weeks. This darn room is like a prison without it.

"The man called Mon. morning and said 2 more wks. or he'd sell our storage.

"I am anxious to hear from Mother so she can tell me how you looked and how you were.

"You boys just don't realize how much I miss you all and you all so scattered and no one to wash shirts for or to cook meals for. I fumed around a lot I guess but didn't really mean it. Down deep I really loved doing for you all but my strength ran out so many times and I know I was grouchy. I just feel kind of lost and no incentive to do anything. Just each day for itself to draw a payday till the next one.

"Jerry I need some advice and I want you to really give this serious thought. Dick had a letter from Ann. I kept it a couple days and then opened it as I just couldn't send it on to him, with him in prison, and get him all upset, not knowing when they will let him out. She said her mother told her she had seen Dick in Manheim—that was before the military prison released him and he left Germany and came home, and she said he had told her he was thru with Ann, and so she made Ann write that she was married to someone else and to forget her. Ann said none of this was true and she still loved him and still wore his ring and that she was waiting on her visa to come to Canada so she could be near enough to him for him to go up and see her.

"I am not too sure he is not still in love with her and that he just married Eva on the rebound. Eva is a good, sweet girl but so nondescript and no personality or looks and comes from a sort of trashy family. Dick sure must have been lonesome or something.

"Anyway, did I do right not to send Ann's letter to him, and should I do so now, even if her father was a Nazi colonel? I have worried till I don't know what to do. I will stop before I lay any more on you.

"Guess who I have a date with tomorrow night? Bill Williams, your favorite of all my sweethearts. A card in my box that he will be in Nashville tomorrow night. I have washed my hair and done my nails and fixed something nice to wear. I just hope I don't act too glad to see the big heel. Four years you know and I am 5 lbs. heavier and 4 years older. He may not look so hot himself and wouldn't be surprised if he was real gray.

"Had a letter from John and he is not sure when he is discharged from the Marines. Sure takes them a long time, huh? Maybe he'll out talk them yet.

"Write Dick and slip him a couple bucks when you can. Also your old lady, as she sure is about barefoot.

"Love, Mother.

"P. S. Dick is writing poetry now and darn good too. Mention I told you. It will give him a boost in spirit.

"Do not mention to Dick about the letter to Ann or what I said about Eva."

JOHN'S POLITICAL ACTIVITIES

Sometimes she felt she had a politician-in-residence, John wrote so many letters to presidents, governors, senators, representatives, and mayors, many published as letters to the editor. Personal notes from some high-up fellow in the White House coming in the mail didn't surprise her. Watching TV with John could be a nice jolt when he came on the nightly news, that face of outrage combined with a sudden wily grin, and there sits John in the flesh right across from her. "I forgot to tell you."

Or he might be baking an apple pie to please her, when suddenly he was on. "John, get in here. It's you again—on the news about the Gay Street Bridge being about to fall down." He'd run in, a sort of dance walking, going "ut, ut, ut, ut," a kind of mock delight.

Newspapers in Nashville showed him with his club, the Sunshine Kids, in Governor Duncan's office and later, on the Capitol steps in Washington shaking hands with Duncan when he had become a senator, all John's kids in UT colors, orange uniforms and caps, arrayed behind them.

Where was he tonight? Being fitted with a mic on his collar?

WHAT A FAMILY OF CON MEN

Jerry once told me that I am a con man, too, or is it con woman? I guess they have them, working with the men on what they do, I reckon.

That time I asked him why did he think John and Dickie do the things they do, Jerry said, "Momma, look at it this way, the way you've had to live, all those problems of every kind, including John and Dickie's troubles, all those jobs when you were too sick to hold on to them, all those houses and apartments, moving from one to another, all those men whose help you needed, you had to work cons on all of them.

"Me, too, as a teacher, I con kids into learning, as a writer I con readers into turning the page, techniques, you have them, too, not just John and Dickie and me, and I guess Daddy, Phil, Chuck, but not as much as us boys and you, not Mammy, except as a storyteller, and not Cap. Maybe it came to us through Granny Merritt, a single mom, who had to deal with all that you yourself have had to, and maybe Charlie Merritt, too, a life as an illegitimate.

"That doesn't excuse John and Dickie breaking the law as con men, but it might help you answer the question, why do they do what they do, and now John as a doer of good deeds, and gay, and ex-convict, as a citizen politician, he sure as hell is the greatest con man of us all."

THE OLD HOME PLACE,

LIKE LORETTA LYNN'S

Leafing through the *Knoxville News-Sentinel* on Pearl Harbor Day, she was delighted to come upon an entire front page in the Living Today section devoted to Loretta Lynn. NOSTALGIC BRUSH WITH THE PAST/ LORETTA LYNN SANG HER WAY FROM LOG CABIN TO REGAL MANSION. What struck her was the crude painting of a log cabin Loretta claimed to've been born in, contrasted with a color photo of a six-column, two-story mansion that was not half as beautiful and impressive as Jerry's mansion on Park Boulevard in Baton Rouge. And that cabin. Just like Granny Merritt's the way it looked when she and Mother and Daddy and Phil and Chuck returned to Knoxville and had to live in that one small room. Only two rooms and a kitchen. In the margin of the clipping, she drew a picture of Granny's house the way it used to be and wrote, "A window here, in the bedroom, a window in the front room here, where Granny Merritt died and where you and Dickie were born." Loretta's was long—Granny's was not. Then to sum up Loretta's life, she dashed off her own phrase above the *Sentinel's* headline: RAGS TO RICHES.

"This is very much like little Granny Merritt's house on Henegar (Mammy added to it little by little). Only had split wooden shingles and no water or electricity. Carried water from the big house next door. Finally had water spigot in our *yard.* Your daddy and I smooched many times on the tiny front porch. Very few houses around us and few trees close by. There was one big oak tree in front of the big house next door—dead end of Henegar back then. Granny tied her hen there, with its chicks loose all around her."

JUST MARRIED

Emily Madden. Hard to believe it's true. No more Emily Merritt. Unless I use all three, Emily Merritt Madden. But that sounds hoity toity, especially for a nineteen-year-old teenager, who looks, I hope, seventeen. Jimmy two years older. What a sweet and loving husband. But I never dreamed he would stash me away in a two-room basement apartment that smells like sweaty socks. Not that I wasn't warned. His sister warned me he was not quite mature enough for marriage. Still counting on handouts from her, his big brother Elmo, and that rich David Madden that owns the meat packing plant. They all say Jimmy's too blasé in all departments. Marriage is serious, especially when children come along. Maybe Mother and Daddy will let us live with them now they added that back room. Or that little house next door may come up for rent.

It wouldn't be so bad if we could get out and be with people. His own kin only blocks away up the hill, and he keeps putting off taking me up there, and none of them seem to want to walk it down here, not even to see what Jimmy's wife looks like. If only Jimmy would learn to dance. And swimming doesn't appeal to him either. Working and loafing and being sweet and charming is all he seems to know how to do.

I doubt he knows what that broom in the corner is. Oh, Emily, don't exaggerate. He did pick up a hammer. I saw him do it. But I never saw him use it.

JERRY AND ROBBIE LIVING

ON A FARM IN BOONE

She opened the envelope from Jerry, addressed in Robbie's handwriting. Photos. That picnic last month at the Blue Mule Hotel where three creeks intersect to form a cross in Valle Crucis near Boone. She handled them, scanned them, then looked closely at each, feeling as if she were still there. A magical place.

Jerry rigged up a table near the driveway in front of the abandoned hotel.

And a tablecloth. Just the three of us under those trees, and within sight of the ruins of other structures, the old barn off to the side and the ponds, stones from the river making low walls on six or seven levels all over the terraced site, a steep cliff behind. Jerry's car parked in the drive in this photo.

And just like Jerry to persuade Robbie to pose for artistic shots on the wraparound porches on both floors, and in front of the entrance, a wall of many panes of glass.

I was nervous the whole time, from when he turned in the drive, because the owner might find us there and point at the sign that said KEEP OFF. NO TRESPASSERS. And call the sheriff.

But it was wonderful. I'll never forget it, and I just know it's one of those places Jerry will use as a setting for one of his stories. Maybe that's what he had in mind taking us there in the first place.

THE BILTMORE SALOON BARTENDER

When she took Miller's back exit into the alley, a roly-poly little fellow was dumping trash from the Biltmore Saloon into the Dempster-Dumpster but stopped a few seconds looking at her before he let it go. She smiled and that got him smiling. She played like that was that and went straight into Miller's Annex to take a look at a special sale on nylons.

With a bag of nylons and some impulse items under her arm, she stepped onto the sidewalk at Market Square and turned the Union Avenue corner, and there that same little fellow was, no taller than she, on the curb smoking a cigar, still wearing his bartender apron, a fresh one as if he wanted to dress up in case she came along. He smiled and waved his cigar-holding hand, setting off a face-brightening smile from her at him.

"You Jimmy's wife?"

"Was. Not anymore."

"Thank goodness. I don't ask out other men's wives."

"I guess I can guess how you know Jimmy."

"He drops in sort of regular, you might say. Would you like a Pabst Blue Ribbon—on me?"

"I don't drink, thank you. Tra la."

"Tra la yourself, and I hope to see you passing by again—soon—tomorrow."

On the streetcar going home, she had a feeling she would be seeing that roly-poly little fellow, just her size, again. Sooner or later.

A month or so later, after a few dancing dates, she invited Clyde to come over for Sunday dinner and she baked a cherry pie. He helped her and Jerry rearrange some storage boxes in her bedroom.

LETTER TO JERRY ABOUT

HER LOVER IN NASHVILLE

"Dear Jerry, Met a handsome jewelry salesman from N.Y. Cocktails, movies, dinner, lunch and Sonja Henie ice show 'for 3 days.' He said I was just like a kid I was so enthralled. It was certainly out of this world. But he has moved on now.

"Your old mom has been having quite a time lately. I've been more places and made more friends in Nashville in 2 months than I did in Knoxville in a year.

"Roy is here for the weekend. We ate waffles and maple syrup till it ran out our ears and then walked up to the War Museum. We spent 2 hrs and still had 3 rooms to go. He does everything so thoroughly. My feet are killing me.

"He is in his room writing his boss (he said) and me in mine writing you. Then we are going for a ride to the Parthenon . . . Then we are going to eat dinner and I'll help him with his tie line. We inventory there and take out the obsolete styles. He is a pleasure to know. Manners to the 9th degree and very well educated—a Mason too.

"Jerry, if you can throw a few dollars my way till payday I will sure appreciate it. I need to get every red cent paid on the storage possible. If you and John both send me 10 or 15 each payday I would soon pay it off and keep up the current storage. . . . A few min. by myself.

"My 20 min. break is up. Back to the cigar counter. Will write later. Bye now."

WRAPPING CHRISTMAS PRESENTS

She nervously wrapped the first Christmas present, the one for Dickie, to send to Texas, maybe too late to get through the prison system to him by Christmas.

She always loved wrapping Christmas presents, but not when her nerves were shot.

She was late getting Mother's present and hoped she would love it. Next is John's, the same problem as Dickie. Federal prison in El Reno, Oklahoma.

And now Jerry had the FBI on his butt for sassing the army. Well, worse than that, refusing to sign some kind of new loyalty oath. Why? Why, oh, why? Please, God, not the stockade. Do I have to mail his present to a stockade in Columbia?

He asked for a book, but didn't get around to telling me which one, so warm socks will have to do, case they clear him, then ship him off to Alaska, which they are threatening to do.

All the Christmases, and now I am an old lady of forty-four. Mays well ship me to the funny farm now. Why wait? Well, I'm a whole lot better off than all those folks in that earthquake in . . . I forget where. Knoxville may not be my first choice, but where they've got earthquakes every time you turn around is not the place for me. You can *have* San Francisco and that one long ago in Naples.

So count your blessings, Emily Madden. Christmas, and none of us go to church. "Away in the manger, no crib for a babe . . ." She cried a while. Then she felt better.

WANTING CLEVELAND
AND A LIFE OF DANCING

The girl she had been in Cleveland never thought of herself as a future mother. She wanted to have fun with friends, male and female, with good-looking boys. Not for a lifetime. Marriage, of course. Children would just happen. Naturally. But dancing and laughing and flirting and being charming seemed her welcome fate in her Cleveland girlhood. Children, three, then four, and an alcoholic husband. Shattered, like the head of her doll she dropped yesterday, the life she'd daydreamed for herself. Suddenly, almost, she had to eke out the fun. Work it in. Find time for it. Seek it out. Demand it of herself. Until it receded more and more into the past, overwhelmed day by day in the present. Until she was nursing people for a living, as a job, but proud of it as a semi-profession, wanting to earn Mother's respect. Never sure of it, ever.

Knoxville, too much of her life was a Knoxville life, making her Cleveland life seem to be just enough of a paradise back then. Comparisons were guaranteed to put her in a funk. Goddamn Knoxville. Where her father shot himself in the lumber yard that had lured him out of Cleveland and back into Granny Merritt's little shacklely house in hillbilly Knoxville.

It hurt to hear Jerry tell me that Mother told him just before she died the true story of Matilda Merritt, not the same one she always told me, only that Daddy was illegitimate. She told Jerry that John Carr raised her in Caryville near Jacksboro or Lafollette. And that his son Franklin got her pregnant and the Merritts paid her to get gone, so she came on down to Knoxville and claimed to be the widow of Franklin Merritt. And how Daddy died. Not that an enemy at Chavannes's lumber and roofing company shot him. Suicide. That he killed himself.

She never told *me* that. So I am left to wonder why.

WONDERING WHO LOVES HER

She never knew whether Mother loved her. Nice to her, nice enough. Most of the time, she supposed. But often hateful, as in that husky mean voice from deep down, she used to say, "To be loved, you must be lovable." She doubted that any of the boys ever saw that side of her. They saw both sides off and on of herself, but probably not of Mother. Phil saw it, suffered it. Cap, too, saw it, poor fellow. Probably not Chuck. Everybody loved Chuck, except Ruth in the end, but that was the alcohol, not him. Dickie. She saw herself in Dickie. She would like to come and go, maybe, like Dickie. Not give a damn. But, no, Dickie was mild-mannered, like Jimmy.

She knew she was jealous of Greg, from the day she called and Mother said, "Well, you'll never guess what John dragged in here." A huge box. Little Greg inside the box. Yes, Mother finally found who she could love, no strings attached. No matter how aggravating Greg could be, Mother tolerated his sass, his goofy ways, while leaving it up to Cap to discipline him.

But not his grandmother Emily. "Emmie" was who she was to her own grandson. Not that she ever would have taken him in. Well, they probably never really could tell, but she loved every one of them, whether she acted hateful or lovable.

One night, she dreamed she wandered all over creation looking for people and places and the cat she had loved, Elmer, her first Siamese, but could not find a single one.

Why, she wondered, did she wake feeling blessed? Maybe because she saw everybody and everywhere so clearly as she set out in search of one after another, and that as she looked, she was so intensely, fully aware of each that her feelings, not finding them, made her feel that actually she *had* found them, each and every one.

She even rolled out of bed early and gladly checked in on her ancient, mean-hearted patient.

LOOKING AT PHOTOS
OF HERSELF WITH THE BOYS

Looking at pictures of herself with John, but usually with Jerry, or herself alone, she saw herself as infant, child, adolescent, looking at the camera, serious, dreamy, sometimes sweet-eyed, or looking very gay, trying to convince the person behind the camera that her charming smile was natural. Not that it was phony. Her eyes and mouth and posture were true to how she felt then and usually felt. She was still from year to year as an adult that way—serious or charming, gay, maybe purely happy, she couldn't remember, except the snapshots when she was with Helen and other girlfriends and boyfriends in groups, out roaming around, having fun somewhere in Cleveland.

Letters from boyfriends and girlfriends expressed very lively times carousing and lovemaking and dancing from age thirty-three or so until about sixty. Lover, dancer. In time, some labels may peel. She never drank beer or whiskey, but a little sip of wine a few times for the glamour of it. So her good times were consciously good. Left alone, she was vulnerable.

Knowing that Mother sometimes sat with Jerry or John, maybe even Dickie, and pored over the loose photographs in her own special, big box, smelling of the same cedar chest where she kept her own collection, she imagined them noticing, commenting on those two expressions. The serious look expressed how she was always, but the cheerful, charming look expressed yes, how she was always, but also how she wanted to be and to be seen. She seldom wondered, as most people seem to, "Who took that picture?" but was happy to assume that in Cleveland, Daddy had been the eye behind the camera eye.

LYING SICK

She knew that because of her many and different illnesses, all the doctor visits, and hospital stays, inclined people, even those who saw the seriousness of the many illnesses that came and went, while some lingered in the shadows, to regard her as a complete hypochondriac, or to believe that hypochondria was one of her character traits. Some said, Mother among them, that her illnesses were to some extent bids for attention, especially when she felt unloved, or not loved enough, despite the good she did for those same people, especially Mother, and she realized some truth in that. She loved so she would be loved, but too she loved because loving made her feel good. She suspected that she indulged herself in illnesses now and then, but she really did suffer from each of them, great or small. The hysterectomy was no self-indulgence. Her pregnancy with Ronny caused so many of her teeth to decay that she had to get them all removed, and the result of that was that the dentures never fit her and pained her almost daily.

Thinking of all that on the bus back to Signal Mountain, recalled to work at Alexian Brothers Rest Home, she suddenly felt sweeping over her the ever-constant will to live, not merely to live, but to enjoy as much of life every day that she could eke out. Dying was always possible, but, damn it to hell, so was joy, the joy of the moment, and so in the moment of that realization, what she felt was not pain or fear of death, but joy. She wanted to tell Mother that, but... Too late now. That was the kind of realization that Jerry, though, would understand.

"GO INTO THE LIGHT, MOMMA"

If John and Dickie followed her passing, Greg and Vivien and Philip and little Rachel could move into the house, keep it in the family, own it outright, free, as she wished. If Gregory passed on, leaving Vivien and the children, Jerry would then have to sell the house and all her worldly goods.

He would have to sell the piano he and she finally found and he paid for. Men with a truck would come into the house and wheel it tightly through the front door and up onto a truck. Jerry would take whatever they offered, because with Jerry the money would not matter. That it was the piano he bought for his mother would be the matter, his mother whose father bought her a piano at last, and in no time quick sold it out from under her fingers when they had to move back to Knoxville and into the little house, where the moving men with the truck would take a deep breath and, letting it out, lift the piano.

Embraced by Jerry and Blake, she thought she heard Jerry say, "Go into the light, Momma, go into the light."

She stepped off, as if into a dance to the music of Glenn Miller.